DATA MINING, BIG DATA ANALYTICS AND DEEP LEARNING. EXAMPLES WITH MATLAB

C. PEREZ

CONTENTS

Chapter 1

DATA MINING, BIG DATA ANALYTICS AND DEEP LEARNING

1.1 INTRODUCTION TO DATA MINING TECHNIQUES

The availability of large volumes of data and the generalized use of computer tools has transformed research and data analysis, orienting it towards certain specialized techniques encompassed under the generic name of Analytics that includes Multivariate Data Analysis (MDA), Data Mining and other Business Intelligence techniques.

Data Mining can be defined as a process of discovering new and significant relationships, patterns and trends when examining large amounts of data. The techniques of Data Mining pursue the automatic discovery of the knowledge contained in the information stored in an orderly manner in large databases. These techniques aim to discover patterns, profiles and trends through the analysis of data using advanced statistical techniques of multivariate data analysis.

The goal is to allow the researcher-analyst to find a useful solution to the problem raised through a better understanding of the existing data.

Data Mining uses two types of techniques: predictive techniques, which trains a model on known input and output data so that it can predict future outputs, and descriptive techniques, which finds hidden patterns or intrinsic structures in input data.

The aim of predictive techniques is to build a model that makes predictions based on evidence in the presence of uncertainty. A predictive algorithm takes a known set of input data and known responses to the data (output) and trains a model to generate reasonable predictions for the response to new data. Data Mining techniques uses neural networks classification and regression techniques to develop predictive models.

- *Classification* techniques predict categorical responses, for example, whether an email is genuine or spam, or whether a tumor is cancerous or benign. Classification models classify input data into categories. Typical applications include medical imaging, image and speech recognition, and credit scoring.
- *Regression* techniques predict continuous responses, for example, changes in temperature or fluctuations in power demand. Typical applications include electricity load forecasting and algorithmic trading.

Descriptive techniques finds hidden patterns or intrinsic structures in data. It is used to draw inferences from datasets consisting of input data without labeled responses. *Clustering* is the most common descriptive technique. It is used for exploratory data analysis to find hidden patterns or groupings in data. Applications for clustering include gene sequence analysis, market research, and object recognition.

1.2 INTRODUCTION TO NEURAL NETWORKS

Neural networks theory is inspired from the natural neural network of human nervous system. Is possible define a neural network as a computing system made up of a number of simple, highly interconnected processing elements, which process information by their dynamic state response to external inputs.

The idea of ANNs is based on the belief that working of human brain by making the right connections, can be imitated using silicon and wires as living neurons and dendrites.

The human brain is composed of 100 billion nerve cells called neurons. They are connected to other thousand cells by Axons. Stimuli from external environment or inputs from sensory organs are accepted by dendrites. These inputs create electric impulses, which quickly travel through the neural network. A neuron can then send the message to other neuron to handle the issue or does not send it forward.

ANNs are composed of multiple nodes, which imitate biological neurons of human brain. The neurons are connected by links and they interact with each other. The nodes can take input data and perform simple operations on the data. The result of these operations is passed to other neurons. The output at each node is called its activation or node value.

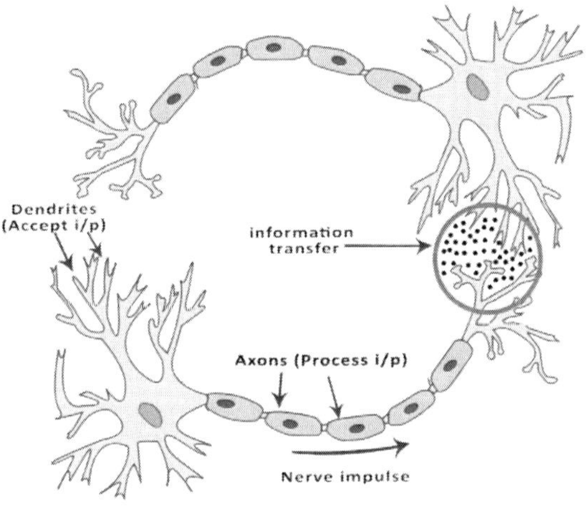

Each link is associated with weight. ANNs are capable of learning, which takes place by altering weight values. The following illustration shows a simple ANN

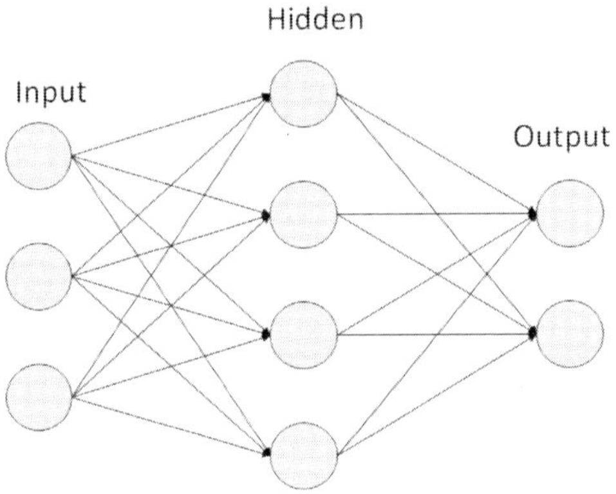

1.3 INTRODUCTION TO BIG DATA ANALYTICS

Big data analytics examines large amounts of data to uncover hidden patterns, correlations and other insights. With today's technology, it's possible to analyze your data and get answers from it almost immediately – an effort that's slower and less efficient with more traditional business intelligence solutions.

The concept of big data has been around for years; most organizations now understand that if they capture all the data that streams into their businesses, they can apply analytics and get significant value from it. But even in the 1950s, decades before anyone uttered the term "big data," businesses were using basic analytics (essentially numbers in a spreadsheet that were manually examined) to uncover insights and trends.

Big data analytics helps organizations harness their data and use it to identify new opportunities. That, in turn, leads to smarter business moves, more efficient operations, higher profits and happier customers. In his report *Big Data in Big Companies*, IIA Director of Research Tom Davenport interviewed more than 50 businesses to understand how they used big data. He found they got value in the following ways:

- **Cost reduction.** Big data technologies such as Hadoop and cloud-based analytics bring significant cost advantages when it comes to storing large amounts of data – plus they can identify more efficient ways of doing business.
- **Faster, better decision making.** With the speed of Hadoop and in-memory analytics, combined with the ability to analyze new sources of data, businesses are able to analyze information immediately – and make decisions based on what they've learned.
- **New products and services.** With the ability to gauge customer needs and satisfaction through analytics comes the power to give customers what they want. Davenport points out that with big data analytics, more companies are creating new products to meet customers' needs.

The new benefits that big data analytics brings to the table, however, are speed and efficiency. Whereas a few years ago a business would have gathered information, run analytics and unearthed information that could be used for future decisions, today that business can identify insights for immediate decisions. The ability to work faster – and stay agile – gives organizations a competitive edge they didn't have before

There's no single technology that encompasses big data analytics. Of course, there's advanced analytics that can be applied to big data, but in reality several types of technology work together to help you get the most value from your information. Here are the biggest players:

Data management. Data needs to be high quality and well-governed before it can be reliably analyzed. With data constantly flowing in and out of an organization, it's important to establish repeatable processes to build and maintain standards for data quality. Once data is reliable, organizations should establish a master data management program that gets the entire enterprise on the same page.

Data mining. Data mining technology helps you examine large amounts of data to discover patterns in the data – and this information can be used for further analysis to help answer complex business questions. With data mining software, you can sift through all the chaotic and repetitive noise in data, pinpoint what's relevant, use that information to assess likely outcomes, and then accelerate the pace of making informed decisions.

Hadoop. This open source software framework can store large amounts of data and run applications on clusters of commodity hardware. It has become a key technology to doing business due to the constant increase of data volumes and varieties, and its distributed computing model processes big data fast. An additional benefit is that Hadoop's open source framework is free and uses commodity hardware to store large quantities of data.

In-memory analytics. By analyzing data from system memory (instead of from your hard disk drive), you can derive immediate insights from your data and act on them quickly. This technology is able to remove data prep and analytical processing latencies to test new scenarios and create models; it's not only an easy way for organizations to stay agile and make better business decisions, it also enables them to run iterative and interactive analytics scenarios.

Predictive analytics. Predictive analytics technology uses data, statistical algorithms and machine-learning techniques to identify the likelihood of future outcomes based on historical data. It's all about providing a best assessment on what will happen in the future, so organizations can feel more confident that they're making the best possible business decision. Some of the most common applications of predictive analytics include fraud detection, risk, operations and marketing.

Text mining. With text mining technology, you can analyze text data from the web, comment fields, books and other text-based sources to uncover insights you hadn't noticed before. Text mining uses machine learning or natural language processing technology to comb through documents – emails, blogs, Twitter feeds, surveys, competitive intelligence and more – to help you analyze large amounts of information and discover new topics and term relationships.

1.4 BIG DATA ANALYTICS AND MATLAB

Big data analytics is the process of collecting, organizing and analyzing large sets of data (*called* big data) to discover patterns and other useful information. Big data analytics can help organizations to better understand the information contained within the data and will also help identify the data that is most important to the business and future business decisions. Analysts working with big data basically want the *knowledge* that comes from analyzing the data.

To analyze such a large volume of data, big data analytics is typically performed using specialized software tools and applications for predictive analytics, data mining, text mining, forecasting and data optimization. Collectively these processes are separate but highly integrated functions of high-performance analytics. Using big data tools and software enables an organization to process extremely large volumes of data that a business has collected to determine which data is relevant and can be analyzed to drive better business decisions in the future. Among all these tools highlights MATLAB.

MATLAB implements various toolboxes for working on big data analytics, such as Statistics Toolbox and Neural Network Toolbox (Deep Learning Toolbox from version 18) (Deep Learning Toolbox from version 18).

1.5 DEEP LEARNING

Deep learning (also known as *deep structured learning, hierarchical learning* or *deep machine learning*) is a branch of machine learning based on a set of algorithms that attempt to model high level abstractions in data. In a simple case, there might be two sets of neurons: ones that receive an input signal and ones that send an output signal. When the input layer receives an input it passes on a modified version of the input to the next layer. In a deep network, there are many layers between the input and output (and the layers are not made of neurons but it can help to think of it that way), allowing the algorithm to use multiple processing layers, composed of multiple linear and non-linear transformations.

Deep learning is part of a broader family of machine learning methods based on learning representations of data. An observation (e.g., an image) can be represented in many ways such as a vector of intensity values per pixel, or in a more abstract way as a set of edges, regions of particular shape, etc. Some representations are better than others at simplifying the learning task (e.g., face recognition or facial expression recognition). One of the promises of deep learning is replacing handcrafted features with efficient algorithms for unsupervised or semi-supervised feature learning and hierarchical feature extraction. Research in this area attempts to make better representations and create models to learn these representations from large-scale unlabeled data. Some of the representations are inspired by advances in neuroscience and are loosely based on interpretation of information processing and communication patterns in a nervous system, such as neural coding which attempts to define a relationship between various stimuli and associated neuronal responses in the brain.

Various deep learning architectures such as deep neural networks, convolutional deep neural networks, deep belief networks and recurrent neural networks have been applied to fields like computer vision, automatic speech recognition, natural language processing, audio recognition and bioinformatics where they have been shown to produce state-of-the-art results on various tasks.

Deep learning has been characterized as a buzzword, or a rebranding of neural networks.

1.5.1 Definitions

Deep learning is characterized as a class of machine learning algorithms that:

- use a cascade of many layers of nonlinear processing units for feature extraction and transformation. Each successive layer uses the output from the previous layer as input. The algorithms may be supervised or unsupervised and applications include pattern analysis (unsupervised) and classification (supervised).
- are based on the (unsupervised) learning of multiple levels of features or representations of the data. Higher level features are derived from lower level features to form a hierarchical representation.
- are part of the broader machine learning field of learning representations of data.
- learn multiple levels of representations that correspond to different levels of abstraction; the levels form a hierarchy of concepts.

These definitions have in common multiple layers of nonlinear processing units and the supervised or unsupervised learning of feature representations in each layer, with the layers forming a hierarchy from low-level to high-level features. The composition of a layer of nonlinear processing units used in a deep learning algorithm depends on the problem to be solved. Layers that have been used in deep learning include hidden layers of an artificial neural network and sets of complicated propositional formulas. They may also include latent variables organized layer-wise in deep generative models such as the nodes in Deep Belief Networks and Deep Boltzmann Machines.

Deep learning algorithms transform their inputs through more layers than shallow learning algorithms. At each layer, the signal is transformed by a processing unit, like an artificial neuron, whose parameters are 'learned' through training. A chain of transformations from input to output is a credit assignment path (CAP). CAPs describe potentially causal connections between input and output and may vary in length – for a feedforward neural network, the depth of the CAPs (thus of the network) is the number of hidden layers plus one (as the output layer is also parameterized), but for recurrent neural networks, in which a signal may propagate through a layer more than once, the CAP is potentially unlimited in length. There is no universally agreed upon threshold of depth dividing shallow learning from deep learning, but most researchers in the field agree that deep learning has multiple nonlinear layers (CAP > 2) and Juergen Schmidhuber considers CAP > 10 to be very deep learning.

1.5.2 Concepts

Deep learning algorithms are based on distributed representations. The underlying assumption behind distributed representations is that observed data are generated by the interactions of factors organized in layers. Deep learning adds the assumption that these layers of factors correspond to levels of abstraction or composition. Varying numbers of layers and layer sizes can be used to provide different amounts of abstraction. Deep learning exploits this idea of hierarchical explanatory factors where higher level, more abstract concepts are learned from the lower level ones. These architectures are often constructed with a greedy layer-by-layer method. Deep learning helps to disentangle these abstractions and pick out which features are useful for learning.

For supervised learning tasks, deep learning methods obviate feature engineering, by translating the data into compact intermediate representations akin to principal components, and derive layered structures which remove redundancy in representation. Many deep learning algorithms are applied to unsupervised learning tasks. This is an important benefit because unlabeled data are usually more abundant than labeled data. Examples of deep structures that can be trained in an unsupervised manner are neural history compressors and deep belief networks.

1.5.3 Deep learning and neural networks

Some of the most successful deep learning methods involve artificial neural networks. Artificial neural networks are inspired by the 1959 biological model proposed by Nobel laureates David H. Hubel & Torsten Wiesel, who found two types of cells in the primary visual cortex: simple cells and complex cells. Many artificial neural networks can be viewed as cascading models of cell types inspired by these biological observations. Fukushima's Neocognitron introduced convolutional neural networks partially trained by unsupervised learning with human-directed features in the neural plane. Yann LeCun et al. (1989) applied supervised backpropagation to such architectures. Weng et al. (1992) published convolutional neural networks Cresceptron for 3-D object recognition from images of cluttered scenes and segmentation of such objects from images.

An obvious need for recognizing general 3-D objects is least shift invariance and tolerance to deformation. Max-pooling appeared to be first proposed by Cresceptron to enable the network to tolerate small-to-large deformation in a hierarchical way, while using convolution. Max-pooling helps, but does not guarantee, shift-invariance at the pixel level.

With the advent of the back-propagation algorithm based on automatic differentiation, many researchers tried to train supervised deep artificial neural networks from scratch, initially with little success. Sepp Hochreiter's diploma thesis of 1991 formally identified the reason for this failure as the vanishing gradient problem, which affects many-layered feedforward networks and recurrent neural networks. Recurrent networks are trained by unfolding them into very deep feedforward networks, where a new layer is created for each time step of an input sequence processed by the network. As errors propagate from layer to layer, they shrink exponentially with the number of layers, impeding the tuning of neuron weights which is based on those errors.

To overcome this problem, several methods were proposed. One is Jürgen Schmidhuber's multi-level hierarchy of networks (1992) pre-trained one level at a time by unsupervised learning, fine-tuned by backpropagation. Here each level learns a compressed representation of the observations that is fed to the next level.

Another method is the long short-term memory (LSTM) network of Hochreiter & Schmidhuber (1997). In 2009, deep multidimensional LSTM networks won three ICDAR 2009 competitions in connected handwriting recognition, without any prior knowledge about the three languages to be learned. Sven Behnke in 2003 relied only on the sign of the gradient (Rprop) when training his Neural Abstraction Pyramid to solve problems like image reconstruction and face localization.

Other methods also use unsupervised pre-training to structure a neural network, making it first learn generally useful feature detectors. Then the network is trained further by supervised back-propagation to classify labeled data. The deep model of Hinton et al. (2006) involves learning the distribution of a high-level representation using successive layers of binary or real-valued latent variables. It uses a restricted Boltzmann machine (Smolensky, 1986[87]) to model each new layer of higher level features. Each new layer guarantees an increase on the lower-bound of the log likelihood of the data, thus improving the model, if trained properly. Once sufficiently many layers have been learned, the deep architecture may be used as a generative model by reproducing the data when sampling down the model (an "ancestral pass") from the top level feature activations.[88]Hinton reports that his models are effective feature extractors over high-dimensional, structured data.

In 2012, the Google Brain team led by Andrew Ng and Jeff Dean created a neural network that learned to recognize higher-level concepts, such as cats, only from watching unlabeled images taken from YouTube videos.

Other methods rely on the sheer processing power of modern computers, in particular, GPUs. In 2010, Dan Ciresan and colleagues in Jürgen Schmidhuber's group at the Swiss AI Lab IDSIA showed that despite the above-mentioned "vanishing gradient problem," the superior processing power of GPUs makes plain back-propagation feasible for deep feedforward neural networks with many layers. The method outperformed all other machine learning techniques on the old, famous MNIST handwritten digits problem of Yann LeCun and colleagues at NYU.

At about the same time, in late 2009, deep learning feedforward networks made inroads into speech recognition, as marked by the NIPS Workshop on Deep Learning for Speech Recognition. Intensive collaborative work between Microsoft Research and University of Toronto researchers demonstrated by mid-2010 in Redmond that deep neural networks interfaced with a hidden Markov model with context-dependent states that define the neural network output layer can drastically reduce errors in large-vocabulary speech recognition tasks such as voice search. The same deep neural net model was shown to scale up to Switchboard tasks about one year later at Microsoft Research Asia. Even earlier, in 2007, LSTM trained by CTC started to get excellent results in certain applications. This method is now widely used, for example, in Google's greatly improved speech recognition for all smartphone users.

As of 2011, the state of the art in deep learning feedforward networks alternates convolutional layers and max-pooling layers, topped by several fully connected or sparsely connected layer followed by a final classification layer. Training is usually done without any unsupervised pre-training. Since 2011, GPU-based implementations of this approach won many pattern recognition contests, including the IJCNN 2011 Traffic Sign Recognition Competition, the ISBI 2012 Segmentation of neuronal structures in EM stacks challenge, the ImageNet Competition, and others.

Such supervised deep learning methods also were the first artificial pattern recognizers to achieve human-competitive performance on certain tasks.

To overcome the barriers of weak AI represented by deep learning, it is necessary to go beyond deep learning architectures, because biological brains use both shallow and deep circuits as reported by brain anatomy displaying a wide variety of invariance. Weng argued that the brain self-wires largely according to signal statistics and, therefore, a serial cascade cannot catch all major statistical dependencies. ANNs were able to guarantee shift invariance to deal with small and large natural objects in large cluttered scenes, only when invariance extended beyond shift, to all ANN-learned concepts, such as location, type (object class label), scale, lighting. This was realized in

Developmental Networks (DNs) whose embodiments are Where-What Networks, WWN-1 (2008) through WWN-7.

1.5.4 Deep neural networks

A *deep neural network* (DNN) is an artificial neural network (ANN) with multiple hidden layers of units between the input and output layers. Similar to shallow ANNs, DNNs can model complex non-linear relationships. DNN architectures, e.g., for object detection and parsing, generate compositional models where the object is expressed as a layered composition of image primitives. The extra layers enable composition of features from lower layers, giving the potential of modeling complex data with fewer units than a similarly performing shallow network.

DNNs are typically designed as feedforward networks, but research has very successfully applied recurrent neural networks, especially LSTM, for applications such as language modeling. Convolutional deep neural networks (CNNs) are used in computer vision where their success is well-documented. CNNs also have been applied to acoustic modeling for automatic speech recognition (ASR), where they have shown success over previous models. For simplicity, a look at training DNNs is given here.

A DNN can be discriminatively trained with the *standard backpropagation algorithm.*

1.5.5 Convolutional neural networks

CNNs have become the method of choice for processing visual and other two-dimensional data. A CNN is composed of one or more convolutional layers with fully connected layers (matching those in typical artificial neural networks) on top. It also uses tied weights and pooling layers. In particular, max-pooling is often used in Fukushima's convolutional architecture. This architecture allows CNNs to take advantage of the 2D structure of input data. In comparison with other deep architectures, convolutional neural networks have shown superior results in both image and speech applications. They can also be trained with standard backpropagation. CNNs are easier to train than other regular, deep, feed-forward neural networks and have many fewer parameters to estimate, making them a highly attractive architecture to use. Examples of applications in Computer Vision include DeepDream. See the main article on Convolutional neural networks for numerous additional references.

1.5.6 Recursive neural networks

A recursive neural network is created by applying the same set of weights recursively over a differentiable graph-like structure, by traversing the structure in topological order. Such networks are typically also trained by the reverse mode of automatic differentiation. They were introduced to learn distributed representations of structure, such as logical terms. A special case of recursive neural networks is the RNN itself whose structure corresponds to a linear chain. Recursive neural networks have been applied to natural language processing. The Recursive Neural Tensor Network uses a tensor-based composition function for all nodes in the tree.

1.5.7 Long short-term memory

Numerous researchers now use variants of a deep learning RNN called the Long short-term memory (LSTM) network published by Hochreiter & Schmidhuber in 1997. It is a system that unlike traditional RNNs doesn't have the vanishing gradient problem. LSTM is normally augmented by recurrent gates called forget gates. LSTM RNNs prevent backpropagated errors from vanishing or exploding. Instead errors can flow backwards through unlimited numbers of virtual layers in LSTM RNNs unfolded in space. That is, LSTM can learn "Very Deep Learning" tasks that require memories of events that happened thousands or even millions of discrete time steps ago. Problem-specific LSTM-like topologies can be evolved. LSTM works even when there are long delays, and it can handle signals that have a mix of low and high frequency components.

Today, many applications use stacks of LSTM RNNs and train them by Connectionist Temporal Classification (CTC) to find an RNN weight matrix that maximizes the probability of the label sequences in a training set, given the corresponding input sequences. CTC achieves both alignment and recognition. In 2009, CTC-trained LSTM was the first RNN to win pattern recognition contests, when it won several competitions in connected handwriting recognition. Already in 2003, LSTM started to become competitive with traditional speech recognizers on certain tasks. In 2007, the combination with CTC achieved first good results on speech data. Since then, this approach has revolutionised speech recognition. In 2014, the Chinese search giant Baidu used CTC-trained RNNs to break the Switchboard Hub5'00 speech recognition benchmark, without using any traditional speech processing methods, LSTM also improved large-vocabulary speech recognition, text-to-speech synthesis, also for Google Android, and photo-real talking heads. In 2015, Google's speech recognition reportedly experienced a dramatic performance jump of 49% through CTC-trained LSTM, which is now available through Google Voice to billions of smartphone users.

LSTM has also become very popular in the field of Natural Language Processing. Unlike previous models based on HMMs and similar concepts, LSTM can learn to recognise context-sensitive languages. LSTM improved machine translation, Language modeling and Multilingual Language Processing. LSTM combined with Convolutional Neural Networks (CNNs) also improved automatic image captioning and a plethora of other applications.

1.5.8 Deep belief networks

A deep belief network (DBN) is a probabilistic, generative model made up of multiple layers of hidden units. It can be considered a composition of simple learning modules that make up each layer. A DBN can be used to generatively pre-train a DNN by using the learned DBN weights as the initial DNN weights. Back-propagation or other discriminative algorithms can then be applied for fine-tuning of these weights. This is particularly helpful when limited training data are available, because poorly initialized weights can significantly hinder the learned model's performance. These pre-trained weights are in a region of the weight space that is closer to the optimal weights than are randomly chosen initial weights. This allows for both improved modeling and faster convergence of the fine-tuning phase.

A DBN can be efficiently trained in an unsupervised, layer-by-layer manner, where the layers are typically made of restricted Boltzmann machines (RBM). An RBM is an undirected, generative energy-based model with a "visible" input layer and a hidden layer, and connections between the layers but not within layers. The training method for RBMs proposed by Geoffrey Hinton for use with training "Product of Expert" models is called contrastive divergence (CD). CD provides an approximation to the maximum likelihood method that would ideally be applied for learning the weights of the RBM

1.5.9 Convolutional deep belief networks

A recent achievement in deep learning is the use of convolutional deep belief networks (CDBN). CDBNs have structure very similar to a convolutional neural networks and are trained similar to deep belief networks. Therefore, they exploit the 2D structure of images, like CNNs do, and make use of pre-training like deep belief networks. They provide a generic structure which can be used in many image and signal processing tasks. Recently, many benchmark results on standard image datasets like CIFAR have been obtained using CDBNs.

1.5.10 Large memory storage and retrieval neural networks

Large memory storage and retrieval neural networks (LAMSTAR) are fast deep learning neural networks of many layers which can use many filters simultaneously. These filters may be nonlinear, stochastic, logic, non-stationary, or even non-analytical. They are biologically motivated and continuously learning.

A LAMSTAR neural network may serve as a dynamic neural network in spatial or time domain or both. Its speed is provided by Hebbian link-weights (Chapter 9 of in D. Graupe, 2013, which serve to integrate the various and usually different filters (preprocessing functions) into its many layers and to dynamically rank the significance of the various layers and functions relative to a given task for deep learning. This grossly imitates biological learning which integrates outputs various preprocessors (cochlea, retina, etc.) and cortexes (auditory, visual, etc.) and their various regions. Its deep learning capability is further enhanced by using inhibition, correlation and by its ability to cope with incomplete data, or "lost" neurons or layers even at the midst of a task. Furthermore, it is fully transparent due to its link weights. The link-weights also allow dynamic determination of innovation and redundancy, and facilitate the ranking of layers, of filters or of individual neurons relative to a task.

LAMSTAR has been applied to many medical and financial predictions (see Graupe, 2013] Section 9C), adaptive filtering of noisy speech in unknown noise,[152]still-image recognition (Graupe, 2013 Section 9D), video image recognition, software security,[156] adaptive control of non-linear systems, and others. LAMSTAR had a much faster computing speed and somewhat lower error than a convolutional neural network based on ReLU-function filters and max pooling, in a comparative character recognition study.

These applications demonstrate delving into aspects of the data that are hidden from shallow learning networks or even from the human senses (eye, ear), such as in the cases of predicting onset of sleep apnea events,[149] of an electrocardiogram of a fetus as recorded from skin-surface electrodes placed on the mother's abdomen early in pregnancy,[150] of financial prediction (Section 9C in Graupe, 2013), or in blind filtering of noisy speech.

LAMSTAR was proposed in 1996 (A U.S. Patent 5,920,852 A) and was further developed by D Graupe and H Kordylewski 1997-2002. A modified version, known as LAMSTAR 2, was developed by N C Schneider and D Graupe in 2008.

1.5.11 Deep Boltzmann machines

A deep Boltzmann machine (DBM) is a type of binary pairwise Markov random field (undirected probabilistic graphical model) with multiple layers of hidden random variables. It is a network of symmetrically coupled stochastic binary units.

Like DBNs, DBMs can learn complex and abstract internal representations of the input in tasks such as object or speech recognition, using limited labeled data to fine-tune the representations built using a large supply of unlabeled sensory input data. However, unlike DBNs and deep convolutional neural networks, they adopt the inference and training procedure in both directions, bottom-up and top-down pass, which allow the DBMs to better unveil the representations of the ambiguous and complex input structures.

However, the speed of DBMs limits their performance and functionality. Because exact maximum likelihood learning is intractable for DBMs, we may perform approximate maximum likelihood learning. Another option is to use mean-field inference to estimate data-dependent expectations, and approximation the expected sufficient statistics of the model by using Markov chain Monte Carlo (MCMC). This approximate inference, which must be done for each test input, is about 25 to 50 times slower than a single bottom-up pass in DBMs. This makes the joint optimization impractical for large data sets, and seriously restricts the use of DBMs for tasks such as feature representation.

1.5.12 Encoder–decoder networks

An encoder–decoder framework is a framework based on neural networks that aims to map highly structured input to highly structured output. It was proposed recently in the context of machine translation where the input and output are written sentences in two natural languages. In that work, an LSTM recurrent neural network (RNN) or convolutional neural network (CNN) was used as an encoder to summarize a source sentence, and the summary was decoded using a conditional recurrent neural network language model to produce the translation. All these systems have the same building blocks: gated RNNs and CNNs, and trained attention mechanisms.

1.5.13 Deep learning applications

Deep ñearning is used in various facets of science. The most common applications are the following:

- Automatic speech recognition
- Image recognition
- Natural language processing
- Drug discovery and toxicology
- Customer relationship management
- Recommendation systems
- Biomedical informatics

1.6 DEEP LEARNING WITH MATLAB: NEURAL NETWORK TOOLBOX (DEEP LEARNING TOOLBOX FROM VERSION 18)

MATLAB has the tool Neural Network Toolbox (Deep Learning Toolbox from version 18) that provides algorithms, functions, and apps to create, train, visualize, and simulate neural networks. You can perform classification, regression, clustering, dimensionality reduction, time-series forecasting, and dynamic system modeling and control.

The toolbox includes convolutional neural network and autoencoder deep learning algorithms for image classification and feature learning tasks. To speed up training of large data sets, you can distribute computations and data across multicore processors, GPUs, and computer clusters using Parallel Computing Toolbox.

The more important features are the following:

- Deep learning, including convolutional neural networks and autoencoders
- Parallel computing and GPU support for accelerating training (with Parallel Computing Toolbox)
- Supervised learning algorithms, including multilayer, radial basis, learning vector quantization (LVQ), time-delay, nonlinear autoregressive (NARX), and recurrent neural network (RNN)
- Unsupervised learning algorithms, including self-organizing maps and competitive layers
- Apps for data-fitting, pattern recognition, and clustering
- Preprocessing, postprocessing, and network visualization for improving training efficiency and assessing network performance
- Simulink® blocks for building and evaluating neural networks and for control systems applications

Neural networks are composed of simple elements operating in parallel. These elements are inspired by biological nervous systems. As in nature, the connections between elements largely determine the network function. You can train a neural network to perform a particular function by adjusting the values of the connections (weights) between elements.

Typically, neural networks are adjusted, or trained, so that a particular input leads to a specific target output. The next figure illustrates such a situation. Here, the network is adjusted, based on a comparison of the output and the target, until the network output matches the target. Typically, many such input/target pairs are needed to train a network.

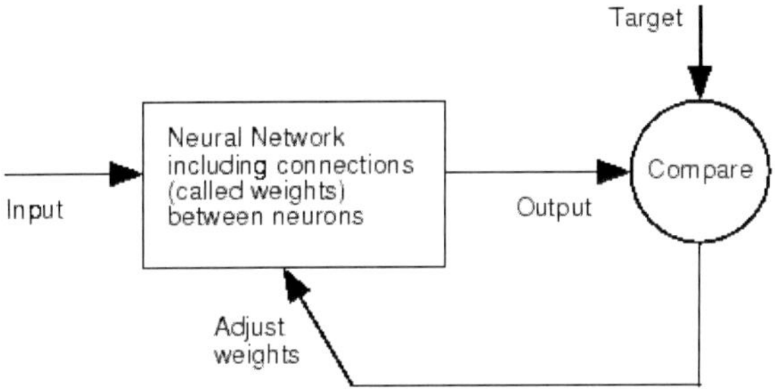

Neural networks have been trained to perform complex functions in various fields, including pattern recognition, identification, classification, speech, vision, and control systems.

Neural networks can also be trained to solve problems that are difficult for conventional computers or human beings. The toolbox emphasizes the use of neural network paradigms that build up to—or are themselves used in— engineering, financial, and other practical applications.

1.7 USING NEURAL NETWORK TOOLBOX (DEEP LEARNING TOOLBOX FROM VERSION 18)

There are four ways you can use the Neural Network Toolbox (Deep Learning Toolbox from version 18) software.

- The first way is through its tools. You can open any of these tools from a master tool started by the command nnstart. These tools provide a convenient way to access the capabilities of the toolbox for the following tasks:

    - Function fitting (*nftool*)
    - Pattern recognition (*nprtool*)

  - Data clustering (*nctool*)
  - Time-series analysis (*ntstool*)

- The second way to use the toolbox is through basic command-line operations. The command-line operations offer more flexibility than the tools, but with some added complexity. If this is your first experience with the toolbox, the tools provide the best introduction. In addition, the tools can generate scripts of documented MATLAB code to provide you with templates for creating your own customized command-line functions. The process of using the tools first, and then generating and modifying MATLAB scripts, is an excellent way to learn about the functionality of the toolbox.

- The third way to use the toolbox is through customization. This advanced capability allows you to create your own custom neural networks, while still having access to the full functionality of the toolbox. You can create networks with arbitrary connections, and you still be able to train them using existing toolbox training functions (as long as the network components are differentiable).

- The fourth way to use the toolbox is through the ability to modify any of the functions contained in the toolbox. Every computational component is written in MATLAB code and is fully accessible.

These four levels of toolbox usage span the novice to the expert: simple tools guide the new user through specific applications, and network customization allows researchers to try novel architectures with minimal effort. Whatever your level of neural network and MATLAB knowledge, there are toolbox features to suit your needs.

1.8 AUTOMATIC SCRIPT GENERATION

The tools themselves form an important part of the learning process for the Neural Network Toolbox (Deep Learning Toolbox from version 18) software. They guide you through the process of designing neural networks to solve problems in four important application areas, without requiring any background in neural networks or sophistication in using MATLAB. In addition, the tools can automatically generate both simple and advanced MATLAB scripts that can reproduce the steps performed by the tool, but with the option to override default settings. These scripts can provide you with templates for creating customized code, and they can aid you in becoming familiar with the command-line functionality of the toolbox. It is highly recommended that you use the automatic script generation facility of these tools.

1.9 NEURAL NETWORK TOOLBOX (DEEP LEARNING TOOLBOX FROM VERSION 18) APPLICATIONS

It would be impossible to cover the total range of applications for which neural networks have provided outstanding solutions. The remaining sections of this topic describe only a few of the applications in function fitting, pattern recognition, clustering, and time-series analysis. The following table provides an idea of the diversity of applications for which neural networks provide state-of-the-art solutions.

Industry	**Business Applications**
Aerospace	High-performance aircraft autopilot, flight path simulation, aircraft control systems, autopilot enhancements, aircraft component simulation, and aircraft component fault detection
Automotive	Automobile automatic guidance system, and warranty activity analysis
Banking	Check and other document reading and credit application evaluation
Defense	Weapon steering, target tracking, object discrimination, facial recognition, new kinds of sensors, sonar, radar and image signal processing including data compression, feature extraction and noise suppression, and signal/image identification
Electronics	Code sequence prediction, integrated circuit chip layout, process control, chip failure analysis, machine vision, voice synthesis, and nonlinear modeling
Entertainment	Animation, special effects, and market forecasting
Financial	Real estate appraisal, loan advising, mortgage screening, corporate bond rating, credit-line use analysis, credit card activity tracking, portfolio trading program, corporate financial analysis, and currency price prediction
Industrial	Prediction of industrial processes, such as the output gases of furnaces, replacing complex and costly equipment used for this purpose in the past
Insurance	Policy application evaluation and product optimization
Manufacturing	Manufacturing process control, product design and analysis, process and machine diagnosis, real-time particle identification, visual quality inspection systems, beer testing, welding quality analysis, paper quality prediction, computer-chip quality analysis, analysis of grinding operations, chemical product design analysis, machine maintenance analysis, project bidding, planning and management, and dynamic modeling of chemical process system
Medical	Breast cancer cell analysis, EEG and ECG analysis, prosthesis design, optimization of transplant times, hospital expense

Industry	Business Applications
	reduction, hospital quality improvement, and emergency-room test advisement
Oil and gas	Exploration
Robotics	Trajectory control, forklift robot, manipulator controllers, and vision systems
Securities	Market analysis, automatic bond rating, and stock trading advisory systems
Speech	Speech recognition, speech compression, vowel classification, and text-to-speech synthesis
Telecommunications	Image and data compression, automated information services, real-time translation of spoken language, and customer payment processing systems
Transportation	Truck brake diagnosis systems, vehicle scheduling, and routing systems

1.10 NEURAL NETWORK DESIGN STEPS

The standard steps for designing neural networks to solve problems are the following:

1. Collect data
2. Create the network
3. Configure the network
4. Initialize the weights and biases
5. Train the network
6. Validate the network
7. Use the network

There are four typical neural networks application areas: function fitting, pattern recognition, clustering, and time-series analysis.

Chapter 2

CONVOLUTIONAL NEURAL NETWORKS WITH MATLAB. FUNCTIONS

2.1 PERFORM CLASSIFICATION, FEATURE EXTRACTION, AND TRANSFER LEARNING USING CONVOLUTIONAL NEURAL NETWORKS (CNNS, CONVNETS)

Convolution neural networks (CNNs or ConvNets) are essential tools for deep learning, and are especially suited for image recognition. You can construct a CNN architecture, train a network, and use the trained network to predict class labels. You can also extract features from a pre-trained network, and use these features to train a linear classifier. Neural Network Toolbox (Deep Learning Toolbox from version 18) also enables you to perform transfer learning; that is, retrain the last fully connected layer of an existing CNN on new data.

2.2 CONSTRUCT NETWORK ARCHITECTURE. FUNCTIONS

MATLAB has the following functions:

`imageInputLayer`	Image input layer
`convolution2dLayer`	Convolutional layer
`reluLayer`	Rectified Linear Unit (ReLU) layer
`crossChannelNormalizationLayer`	Channel-wise local response normalization layer
`averagePooling2dLayer`	Average pooling layer object

`maxPooling2dLayer`	Max pooling layer
`fullyConnectedLayer`	Fully connected layer
`dropoutLayer`	Dropout layer
`softmaxLayer`	Softmax layer
`classificationLayer`	Create a classification output layer

2.2.1 Create an image input layer: imageInputLayer

Syntax

- `inputlayer = imageInputLayer(inputSize)`
- `inputlayer = imageInputLayer(inputSize,Name,Value)`

Description

`inputlayer = imageInputLayer(inputSize)` returns an image input layer.

`inputlayer = imageInputLayer(inputSize,Name,Value)` returns an image input layer, with additional options specified by one or more `Name,Value` pair arguments. For example, you can specify a name for the layer.

Examples: Create Image Input Layer

Create an image input layer for 28-by-28 color images. Specify that the software flips the images from left to right at training time with a probability of 0.5.

```
inputlayer = imageInputLayer([28 28
3],'DataAugmentation','randfliplr')
```

```
inputlayer =

  ImageInputLayer with properties:

                Name: ''
           InputSize: [28 28 3]
    DataAugmentation: 'randfliplr'
       Normalization: 'zerocenter'
```

Input Arguments

`inputSize` — Size of input data

row vector of two or three integer numbers

Size of the input data, specified as a row vector of two integer numbers corresponding to `[height,width]` or three integer numbers corresponding to `[height,width,channels]`.
If the `inputSize` is a vector of two numbers, then the software sets the channel size to 1.
Example: `[200,200,3]`
Data Types: `single` | `double`

Name-Value Pair Arguments

Specify optional comma-separated pairs of `Name,Value` arguments. `Name` is the argument name and `Value` is the corresponding value. `Name` must appear inside single quotes (`' '`). You can specify several name and value pair arguments in any order as `Name1,Value1,...,NameN,ValueN`.

Example: `'DataAugmentation','randcrop','Normalization','none','Name','input'` specifies that the software takes a random crop of the image at training time, does not normalize the data, and assigns the name of the layer as `input`.

`'DataAugmentation'` — Data augmentation transforms
`'none'` (default) | `'randcrop'` | `'randfliplr'` | cell array of `'randcrop'` and `'randfliplr'`

Data augmentation transforms to use during training, specified as the comma-separated pair consisting of `'DataAugmentation'` and one of the following.

- `'none'` — No data augmentation
- `'randcrop'` — Take a random crop from the training image. The random crop has the same size as the `inputSize`.
- `'randfliplr'` — Randomly flip the input images from left to right with a 50% chance in the vertical axis.
- Cell array of `'randcrop'` and `'randfliplr'`. The software applies the augmentation in the order specified in the cell array.

Augmentation of image data is another way of reducing overfitting

Example: `'DataAugmentation',{'randfliplr','randcrop'}`

Data Types: `char` | `cell`

`'Normalization'` — Data transformation
`'zerocenter'` (default) | `'none'`

Data transformation to apply every time data is forward-propagated through the input layer, specified as the comma-separated pair consisting of `'Normalization'` and one of the following.

- `'zerocenter'` — The software subtracts its mean from the training set.
- `'none'` — No transformation.

Example: `'Normalization','none'`

Data Types: `char`

`'Name'` — Name for the layer
`''` (default) | character vector

Name for the layer, specified as the comma-separated pair consisting of `Name` and a character vector.

Example: `'Name','inputlayer'`
Data Types: `char`

Output Arguments

`inputlayer` — Input layer for the image data

`ImageInputLayer` object

Input layer for the image data, returned as an `ImageInputLayer` object.
For information on concatenating layers to construct convolutional neural network architecture, see `Layer`.

2.2.2 Create 2-D convolutional layer: convolution2dLayer

Syntax

- `convlayer = convolution2dLayer(filterSize,numFilters)`
- `convlayer = convolution2dLayer(filterSize,numFilters,Name,Value)`

Description

`convlayer = convolution2dLayer(filterSize,numFilters)` returns a layer for 2-D convolution.

`convlayer = convolution2dLayer(filterSize,numFilters,Name,Value)` returns the convolutional layer, with additional options specified by one or more `Name,Value` pair arguments.

Examples:

Create convolutional layer

Create a convolutional layer with 96 filters, each with a height and width of 11. Use a stride (step size) of 4 in the horizontal and vertical directions.

```
convlayer = convolution2dLayer(11,96,'Stride',4);
```

Specify Initial Weight and Biases in Convolutional Layer

Create a convolutional layer with 32 filters, each with a height and width of 5. Pad the input image with 2 pixels along its border. Set the learning rate factor for the bias to 2. Manually initialize the weights from a Gaussian distribution with a standard deviation of 0.0001.

```
layer =
convolution2dLayer(5,32,'Padding',2,'BiasLearnRateFactor',2);
```

Suppose the input has color images. Manually initialize the weights from a Gaussian distribution with standard deviation of 0.0001.

```
layer.Weights = randn([5 5 3 32])*0.0001;
```

The size of the local regions in the layer is 5-by-5. The number of color channels for each region is 3. The number of feature maps is 32 (the number of filters). Therefore, there are 5*5*3*32 weights in the layer.

`randn([5 5 3 32])` returns a 5-by-5-by-3-by-32 array of values from a Gaussian distribution with a mean of 0 and a standard deviation of 1. Multiplying the values by 0.0001 sets the standard deviation of the Gaussian distribution equal to 0.0001. Similarly, initialize the biases from a Gaussian distribution with a mean of 1 and a standard deviation of 0.00001.

```
layer.Bias = randn([1 1 32])*0.00001+1;
```

There are 32 feature maps, and therefore 32 biases. `randn([1 1 32])` returns a 1-by-1-by-32 array of values from a Gaussian distribution with a mean of 0 and a standard deviation of 1. Multiplying the values by 0.00001 sets the standard deviation of values equal to 0.00001, and adding 1 sets the mean of the Gaussian distribution equal to 1.

Convolution That Fully Covers the Input Image

Suppose the size of the input image is 28-by-28-1. Create a convolutional layer with 16 filters that have a height of 6 and a width of 4, that traverses the image with a stride of 4 both horizontally and vertically. Make sure the convolution covers the images completely.

For the convolution to fully cover the input image, both the horizontal and vertical output dimensions must be integer numbers. For the horizontal output dimension to be an integer, one row zero padding is required on the top and bottom of the image: (28 – 6+ 2*1)/4 + 1 = 7. For the vertical output dimension to be an integer, no zero padding is required: (28 – 4+ 2*0)/4 + 1 = 7. Construct the convolutional layer as follows:

```
convlayer = convolution2dLayer([6 4],16,'Stride',4,'Padding',[1
0]);
```

Input Arguments

FILTERSIZE — height and width of filters integer value | vector of two integer values

Height and width of the filters, specified as an integer value or a vector of two integer values. `filterSize` defines the size of the local regions to which the neurons connect in the input.

- If `filterSize` is a scalar value, then the filters have the same height and width.
- If `filterSize` is a vector, then it must be of the form [*h* *w*], where *h* is the height and *w* is the width.

Example: `[5,5]`
Data Types: `single` | `doublé`

NUMFILTERS — Number of filters integer value

Number of filters, specified as an integer value. `numFilters` represents the number of neurons in the convolutional layer that connect to the same region in the input. This parameter determines the number of channels (feature maps) in the output of the convolutional layer.

Data Types: `single` | `doublé`

Output Arguments

CONVLAYER — 2-D convolutional layer Convolution2DLayer object

2-D convolutional layer for convolutional neural networks, returned as a `Convolution2DLayer` object.

Convolutional Layer

A convolutional layer consists of neurons that connect to small regions of the input or the layer before it. These regions are called *filters*. You can specify the size of these regions using the `filterSize` input argument.

For each region, the software computes a dot product of the weights and the input, and then adds a bias term. The filter then moves along the input vertically and horizontally, repeating the same computation for each region, i.e., convolving the input. The step size with which it moves is called a *stride*. You can specify this step size with the `Stride` name-value pair argument. These local regions that the neurons connect to might overlap depending on the `filterSize` and `Stride`.

The number of weights used for a filter is *h*w*c*, where *h* is the height, and *w* is the width of the filter size, and *c* is the number of channels in the input (for example, if the input is a color image, the number of channels is three). As a filter moves along the input, it uses the same set of weights and bias for the convolution, forming a feature map. The convolution layer usually has multiple feature maps, each with a different set of weights and a bias. The number of feature maps is determined by the number of filters.

The total number of parameters in a convolutional layer is ((*h*w*c* + 1)**Number of Filters*), where 1 is for the bias.

The output height and width of the convolutional layer is (*Input Size* – *Filter Size* + 2**Padding*)/*Stride* + 1. This value must be an integer for the whole image to be fully covered. If the combination of these parameters does not lead the image to be fully covered, the software by default ignores the remaining part of the image along the right and bottom edge in the convolution.

The total number of neurons in a feature map, say *Map Size*, is the product of the output height and width. The total number of neurons (output size) in a convolutional layer, then, is *Map Size*Number of Filters*.

For example, suppose that the input image is a 28-by-28-by-3 color image. For a convolutional layer with 16 filters, and a filter size of 8-by-8, the number of weights per filter is 8*8*3 = 192, and the total number of parameters in the layer is (192+1) * 16 = 3088. Assuming stride is 4 in each direction, the total number of neurons in each feature map is 6-by-6 ((28 – 8+0)/4 + 1 = 6). Then, the total number of neurons in the layer is 6*6*16 = 256. Usually, the results from these neurons pass through some form of nonlinearity, such as rectified linear units (ReLU).

2.2.3 Create a Rectified Linear Unit (ReLU) layer: reluLayer

Syntax

- `layer = reluLayer()`
- `layer = reluLayer(Name,Value)`

Description

`layer = reluLayer()` returns a rectified linear unit (ReLU) layer. It performs a threshold operation to each element, where any input value less than zero is set to zero, i.e.,

$$f(x) = \begin{cases} x, & x \geq 0 \\ 0, & x < 0 \end{cases}.$$

The ReLU layer does not change the size of its input.

`layer = reluLayer(Name,Value)` returns a ReLU layer, with the additional option specified by the `Name,Value` pair argument.

Examples

Create a rectified linear unit layer with the name `relu1`.

```
layer = reluLayer('Name','relu1');
```

2.2.4 Create a local response normalization layer: crossChannelNormalizationLayer

Syntax

- `localnormlayer = crossChannelNormalizationLayer(windowChannelSize)`
- `localnormlayer = crossChannelNormalizationLayer(windowChannelSize,Name,Value)`

Description

`localnormlayer = crossChannelNormalizationLayer(windowChannelSize)` returns a local response normalization layer, which carries out channel-wise normalization [1].

`localnormlayer = crossChannelNormalizationLayer(windowChannelSize,Name,Value)` returns a local response normalization layer, with additional options specified by one or more `Name,Value` pair arguments.

Examples

Create a local response normalization layer for channel-wise normalization, where a window of five channels will be used to normalize each element, and the additive constant for the normalizer (*K*) is 1.

```
localnormlayer = crossChannelNormalizationLayer(5,'K',1);
```

2.2.5 Create an average pooling layer: averagePooling2dLayer

Syntax

- `avgpoollayer = averagePooling2dLayer(poolSize)`
- `avgpoollayer = averagePooling2dLayer(poolSize,Name,Value)`

Description

`avgpoollayer = averagePooling2dLayer(poolSize)` returns a layer that performs average pooling, dividing the input into rectangular regions and computing the average of each region. `poolSize` specifies the dimensions of the rectangular region.

`avgpoollayer = averagePooling2dLayer(poolSize,Name,Value)` returns the average pooling layer, with additional options specified by one or more `Name,Value` pair arguments.

Examples:

Average Pooling Layer with Non-Overlapping Pooling Regions

Create an average pooling layer with non-overlapping pooling regions, which down-samples by a factor of 2.

```
avgpoollayer = averagePooling2dLayer(2,'Stride',2);
```

The height and width of the rectangular region (pool size) are both 2. This layer creates pooling regions of size [2,2] and takes the average of the four elements in each region. Because the stride (step size for moving along the images vertically and horizontally) is also [2,2] the pooling regions do not overlap.

Average Pooling Layer with Overlapping Pooling Regions

Create an average pooling layer with overlapping pooling regions. Also add padding for the top and bottom of the input.

```
avgpoollayer = averagePooling2dLayer([3,2],'Stride',2,'Padding',[1
0]);
```

The height and width of the rectangular region (pool size) are 3 and 2. This layer creates pooling regions of size [3,2] and takes the average of the six elements in each region. Because the stride is [2,2], the pooling regions overlap.

A value of `1` for the `Padding` name-value pair indicates that software also adds a row of zeros to the top and bottom of the input data. `0` indicates that no padding is added to the right and left of the input data.

2.2.6 Create max pooling layer: maxPooling2dLayer

Syntax

- `maxpoollayer = maxPooling2dLayer(poolSize)`
- `maxpoollayer = maxPooling2dLayer(poolSize,Name,Value)`

Description

`maxpoollayer = maxPooling2dLayer(poolSize)` returns a layer that performs max pooling, dividing the input into rectangular regions and returning the maximum value of each region. `poolSize` specifies the dimensions of a pooling region.

`maxpoollayer = maxPooling2dLayer(poolSize,Name,Value)` returns the max pooling layer, with additional options specified by one or more `Name,Value` pair arguments.

Examples:

Max Pooling Layer with Non-Overlapping Pooling Regions

Create a max pooling layer with non-overlapping pooling regions, which down-samples by a factor of 2.

```
maxpoollayer = maxPooling2dLayer(2,'Stride',2);
```

The height and width of the rectangular region (pool size) are both 2. This layer creates pooling regions of size [2,2] and returns the maximum of the four elements in each region. Because the stride (step size for moving along the images vertically and horizontally) is also [2,2], the pooling regions do not overlap.

Max Pooling Layer with Overlapping Pooling Regions

Create a max pooling layer with overlapping pooling regions. Also add padding for the top and bottom of the input.

```
maxpoollayer = maxPooling2dLayer([3,2],'Stride',2,'Padding',[1 0]);
```

The height and width of the rectangular region (pool size) are 3 and 2. This layer creates pooling regions of size [3,2] and returns the maximum of the six elements in each region. Because the stride (step size for moving along the images vertically and horizontally) is [2,2], the pooling regions overlap.

The value 1 for the `Padding` name-value pair indicates that the software adds a row of zeros to the top and bottom of the input data. `0` indicates that no padding is added to the right and left of the input data.

2.2.7 Create fully connected layer: fullyConnectedLayer

Syntax

- `fullconnectlayer = fullyConnectedLayer(outputSize)`
- `fullconnectlayer = fullyConnectedLayer(outputSize,Name,Value)`

Description

`fullconnectlayer = fullyConnectedLayer(outputSize)` returns a fully connected layer, in which the software multiplies the input by a weight matrix and then adds a bias vector.

`fullconnectlayer = fullyConnectedLayer(outputSize,Name,Value)` returns a fully connected layer with additional options specified by one or more `Name,Value` pair arguments.

Examples:

Create Fully Connected Layer

Create a fully connected layer with an output size of 10.

```
fullconnectlayer = fullyConnectedLayer(10);
```

The software determines the input size at training time.

Specify Initial Weight and Biases in Fully Connected Layer

Create a fully connected layer with an output size of 10. Set the learning rate factor for the bias to 2. Manually initialize the weights from a Gaussian distribution with a standard deviation of 0.0001.

```
layers = [imageInputLayer([28 28 1],'Normalization','none');
          convolution2dLayer(5,20,'NumChannels',1);
          reluLayer();
```

```
        maxPooling2dLayer(2,'Stride',2);
        fullyConnectedLayer(10);
        softmaxLayer();
        classificationLayer()];
```

To initialize the weights of the fully connected layer, you must know the layer's input size. The input size is equal to the output size of the preceding max pooling layer, which, in turn, depends on the output size of the convolutional layer.

For one direction in a channel (feature map) of the convolutional layer, the output is ((28 – 5 + 2*0)/1) +1 = 24. The max pooling layer has nonoverlapping regions, so it down-samples by 2 in each direction, i.e., 24/2 = 12. For one channel of the convolutional layer, the output of the max pooling layer is 12 * 12 = 144. There are 20 channels in the convolutional layer, so the output of the max pooling layer is 144 * 20 = 2880. This is the size of the input to the fully connected layer.

The formula for overlapping regions gives the same result: For one direction of a channel, the output is (((24 – 2 +0)/2) + 1 = 12. For one channel, the output is 144, and for all 20 channels in the convolutional layer, the output of the max pooling layer is 2880.

Initialize the weights of the fully connected layer from a Gaussian distribution with a mean of 0 and a standard deviation of 0.0001.

```
layers(5).Weights = randn([10 2880])*0.0001;
```

`randn([10 2880])` returns a 10-by-2880 matrix of values from a Gaussian distribution with mean 0 and standard deviation 1. Multiplying the values by 0.0001 sets the standard deviation of the Gaussian distribution equal to 0.0001. Similarly, initialize the biases from a Gaussian distribution with a mean of 1 and a standard deviation of 0.0001.

```
layers(5).Bias = randn([10 1])*0.0001+1;
```

The size of the bias vector is equal to the output size of the fully connected layer, which is 10. `randn([10 1])` returns a 10-by-1 vector of values from a Gaussian distribution with a mean of 0 and a standard deviation of 1. Multiplying the values by 0.00001 sets the standard deviation of values equal to 0.00001, and adding 1 sets the mean of the Gaussian distribution equal to 1.

2.2.8 Create a dropout layer: dropoutLayer

Syntax

- `droplayer = dropoutLayer()`
- `droplayer = dropoutLayer(probability)`
- `droplayer = dropoutLayer(___,Name,Value)`

Description

`droplayer = dropoutLayer()` returns a dropout layer, which randomly sets input elements to zero with a probability of 0.5. Dropout layer only works at training time.

`droplayer = dropoutLayer(probability)` returns a dropout layer, which randomly sets input elements to zero with a probability specified by `probability`.

`droplayer = dropoutLayer(___,Name,Value)` returns the dropout layer, with the additional option specified by the `Name,Value` pair argument.

Examples

Create a dropout layer, which randomly sets about 40% of the input to zero. Assign the name of the layer as `dropout1`.

```
droplayer = dropoutLayer(0.4,'Name','dropout1');
```

2.2.9 Create a softmax layer softmaxLayer

Syntax

- `smlayer = softmaxLayer()`
- `smlayer = softmaxLayer(Name,Value)`

Description

`smlayer = softmaxLayer()` returns a softmax layer for classification problems. The softmax layer uses the softmax activation function.

`smlayer = softmaxLayer(Name,Value)` returns a softmax layer, with the additional option specified by the `Name,Value` pair argument.

Examples

Create Softmax Layer with Specified Name

Create a softmax layer with the name `sml1`.

```
smlayer = softmaxLayer('Name','sml1');
```

2.2.10 Create a classification output layer: classificationLayer

Syntax

- `coutputlayer = classificationLayer()`

- `coutputlayer = classificationLayer(Name,Value)`

Description

`coutputlayer = classificationLayer()` returns a classification output layer for a neural network. The classification output layer holds the name of the loss function that the software uses for training the network for multi-class classification, the size of the output, and the class labels.

`coutputlayer = classificationLayer(Name,Value)` returns the classification output layer, with the additional option specified by the `Name,Value` pair argument.

Examples

Create a classification output layer with the name `'coutput'`.

```
coutputlayer = classificationLayer('Name','coutput')
coutputlayer =

  ClassificationOutputLayer with properties:

      OutputSize: 'auto'
    LossFunction: 'crossentropyex'
      ClassNames: {}
            Name: 'coutput'
```

The software determines the output layer automatically during training. The default loss function for classification is cross entropy for *k* mutually exclusive classes.

2.3 TRAIN NETWORKS. FUNCTIONS

MATLAB has the following functions:

`trainingOptions`	Options for training neural network
`trainNetwork`	Train a network

2.3.1 Train network: trainNetwork

Syntax

- `trainedNet = trainNetwork(imds,layers,options)`
- `trainedNet = trainNetwork(X,Y,layers,options)`
- `[trainedNet,traininfo] = trainNetwork(__)`

Description

NOTE: `trainNetwork` requires the Parallel Computing Toolbox and a CUDA®-enabled NVIDIA®GPU with compute capability 3.0 or higher.

`trainedNet = trainNetwork(imds,layers,options)` returns a trained network defined by the convolutional neural network (ConvNet) architecture, `layers`, for the input image data, `imds`, using the training options, `options`.

`trainedNet = trainNetwork(X,Y,layers,options)` returns a trained network for the predictors in `X` and responses in `Y`.

`[trainedNet,traininfo] = trainNetwork(__)` also returns information on the training for any of the above input arguments.

Examples:

Train a Convolutional Neural Network Using Data in ImageDatastore

Load the sample data as an `ImageDatastore` object.

```
digitDatasetPath =
fullfile(matlabroot,'toolbox','nnet','nndemos',...
    'nndatasets','DigitDataset');
digitData = imageDatastore(digitDatasetPath,...
        'IncludeSubfolders',true,'LabelSource','foldernames');
```

The data store contains 10000 synthetic images of digits 0-9. The images are generated by applying random transformations to digit images created using different fonts. Each digit image is 28-by-28 pixels.

Display some of the images in the datastore.

```
for i = 1:20
    subplot(4,5,i);
    imshow(digitData.Files{i});
end
```

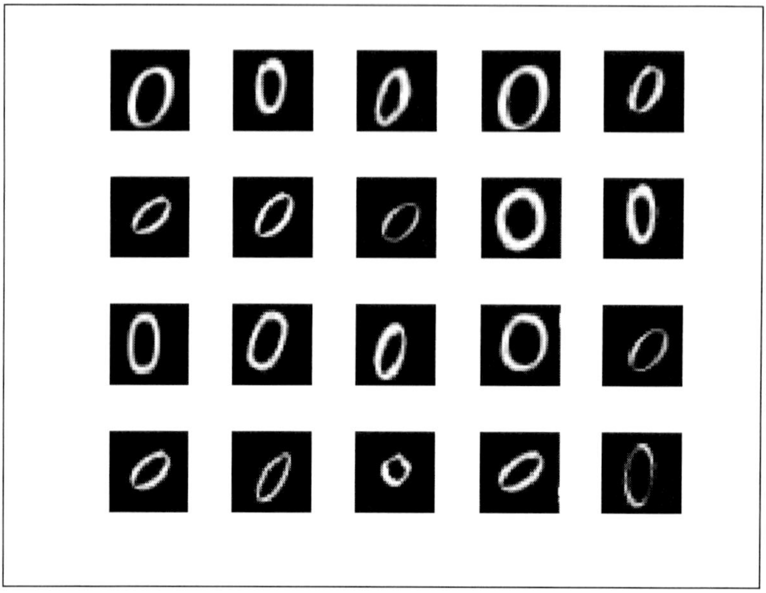

Check the number of images in each digit category.

```
digitData.countEachLabel
ans =

    Label    Count
    _____    _____

    0          988
    1         1026
    2         1003
    3          993
    4          991
    5         1017
    6          992
    7          999
    8         1003
    9          988
```

The data contains an unequal number of images per category.

To balance the number of images for each digit in the training set, first find the minimum number of images in a category.

```
minSetCount = min(digitData.countEachLabel{:,2})
```

```
minSetCount =

   988
```

Divide the dataset so that each category in the training set has 494 images and the testing set has the remaining images from each label.

```
trainingNumFiles = round(minSetCount/2);
rng(1) % For reproducibility
[trainDigitData,testDigitData] = splitEachLabel(digitData,...
                                 trainingNumFiles,'randomize');
```

`splitEachLabel` splits the image files in `digitData` into two new datastores, `trainDigitData` and `testDigitData`.

Define the convolutional neural network architecture.

```
layers = [imageInputLayer([28 28 1]);
          convolution2dLayer(5,20);
          reluLayer();
          maxPooling2dLayer(2,'Stride',2);
          fullyConnectedLayer(10);
          softmaxLayer();
          classificationLayer()];
```

Set the options to default settings for the stochastic gradient descent with momentum. Set the maximum number of epochs at 20, and start the training with an initial learning rate of 0.001.

```
options = trainingOptions('sgdm','MaxEpochs',20,...
        'InitialLearnRate',0.001);
```

Train the network.

```
convnet = trainNetwork(trainDigitData,layers,options);
```

Epoch	Iteration	Time Elapsed (seconds)	Mini-batch Loss	Mini-batch Accuracy	Base Learning Rate
2	50	0.72	0.2232	92.97%	0.001000
3	100	1.37	0.0182	99.22%	0.001000
4	150	1.99	0.0141	100.00%	0.001000
6	200	2.64	0.0023	100.00%	0.001000
7	250	3.27	0.0004	100.00%	0.001000
8	300	3.91	0.0001	100.00%	0.001000
10	350	4.56	0.0002	100.00%	0.001000
11	400	5.19	0.0003	100.00%	0.001000
12	450	5.82	0.0001	100.00%	0.001000
14	500	6.46	0.0001	100.00%	0.001000
15	550	7.09	0.0001	100.00%	0.001000
16	600	7.72	0.0001	100.00%	0.001000
18	650	8.37	0.0001	100.00%	0.001000
19	700	9.00	0.0001	100.00%	0.001000
20	750	9.62	0.0001	100.00%	0.001000

Run the trained network on the test set that was not used to train the network and predict the image labels (digits).

```
YTest = classify(convnet,testDigitData);
TTest = testDigitData.Labels;
```

Calculate the accuracy.

```
accuracy = sum(YTest == TTest)/numel(TTest)
accuracy =

    0.9984
```

Accuracy is the ratio of the number of true labels in the test data matching the classifications from classify, to the number of images in the test data. In this case about 99.8% of the digit estimations match the true digit values in the test set.

Construct and Train a Convolutional Neural Network

Load the sample data.

```
load lettersTrainSet
```

XTrain contains 1500 28-by-28 grayscale images of the letters A, B, and C in a 4-D array. There is equal numbers of each letter in the data set. TTrain contains the categorical array of the letter labels.

Display some of the letter images.

```
figure;
for j = 1:20
    subplot(4,5,j);
    selectImage = datasample(XTrain,1,4);
    imshow(selectImage,[]);
end
```

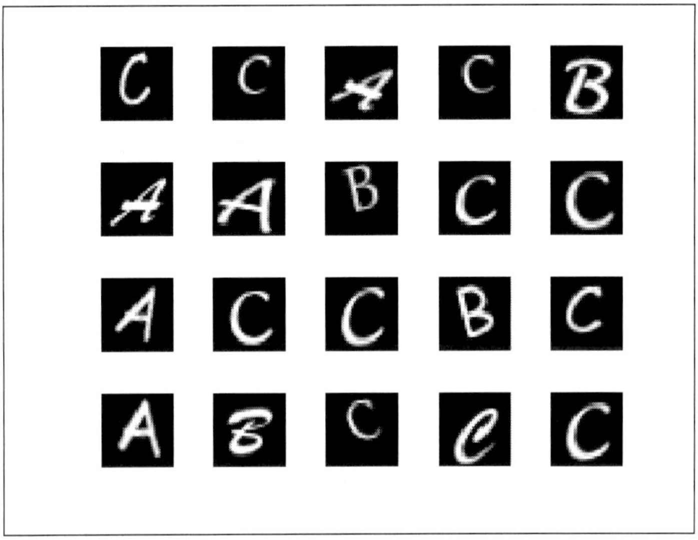

Define the convolutional neural network architecture.

```
layers = [imageInputLayer([28 28 1]);
          convolution2dLayer(5,16);
          reluLayer();
          maxPooling2dLayer(2,'Stride',2);
          fullyConnectedLayer(3);
          softmaxLayer();
          classificationLayer()];
```

Set the options to default settings for the stochastic gradient descent with momentum.

```
options = trainingOptions('sgdm');
```

Train the network.

```
rng('default') % For reproducibility
net = trainNetwork(XTrain,TTrain,layers,options);
```

Epoch	Iteration	Time Elapsed (seconds)	Mini-batch Loss	Mini-batch Accuracy	Base Learning Rate
5	50	0.50	0.2175	98.44%	0.010000
10	100	1.01	0.0238	100.00%	0.010000
14	150	1.52	0.0108	100.00%	0.010000
19	200	2.03	0.0088	100.00%	0.010000
23	250	2.53	0.0048	100.00%	0.010000
28	300	3.04	0.0035	100.00%	0.010000

Run the trained network on a test set that was not used to train the network and predict the image labels (letters).

```
load lettersTestSet;
```

XTest contains 1500 28-by-28 grayscale images of the letters A, B, and C in a 4-D array. There is again equal numbers of each letter in the data set. TTest contains the categorical array of the letter labels.

```
YTest = classify(net,XTest);
```

Compute the confusion matrix.

```
targets(:,1)=(TTest=='A');
targets(:,2)=(TTest=='B');
targets(:,3)=(TTest=='C');
outputs(:,1)=(YTest=='A');
outputs(:,2)=(YTest=='B');
outputs(:,3)=(YTest=='C');

plotconfusion(double(targets'),double(outputs'))
```

2.3.2 Options for training neural network. trainingOptions

Syntax

- `options = trainingOptions(solverName)`
- `options = trainingOptions(solverName,Name,Value)`

Description

`options = trainingOptions(solverName)` returns a set of training options for the solver specified by `solverName`.

`options = trainingOptions(solverName,Name,Value)` returns a set of training options, with additional options specified by one or more `Name,Value` pair arguments.

Examples

Create a set of options for training a network using stochastic gradient descent with momentum. Reduce the learning rate by a factor of 0.2 every 5 epochs. Set the maximum number of epochs for training at 20, and use a mini-batch with 300 observations at each iteration. Specify a path for saving checkpoint networks after every epoch.

```
options = trainingOptions('sgdm',...
      'LearnRateSchedule','piecewise',...
```

```
    'LearnRateDropFactor',0.2,...
    'LearnRateDropPeriod',5,...
    'MaxEpochs',20,...
    'MiniBatchSize',300,...
    'CheckpointPath','C:\TEMP\checkpoint');
```

2.4 EXTRACT FEATURES AND PREDICT OUTCOMES. FUNCTIONS

MATLAB has the following functions:

`activations`	Compute network layer activations
`predict`	Predict responses using a trained network
`classify`	Classify data using a trained network

2.4.1 Compute network layer activations: activations

Syntax

- `features = activations(net,X,layer)`
- `features = activations(net,X,layer,Name,Value)`

Description

`features = activations(net,X,layer)` returns network activations for a specific layer using the trained network `net` and the data in `X`.

`features = activations(net,X,layer,Name,Value)` returns network activations for a specific layer with additional options specified by one or more `Name,Value` pair arguments.

For example, you can specify the format of the output `trainedFeatures`.

Example: Extract Features from Trained Convolutional Neural Network

NOTE: Training a convolutional neural network requires Parallel Computing Toolbox™ and a CUDA®-enabled NVIDIA® GPU with compute capability 3.0 or higher.

Load the sample data.

```
[XTrain,TTrain] = digitTrain4DArrayData;
```

digitTrain4DArrayData loads the digit training set as 4-D array data. XTrain is a 28-by-28-by-1-by-4940 array, where 28 is the height and 28 is the width of the images. 1 is the number of channels and 4940 is the number of synthetic images of handwritten digits. TTrain is a categorical vector containing the labels for each observation.

Construct the convolutional neural network architecture.

```
layers = [imageInputLayer([28 28 1]);
          convolution2dLayer(5,20);
          reluLayer();
          maxPooling2dLayer(2,'Stride',2);
          fullyConnectedLayer(10);
          softmaxLayer();
          classificationLayer()];
```

Set the options to default settings for the stochastic gradient descent with momentum.

```
options = trainingOptions('sgdm');
```

Train the network.

```
rng('default')
net = trainNetwork(XTrain,TTrain,layers,options);
```

Epoch	Iteration	Time Elapsed (seconds)	Mini-batch Loss	Mini-batch Accuracy	Base Learning Rate
2	50	0.45	2.2301	47.66%	0.010000
3	100	0.88	0.9880	75.00%	0.010000
4	150	1.31	0.5558	82.03%	0.010000
6	200	1.75	0.4022	89.06%	0.010000
7	250	2.17	0.3750	88.28%	0.010000
8	300	2.61	0.3368	91.41%	0.010000
10	350	3.04	0.2589	96.09%	0.010000
11	400	3.47	0.1396	98.44%	0.010000
12	450	3.90	0.1802	96.09%	0.010000
14	500	4.33	0.0892	99.22%	0.010000
15	550	4.76	0.1221	96.88%	0.010000
16	600	5.19	0.0961	98.44%	0.010000
18	650	5.62	0.0856	99.22%	0.010000
19	700	6.05	0.0651	100.00%	0.010000
20	750	6.49	0.0582	98.44%	0.010000
22	800	6.92	0.0808	98.44%	0.010000
23	850	7.35	0.0521	99.22%	0.010000
24	900	7.77	0.0248	100.00%	0.010000
25	950	8.20	0.0241	100.00%	0.010000
27	1000	8.63	0.0253	100.00%	0.010000
28	1050	9.07	0.0260	100.00%	0.010000
29	1100	9.49	0.0246	100.00%	0.010000

Make predictions, but rather than taking the output from the last layer, specify the second ReLU layer (the sixth layer) as the output layer.

```
trainFeatures = activations(net,XTrain,6);
```

These predictions from an inner layer are known as *activations* or *features* . `activations` method, by default, uses a CUDA-enabled GPU with compute ccapability 3.0, when available. You can also choose to run activations on a CPU using the `'ExecutionEnvironment','cpu'` name-value pair argument.
You can use the returned features to train a support vector machine using the Statistics and Machine Learning Toolbox™ function `fitcecoc`.

```
svm = fitcecoc(trainFeatures,TTrain);
```

Load the test data.

```
[XTest,TTest]= digitTest4DArrayData;
```

Extract the features from the same ReLU layer (the sixth layer) for test data and use the returned features to train a support vector machine.

```
testFeatures = activations(net,XTest,6);
testPredictions = predict(svm,testFeatures);
```

Plot the confusion matrix. Convert the data into the format plotconfusion accepts

```
ttest = dummyvar(double(TTest))'; % dummyvar requires Statistics
and Machine Learning Toolbox
tpredictions = dummyvar(double(testPredictions))';
plotconfusion(ttest,tpredictions);
```

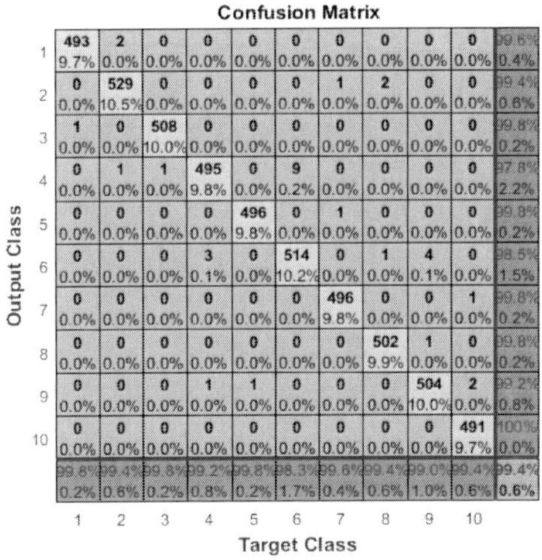

The overall accuracy for the test data using the trained network `net` is 99.4%. Manually compute the overall accuracy.

```
accuracy = sum(TTest == testPredictions)/numel(TTest)
```

```
accuracy =

    0.9937
```

2.4.2 Predict responses using a trained network: predict

Syntax

```
YPred = predict(net,X)
YPred = predict(net,X,Name,Value)
```

Description

`YPred = predict(net,X)` predicts responses for data in `X` using the trained network `net`.

`YPred = predict(net,X,Name,Value)` predicts responses with the additional option specified by the `Name,Value` pair argument.

Examples: Predict Output Scores Using a Trained ConvNet

NOTE: Training a convolutional neural network requires Parallel Computing Toolbox and a CUDA®-enabled NVIDIA® GPU with compute capability 3.0 or higher.

Load the sample data.

```
[XTrain,TTrain] = digitTrain4DArrayData;
```

`digitTrain4DArrayData` loads the digit training set as 4-D array data. `XTrain` is a 28-by-28-by-1-by-4940 array, where 28 is the height and 28 is the width of the images. 1 is the number of channels and 4940 is the number of synthetic images of handwritten digits. `TTrain` is a categorical vector containing the labels for each observation.
Construct the convolutional neural network architecture.

```
layers = [imageInputLayer([28 28 1]);
          convolution2dLayer(5,20);
          reluLayer();
          maxPooling2dLayer(2,'Stride',2);
          fullyConnectedLayer(10);
```

```
        softmaxLayer();
        classificationLayer()];
```

Set the options to default settings for the stochastic gradient descent with momentum.

```
options = trainingOptions('sgdm');
```

Train the network.

```
rng(1)
net = trainNetwork(XTrain,TTrain,layers,options);
```

Epoch	Iteration	Time Elapsed (seconds)	Mini-batch Loss	Mini-batch Accuracy	Base Learning Rate
2	50	0.42	2.2315	51.56%	0.010000
3	100	0.83	1.0606	68.75%	0.010000
4	150	1.25	0.6321	82.03%	0.010000
6	200	1.67	0.3873	85.16%	0.010000
7	250	2.09	0.4310	89.84%	0.010000
8	300	2.52	0.3524	90.63%	0.010000
10	350	2.94	0.2313	96.88%	0.010000
11	400	3.36	0.2115	94.53%	0.010000
12	450	3.78	0.1681	96.88%	0.010000
14	500	4.21	0.1171	100.00%	0.010000
15	550	4.64	0.0920	99.22%	0.010000
16	600	5.06	0.1015	99.22%	0.010000
18	650	5.49	0.0682	98.44%	0.010000
19	700	5.92	0.0927	99.22%	0.010000
20	750	6.35	0.0685	98.44%	0.010000
22	800	6.77	0.0496	99.22%	0.010000
23	850	7.20	0.0483	99.22%	0.010000
24	900	7.64	0.0492	99.22%	0.010000
25	950	8.06	0.0390	100.00%	0.010000
27	1000	8.49	0.0315	100.00%	0.010000
28	1050	8.92	0.0187	100.00%	0.010000
29	1100	9.35	0.0338	100.00%	0.010000

Run the trained network on a test set and predict the scores.

```
[XTest,TTest]= digitTest4DArrayData;
YTestPred = predict(net,XTest);
```

`predict`, by default, uses a CUDA-enabled GPU with compute ccapability 3.0, when available. You can also choose to run `predict` on a CPU using the `'ExecutionEnvironment','cpu'` name-value pair argument.
Display the first 10 images in the test data and compare to the predictions from `predict`.

```
TTest(1:10,:)

ans =
```

```
     0
     0
     0
     0
     0
     0
     0
     0
     0
     0

YTestPred(1:10,:)

ans =

  10×10 single matrix

  Columns 1 through 7

    1.0000    0.0000    0.0000    0.0000    0.0000    0.0000    0.0000
    1.0000    0.0000    0.0000    0.0000    0.0000    0.0000    0.0000
    0.9998    0.0000    0.0000    0.0000    0.0001    0.0000    0.0000
    0.9981    0.0000    0.0005    0.0000    0.0000    0.0000    0.0000
    0.9898    0.0032    0.0037    0.0000    0.0000    0.0000    0.0002
    0.9987    0.0000    0.0013    0.0000    0.0000    0.0000    0.0000
    1.0000    0.0000    0.0000    0.0000    0.0000    0.0000    0.0000
    0.9922    0.0000    0.0000    0.0000    0.0000    0.0000    0.0000
    0.9930    0.0000    0.0000    0.0000    0.0000    0.0000    0.0000
    0.9846    0.0000    0.0000    0.0000    0.0000    0.0000    0.0080

  Columns 8 through 10

    0.0000    0.0000    0.0000
    0.0000    0.0000    0.0000
    0.0000    0.0000    0.0001
    0.0000    0.0011    0.0004
    0.0015    0.0014    0.0001
    0.0000    0.0000    0.0000
    0.0000    0.0000    0.0000
    0.0000    0.0000    0.0078
    0.0000    0.0000    0.0070
    0.0000    0.0000    0.0073
```

`TTest` contains the digits corresponding to the images in `XTest`. The columns of `YTestPred` contain `predict`'s estimation of a probability that an image contains a particular digit. That is, the first column contains the probability estimate that the given image is digit 0, the second column contains the probability estimate that the image is digit 1, the third column contains the probability estimate that the image is digit 2, and so on. You can see that `predict`'s estimation of probabilities for the correct digits are almost 1 and the probability for any other digit is almost 0. `predict` correctly estimates the first 10 observations as digit 0.

2.4.3 Classify data using a trained network: classify

Syntax

```
[Ypred,scores] = classify(net,X)
[Ypred,scores] = classify(net,X,Name,Value)
```

Description

`[Ypred,scores] = classify(net,X)` estimates the classes for the data in `X` using the trained network, `net`.

`[Ypred,scores] = classify(net,X,Name,Value)` estimates the classes with the additional option specified by the `Name,Value` pair argument.

Examples: Classify Images Using Trained ConvNet

NOTE: Training a convolutional neural network requires Parallel Computing Toolbox™ and a CUDA®-enabled NVIDIA® GPU with compute capability 3.0 or higher.

Load the sample data.

```
[XTrain,TTrain] = digitTrain4DArrayData;
```

`digitTrain4DArrayData` loads the digit training set as 4-D array data. `XTrain` is a 28-by-28-by-1-by-4940 array, where 28 is the height and 28 is the width of the images. 1 is the number of channels and 4940 is the number of synthetic images of handwritten digits. `TTrain` is a categorical vector containing the labels for each observation.

Construct the convolutional neural network architecture.

```
layers = [imageInputLayer([28 28 1]);
          convolution2dLayer(5,20);
          reluLayer();
          maxPooling2dLayer(2,'Stride',2);
          fullyConnectedLayer(10);
          softmaxLayer();
          classificationLayer()];
```

Set the options to default settings for the stochastic gradient descent with momentum.

```
options = trainingOptions('sgdm');
```

Train the network.

```
rng('default')
net = trainNetwork(XTrain,TTrain,layers,options);
```

Epoch	Iteration	Time Elapsed (seconds)	Mini-batch Loss	Mini-batch Accuracy	Base Learning Rate
2	50	0.42	2.2301	47.66%	0.010000
3	100	0.83	0.9880	75.00%	0.010000
4	150	1.24	0.5558	82.03%	0.010000
6	200	1.66	0.4023	89.06%	0.010000
7	250	2.08	0.3750	88.28%	0.010000
8	300	2.50	0.3368	91.41%	0.010000
10	350	2.93	0.2589	96.09%	0.010000
11	400	3.35	0.1396	98.44%	0.010000
12	450	3.77	0.1802	96.09%	0.010000
14	500	4.19	0.0892	99.22%	0.010000
15	550	4.62	0.1221	96.88%	0.010000
16	600	5.05	0.0961	98.44%	0.010000
18	650	5.48	0.0857	99.22%	0.010000
19	700	5.90	0.0651	100.00%	0.010000
20	750	6.33	0.0582	98.44%	0.010000
22	800	6.76	0.0808	98.44%	0.010000
23	850	7.19	0.0521	99.22%	0.010000
24	900	7.61	0.0248	100.00%	0.010000
25	950	8.03	0.0241	100.00%	0.010000
27	1000	8.46	0.0253	100.00%	0.010000
28	1050	8.88	0.0260	100.00%	0.010000
29	1100	9.31	0.0246	100.00%	0.010000

Run the trained network on a test set.

```
[XTest,TTest]= digitTest4DArrayData;
YTestPred = classify(net,XTest);
```

Display the first 10 images in the test data and compare to the classification from `classify`.

```
[TTest(1:10,:) YTestPred(1:10,:)]
ans =

     0      0
     0      0
     0      0
     0      0
     0      0
     0      0
     0      0
     0      0
     0      0
     0      0
```

The results from `classify` match the true digits for the first ten images. Calculate the accuracy over all test data.

```
accuracy = sum(YTestPred == TTest)/numel(TTest)
accuracy =

    0.9929
```

Chapter 3

CONVOLUTIONAL NEURAL NETWORKS WITH MATLAB. CLASSES

3.1 INTRODUCTION

Convolution neural networks (CNNs or ConvNets) are essential tools for deep learning, and are especially suited for image recognition. You can construct a CNN architecture, train a network, and use the trained network to predict class labels. You can also extract features from a pre-trained network, and use these features to train a linear classifier. Neural Network Toolbox (Deep Learning Toolbox from version 18) also enables you to perform transfer learning; that is, retrain the last fully connected layer of an existing CNN on new data.

3.2 CONSTRUCT NETWORK ARCHITECTURE. CLASSES

MATLAB has the following classes:

Layer	Network layer

3.2.1 Network layer: layer

Description

Network layer class containing the layer information. Each layer in the architecture of a convolutional neural network is of `Layer` class.

Construction

To define the architecture of a convolutional neural network, create a vector of layers directly.

Copy Semantics

Value. To learn how value classes affect copy operations, see the following paragraphs:

Two Copy Behaviors

There are two fundamental kinds of MATLAB® objects — handles and values.

Value objects behave like MATLAB fundamental types with respect to copy operations. Copies are independent values. Operations that you perform on one object do not affect copies of that object.

Handle objects are referenced by their handle variable. Copies of the handle variable refer to the same object. Operations that you perform on a handle object are visible from all handle variables that reference that object.

Value Object Copy Behavior

MATLAB numeric variables are value objects. For example, when you copy a to the variable b, both variables are independent of each other. Changing the value of a does not change the value of b:

```
a = 8;
b = a;
```

Now reassign a. b is unchanged:

```
a = 6;
b
b =
     8
```

Clearing a does not affect b:

```
clear a
b
b =
     8
```

Value Object Properties

The copy behavior of values stored as properties in value objects is the same as numeric variables. For example, suppose `vobj1` is a value object with property `a`:

```
vobj1.a = 8;
```

If you copy `vobj1` to `vobj2`, and then change the value of `vobj1` property `a`, the value of the copied object's property, `vobj2.a`, is unaffected:

```
vobj2 =vobj1;
vobj1.a = 5;
vobj2.a
ans =
     8
```

Handle Object Copy Behavior

Here is a handle class called `HdClass` that defines a property called `Data`.

```
classdef HdClass < handle
   properties
      Data
   end
   methods
      function obj = HdClass(val)
         if nargin > 0
            obj.Data = val;
         end
      end
   end
end
```

Create an object of this class:

```
hobj1 = HdClass(8)
```

Because this statement is not terminated with a semicolon, MATLAB displays information about the object:

```
hobj1 =

  HdClass with properties:

    Data: 8
```

The variable `hobj1` is a handle that references the object created.
Copying `hobj1` to `hobj2` results in another handle referring to the same object:

```
hobj2 = hobj1
hobj2 =

  HdClass with properties:
```

```
    Data: 8
```

Because handles reference the object, copying a handle copies the handle to a new variable name, but the handle still refers to the same object. For example, given that `hobj1` is a handle object with property `Data`:

```
hobj1.Data
ans =

     8
```

Change the value of `hobj1`'s `Data` property and the value of the copied object's `Data` property also changes:

```
hobj1.Data = 5;
hobj2.Data
ans =

     5
```

Because `hobj2` and `hobj1` are handles to the same object, changing the copy, `hobj2`, also changes the data you access through handle `hobj1`:

```
hobj2.Data = 17;
hobj1.Data
ans =

    17
```

Reassigning Handle Variables

Reassigning a handle variable produces the same result as reassigning any MATLAB variable. When you create an object and assign it to `hobj1`:

```
hobj1 = HdClass(3.14);
```

`hobj1` references the new object, not the same object referenced previously (and still referenced by `hobj2`).

Clearing Handle Variables

When you clear a handle from the workspace, MATLAB removes the variable, but does not remove the object referenced by the other handle. However, if there are no references to an object, MATLAB destroys the object.

Given `hobj1` and `hobj2`, which both reference the same object, you can clear either handle without affecting the object:

```
hobj1.Data = 2^8;

clear hobj1

hobj2
```

```
hobj2 =

  HdClass with properties:

    Data: 256
```

If you clear both `hobj1` and `hobj2`, then there are no references to the object. MATLAB destroys the object and frees the memory used by that object.

Deleting Handle Objects

To remove an object referenced by any number of handles, use `delete`. Given `hobj1` and `hobj2`, which both refer to the same object, delete either handle. MATLAB deletes the object:

```
hobj1 = HdClass(8);

hobj2 = hobj1;

delete(hobj1)

hobj2
```

```
hobj2 =

  handle to deleted HdClass
```

Use `clear` to remove the variable from the workspace.

Modifying Objects

When you pass an object to a function, MATLAB passes a copy of the object into the function workspace. If the function modifies the object, MATLAB modifies only the copy of the object that is in the function workspace. The differences in copy behavior between handle and value classes are important in such cases:

- Value object — The function must return the modified copy of the object. To modify the object in the caller's workspace, assign the function output to a variable of the same name
- Handle object — The copy in the function workspace refers to the same object. Therefore, the function does not have to return the modified copy.

Testing for Handle or Value Class

To determine if an object is a handle object, use the `isa` function. If `obj` is an object of some class, this statement determines if `obj` is a handle:

```
isa(obj,'handle')
```

For example, the `containers.Map` class creates a handle object:

```
hobj = containers.Map({'Red Sox','Yankees'},{'Boston','New York'});
isa(hobj,'handle')
ans =

     1
```

`hobj` is also a `containers.Map` object:

```
isa(hobj,'containers.Map')

ans =

     1
```

Querying the class of `hobj` shows that it is a `containers.Map` object:

```
class(hobj)
ans =

containers.Map
```

The `class` function returns the specific class of an object.

Indexing

You can access the properties of a layer in the network architecture by indexing into the vector of layers and using dot notation. For example, an image input layer is the first layer in a convolutional neural network. To access the `InputSize` property of the image input layer, use `layers(1).InputSize`.

Examples:

Construct Network Architecture

Define a convolutional neural network architecture for classification, with only one convolutional layer, a ReLU layer, and a fully connected layer.

```
cnnarch = [
        imageInputLayer([28 28 3])
        convolution2dLayer([5 5],10)
        reluLayer()
        fullyConnectedLayer(10)
        softmaxLayer()
        classificationLayer()
                ];
```

Alternatively you can create the layers individually and then concatenate them.

```
input = imageInputLayer([28 28 3]);
conv = convolution2dLayer([5 5],10);
```

```
relu = reluLayer();
fcl = fullyConnectedLayer(10);
sml = softmaxLayer();
col = classificationLayer();
cnnarch = [input;conv;relu;fcl;sml;col];
```

`cnnarch` is a 6-by-1 vector of layers.
Display the class for this vector of layers.

```
class (cnnarch)
```

```
nnet.cnn.layer.Layer
```

`cnnarch` is a `Layer` object.

Access Layers and Properties in a Layer Array

Define a convolutional neural network architecture for classification, with only one convolutional layer, a ReLU layer, and a fully connected layer.

```
layers = [imageInputLayer([28 28 3])
        convolution2dLayer([5 5],10)
        reluLayer()
        fullyConnectedLayer(10)
        softmaxLayer()
        classificationLayer()];
```

Display the image input layer.

```
layers(1)
```

```
ans =

  ImageInputLayer with properties:

                 Name: ''
            InputSize: [28 28 3]
     DataAugmentation: 'none'
        Normalization: 'zerocenter'
```

Extract the input size.

```
layers(1).InputSize
```

```
ans =

    28    28     3
```

Display the stride for the convolutional layer.

```
layers(2).Stride
```

```
ans =

     1     1
```

Access the bias learn rate factor for the fully connected layer.

```
layers(4).BiasLearnRateFactor
```

```
ans =

     1
```

Create a Typical Convolutional Neural Network Architecture

Create a convolutional neural network for classification with two convolutional layers and two fully connected layers. Down-sample the convolutional layers using max pooling with 2-by-2 non-overlapping pooling regions. Use a rectified linear unit as nonlinear activation function for the convolutional layers and fully connected layer. Use local response normalization for the first two convolutional layers. The first convolutional layer has 12 4-by-3 filters and the second convolutional layer has 16 5-by-5 filters. The first fully connected layer has 100 neurons. Suppose the input data are gray images of size 28-by-28, and there are 10 classes. Assign a name to each layer.

```
layers = [imageInputLayer([28 28
1],'Normalization','none','Name','inputl')
          convolution2dLayer([4
3],12,'NumChannels',1,'Name','conv1')
          reluLayer('Name','relu1')
          crossChannelNormalizationLayer(4,'Name','cross1')
          maxPooling2dLayer(2,'Stride',2,'Name','max1')
          convolution2dLayer(5,16,'NumChannels',12,'Name','conv2')
          reluLayer('Name','relu2');
          crossChannelNormalizationLayer(4,'Name','cross2')
          maxPooling2dLayer(2,'Stride',2,'Name','max2')
          fullyConnectedLayer(256,'Name','full1')
          reluLayer('Name','relu4')
          fullyConnectedLayer(10,'Name','full2')
          softmaxLayer('Name','softm')
          classificationLayer('Name','out')];
```

3.3 TRAIN NETWORKS. CLASSES

MATLAB has the following classes:

SeriesNetwork	Series network class
TrainingOptionsSGDM	Training options for stochastic gradient descent with momentum

3.3.1 Series network class: SeriesNetwork

Description

A series network class that contains the layers in the trained network. A series network is a network with layers arranged one after another. There is a single input and a single output.

Construction

`trainedNet = trainNetwork(X,Y,layers,options)` returns a trained network. `trainedNet` is a `SeriesNetwork` object.

For more information on training a convolutional neural network, see `trainNetwork`.

Input Arguments

`X` — Images: 4-D numeric array

`Y` — Class labels: array of categorical responses

`layers` — An array of network layers: `Layer` object

`options` — Training options object

Methods

activations	Compute network layer activations
classify	Classify data using a trained network
predict	Predict responses using a trained network

Copy Semantics

Value. To learn how value classes affect copy operations, see the previous class.

Examples: Construct and Train a Convolutional Neural Network

Load the sample data.

```
[XTrain,TTrain] = digitTrain4DArrayData;
```

`digitTrain4DArrayData` loads the digit training set as 4-D array data. `XTrain` is a 28-by-28-by-1-by-4940 array, where 28 is the height and 28 is the width of the images. 1 is the number of channels and 4940 is the number of synthetic images of handwritten digits. `TTrain` is a categorical vector containing the labels for each observation.

Construct the convolutional neural network architecture.

```
layers = [imageInputLayer([28 28 1]);
          convolution2dLayer(5,20);
          reluLayer();
          maxPooling2dLayer(2,'Stride',2);
          fullyConnectedLayer(10);
          softmaxLayer();
          classificationLayer()];
```

Set the options to default settings for the stochastic gradient descent with momentum.

```
options = trainingOptions('sgdm');
```

Train the network.

```
net = trainNetwork(XTrain,TTrain,layers,options);
```

Epoch	Iteration	Time Elapsed (seconds)	Mini-batch Loss	Mini-batch Accuracy	Base Learning Rate
2	50	0.42	2.2301	47.66%	0.010000
3	100	0.83	0.9880	75.00%	0.010000
4	150	1.26	0.5558	82.03%	0.010000
6	200	1.68	0.4023	89.06%	0.010000
7	250	2.10	0.3750	88.28%	0.010000
8	300	2.53	0.3368	91.41%	0.010000
10	350	2.95	0.2589	96.09%	0.010000
11	400	3.38	0.1396	98.44%	0.010000
12	450	3.80	0.1802	96.09%	0.010000
14	500	4.22	0.0892	99.22%	0.010000
15	550	4.66	0.1221	96.88%	0.010000
16	600	5.08	0.0961	98.44%	0.010000
18	650	5.51	0.0857	99.22%	0.010000
19	700	5.93	0.0651	100.00%	0.010000
20	750	6.35	0.0582	98.44%	0.010000
22	800	6.77	0.0808	98.44%	0.010000
23	850	7.19	0.0521	99.22%	0.010000
24	900	7.61	0.0248	100.00%	0.010000
25	950	8.04	0.0241	100.00%	0.010000
27	1000	8.46	0.0253	100.00%	0.010000
28	1050	8.89	0.0260	100.00%	0.010000
29	1100	9.31	0.0246	100.00%	0.010000

Run the trained network on a test set and predict the image labels (digits).

```
[XTest,TTest]= digitTest4DArrayData;
YTest = classify(net,XTest);
```

Calculate the accuracy.

```
accuracy = sum(YTest == TTest)/numel(TTest)
```

```
    0.9929
```

Tips

- A convolutional neural network model saved with R2016a can only be loaded with a GPU, because in R2016a, the learnable parameters are stored as `gpuArrays`. Once you load the model, you can resave it in R2016b. This saves the learnable parameters as MATLAB arrays. You can then change the execution environment to CPU while running the network.

3.3.2 Training options for stochastic gradient descent with momentum. TrainingOptionsSGDM

Description

Class that is comprising training options such as learning rate information, L2 regularization factor, and mini-batch size for stochastic gradient descent with momentum.

Construction

`options = trainingOptions(solverName)` returns a set of training options for the solver specified by `solverName`.

`options = trainingOptions(solverName,Name,Value)` returns a set of training options, with additional options specified by one or more `Name,Value` pair arguments.

Input Arguments

`solverName` — **Solver to use for training the network (default) | `'sgdm'`**

Properties

`Momentum` — **Contribution of the previous gradient step a scalar value from 0 to 1**

`InitialLearnRate` — **Initial learning rate a scalar value**

`LearnRateScheduleSettings` — **Settings for learning rate schedule, specified by the user structure**

`L2Regularization` — **Factor for L2 regularizer scalar value**

`MaxEpochs` — **Maximum number of epochs an integer value**

`MiniBatchSize` — Size of the mini-batch an integer value

`Verbose` — Indicator to display the information on the training progress
`1` (default) | `0`

Copy Semantics

Value. To learn how value classes affect copy operations, see the previous class documentation.

Examples. Specify Training Options

Create a set of options for training with stochastic gradient descent with momentum. The learning rate will be reduced by a factor of 0.2 every 5 epochs. The training will last for 20 epochs, and each iteration will use a mini-batch with 300 observations.

```
options = trainingOptions('sgdm',...
      'LearnRateSchedule','piecewise',...
      'LearnRateDropFactor',0.2,...
      'LearnRateDropPeriod',5,...
      'MaxEpochs',20,...
      'MiniBatchSize',300);
```

3.4 CONSTRUCT NETWORK ARCHITECTURE. LAYERS

MATLAB has de following clases:

`ImageInputLayer`	Image input layer
`Convolution2DLayer`	Convolutional layer
`ReLULayer`	Rectified Linear Unit (ReLU) layer
`CrossChannelNormalizationLayer`	Channel-wise local response normalization layer
`AveragePooling2DLayer`	Average pooling layer object
`MaxPooling2DLayer`	Max pooling layer
`FullyConnectedLayer`	Fully connected layer
`DropoutLayer`	Dropout layer
`SoftmaxLayer`	Softmax layer
`ClassificationOutputLayer`	Classification output layer

3.4.1 ImageInputLayer class

Description

Image input layer class containing the input size, data transformation, and the layer name.

Construction

`inputlayer = imageInputLayer(inputSize)` returns an image input layer.

`inputlayer = imageInputLayer(inputSize, Name,Value)` returns an image input layer, with additional options specified by one or more `Name,Value` pair arguments.

For more information on the name-value pair arguments, see `imageInputLayer`.

Input Arguments

`inputSize` — Size of input data row vector of two or three integer numbers

Properties

`inputSize` — Size of input data row vector of three integer numbers

`DataAugmentation` — Data augmentation transforms `'none'` (default) | `'randcrop'` | `'randfliplr'` | cell array of `'randcrop'` and `'randfliplr'`

`Normalization` — Data transformation `'zerocenter'` (default) | `'none'`

`Name` — Layer name `''` (default) | character vector

Examples: Create and Display Image Input Layer

Create an image input layer for 28-by-28 color images. Specify that the software flips the images from left to right at training time with a probability of 0.5.

```
inputlayer = imageInputLayer([28 28
3],'DataAugmentation','randfliplr');

inputlayer =

  ImageInputLayer with properties:

                Name: ''
           InputSize: [28 28 3]
```

```
    DataAugmentation: 'randfliplr'
       Normalization: 'zerocenter'
```

Display the input size.

```
inputlayer.InputSize

ans =

    28    28     3
```

3.4.2 Convolution2DLayer class

Description

A convolutional layer class containing filter size, number of channels, layer name, weights and bias data.

Construction

`convlayer = convolutional2dLayer(filterSize,numFilters)` returns a layer for 2-D convolution.

`convlayer = convolutional2dLayer(filterSize,numFilters,Name,Value)` returns the convolutional layer, with additional options specified by one or more `Name,Value`pair arguments.

For more details, see `convolution2dLayer` function reference page.

Input Arguments

`filterSize` — Height and width of filters integer value | vector of two integer values

`numFilters` — Number of filters integer value

Properties

`Stride` — Step size for traversing input `[1 1]` (default) | vector of two scalar values

`Padding` — Size of zero padding applied to borders of input `[0 0]` (default) | vector of two scalar values

`NumChannels` — Number of channels for each filter `'auto'` (default) | integer value

`Weights` — **The layer weights 4-D array**

`Bias` — **The layer biases 3-D array**

`WeightLearnRateFactor` — **Learning rate factor for weights scalar value**

`WeightL2Factor` — **L2 regularization factor for weights scalar value**

`BiasLearnRateFactor` — **Learning rate factor for biases scalar value**

`BiasL2Factor` — **L2 regularization factor for biases scalar value**

`Name` — **Layer name '' (default) | character vector**

Examples Create Convolutional Layer

Create a convolutional layer with 96 filters that have a height and width of 11, and use a stride (step size) of 4 in the horizontal and vertical directions.

```
convlayer = convolution2dLayer(11,96,'Stride',4)

convlayer =

  Convolution2DLayer with properties:

                   Name: ''
             FilterSize: [11 11]
            NumChannels: 'auto'
             NumFilters: 96
                 Stride: [4 4]
                Padding: [0 0]
                Weights: []
                   Bias: []
  WeightLearnRateFactor: 1
         WeightL2Factor: 1
    BiasLearnRateFactor: 1
           BiasL2Factor: 0
```

You can display any of the properties separately by indexing into the object. For example, display the filter size.

```
convlayer.FilterSize

ans =

    11    11
```

3.4.3 ReLULayer class

Description

A rectified linear unit (ReLU) layer class that contains the name of the layer. A ReLU layer performs a threshold operation, where any input value less than zero is set to zero, i.e.

$$f(x) = \begin{cases} x, & x \geq 0 \\ 0, & x < 0 \end{cases}.$$

Construction

`layer = relu()` returns a ReLU layer.

`layer = reluLayer(Name,Value)` returns a ReLU layer, with the additional option specified by the `Name,Value` pair argument.

Properties

`Name` — Layer name `''` (default) | character vector

Layer name, stored as a character vector. If `Name` is set to `''`, then the software automatically assigns a name at training time.
Data Types: `char`

Examples: Create ReLU Layer with Specified Name

Create a rectified linear unit layer with the name `relu1`.

```
layer = reluLayer('Name','relu1');
```

3.4.4 CrossChannelNormalizationLayer class

Description

Channel-wise local response normalization layer class that contains the size of the channel window, the hyperparameters for normalization, and the name of the layer.

Construction

`localnormlayer = crossChannelNormalizationLayer(windowChannelSize)` returns a local response normalization layer, which carries out channel-wise normalization [1].

`localnormlayer = crossChannelNormalizationLayer(windowChannelSize,Name,Value)` returns a local response normalization layer, with additional options specified by one or more `Name,Value` pair arguments.

For more details on the name-value pair arguments, see `crossChannelNormalizationLayer`.

Input Arguments

`windowChannelSize` — The size of the channel window
positive integer

Properties

`windowChannelSize` — The size of the channel window positive integer

`Alpha` — α hyperparameter in the normalization scalar value

`Beta` — β hyperparameter in the normalization 0.75 (default) | scalar value

`K` — *K* hyperparameter in the normalization 2 (default) | scalar value

`Name` — Layer name `''` (default) | character vector

Examples: Create Local Response Normalization Layer

Create a local response normalization layer for channel-wise normalization, where a window of 5 channels will be used to normalize each element, and the additive constant for the normalizer is 1.

```
localnormlayer = crossChannelNormalizationLayer(5,'K',1);

localnormlayer =

  CrossChannelNormalizationLayer with properties:

    WindowChannelSize: 5
                Alpha: 1.0000e-04
                 Beta: 0.7500
                    K: 1
                 Name: ''
```

3.4.5 AveragePooling2DLayer class

Description

Average pooling layer class containing the pool size, the stride size, padding, and the name of the layer. An average pooling layer performs down-sampling by dividing the input into rectangular pooling regions and computing the average of each region. It returns the averages for the pooling regions. The size of the pooling regions is determined by the `poolSize` argument to the `averagePooling2dLayer` function.

Construction

`avgpoollayer = averagePooling2dLayer(poolSize)` creates a layer that performs average pooling. `poolSize` specifies the dimensions of the rectangular region.

`avgpoollayer = averagePooling2dLayer(poolSize, Name,Value)` creates the average pooling layer, with additional options specified by one or more `Name,Value` pair arguments.

For more details, see `averagePooling2dLayer`.

Input Arguments

`poolSize` — Height and width of pooling región scalar value | vector of two scalar values

Properties

`PoolSize` — Height and width of pooling región scalar | vector of two scalar values

`Stride` — Step size for traversing input `[1 1]` (default) | vector of two scalar values

`Padding` — Size of zero padding applied to borders of input `[0 0]` (default) | vector of two scalar values

`Name` — Layer name `''` (default) | character vector

Examples:

Average Pooling Layer with Non-Overlapping Pooling Regions

Create an average pooling layer with non-overlapping pooling regions. Set the layer to down-sample by a factor of 2.

```
avgpoollayer = averagePooling2dLayer(2,'Stride',2)
```

```
avgpoollayer = 

  AveragePooling2DLayer with properties:

    PoolSize: [2 2]
      Stride: [2 2]
     Padding: [0 0]
        Name: ''
```

The height and width of the rectangular region (pool size) are both 2. This layer creates pooling regions of size [2 2] and takes the average of the four elements in each region. Because the step size for traversing the images vertically and horizontally (stride) is also [2 2] the pooling regions do not overlap.

Average Pooling Layer with Overlapping Pooling Regions

Create an average pooling layer with overlapping pooling regions. Add padding for the top and bottom of the input.

```
avgpoollayer = averagePooling2dLayer([3 2],'Stride',2,...
    'Padding',[1 0],'Name','avg1')
```

```
avgpoollayer = 

  AveragePooling2DLayer with properties:

    PoolSize: [3 2]
      Stride: [2 2]
     Padding: [1 0]
        Name: 'avg1'
```

The height and width of the rectangular region (pool size) are 3 and 2. This layer creates pooling regions of size [3 2] and takes the average of the six elements in each region. Because the step size for stride) is [2 2] the pooling regions overlap.

A value of `1` for the `Padding` name-value pair indicates that `averagepooling2dlayer` also adds a row of zeros to the top and bottom of the input data. `0` indicates that no padding is added to the right and left of the input data.

You can display any of the properties by using dot notation. Display the name of the layer.

```
avgpoollayer.Name

ans =

avg1
```

3.4.6 MaxPooling2DLayer class

Description

Max pooling layer class containing the pool size, the stride size, padding, and the name of the layer. A max pooling layer performs down-sampling by dividing the input into rectangular pooling regions, and computing the maximum of each region. The size of the pooling regions is determined by the `poolSize` argument to the `maxPooling2dLayer`function.

Construction

`maxpoollayer = maxPooling2dLayer(poolSize)` returns a layer that performs max pooling, which is dividing the input into rectangular regions and returning the maximum of each region. `poolSize` specifies the dimensions of a pooling region.

`maxpoollayer = maxPooling2dLayer(poolSize,Name,Value)` returns the max pooling layer, with additional options specified by one or more `Name,Value` pair arguments.

For more details on the name-value pair arguments, see `maxPooling2dLayer`.

Input Arguments

`poolSize` — Height and width of pooling región scalar value | vector of two scalar values

Properties

`PoolSize` — Height and width of pooling región scalar | vector of two scalar values

`Stride` — Step size for traversing input `[1 1]` (default) | vector of two scalar values

`Padding` — Size of the padding applied to the borders of the input
`[0,0]` (default) | vector of two scalar values

`Name` — Layer name `''` (default) | character vector

Examples:

Max Pooling Layer with Non-Overlapping Pooling Regions

Create a maxpooling layer with non-overlapping pooling regions, which down-samples by a factor of 2.

```
maxpoollayer = maxPooling2dLayer(2,'Stride',2);
```

```
maxpoollayer =

  MaxPooling2DLayer with properties:

    PoolSize: [2 2]
      Stride: [2 2]
     Padding: [0 0]
        Name: ''
```

The height and width of the rectangular region (pool size) are both 2. This layer creates pooling regions of size [2 2] and returns the maximum of the four elements in each region. Because the step size for traversing the images vertically and horizontally (stride) is also [2 2] the pooling regions do not overlap.

Max Pooling Layer with Overlapping Pooling Regions

Create a max pooling layer with overlapping pooling regions. Also add padding for the top and bottom of the input.

```
maxpoollayer = maxPooling2dLayer([3 2],'Stride',2,...
   'Padding',[1 0],'Name','max1');
```

```
maxpoollayer =

  MaxPooling2DLayer with properties:

    PoolSize: [3 2]
      Stride: [2 2]
     Padding: [1 0]
        Name: 'max1'
```

The height and width of the rectangular region (pool size) are 3 and 2. This layer creates pooling regions of size [3 2] and returns the maximum of the six elements in each region. Because the step size for traversing the images vertically and horizontally (stride) is [2 2] the pooling regions overlap.

`1` in the value for the `Padding` name-value pair indicates that software also adds padding to the top and bottom of the input data. `0` indicates that no padding is added to the right and left of the input data.
You can display any of the properties by indexing into the object. Display the name of the layer.

```
maxpoollayer.Name
```

```
ans =

max1
```

3.4.7 FullyConnectedLayer class

Description

A fully connected layer class containing input and output size, layer name, and weights and bias data.

Construction

`fullconnectlayer = fullyConnectedLayer(outputSize)` returns a fully connected layer, in which the software multiplies the input by a matrix and then adds a bias vector.

`fullconnectlayer = fullyConnectedLayer(outputSize,Name,Value)` returns the fully connected layer, with additional options specified by one or more `Name,Value` pair arguments.

For more details on the name-value pair arguments, see `fullyConnectedLayer`.

Input Arguments

`outputSize` — Size of output for fully connected layer integer value

Properties

`InputSize` — Layer input size a positive integer | `'auto'`

`OutputSize` — Layer output size a positive integer

`Weights` — Layer weights `OutputSize`-by-`InputSize` matrix

`Bias` — Layer biases `OutputSize`-by-1 matrix

`WeightLearnRateFactor` — **Learning rate factor for weights scalar value**

`WeightL2Factor` — **L2 regularization factor for weights scalar value**

`BiasLearnRateFactor` — **Learning rate factor for biases scalar value**

`BiasL2Factor` — **L2 regularization factor for biases scalar value**

`Name` — **Layer name `''` (default) | character vector**

Examples: Create Fully Connected Layer

Create a fully connected layer with an output size of 10.

```
fullclayer = fullyConnectedLayer(10)

    fullclayer =

      FullyConnectedLayer with properties:

                    Weights: []
                       Bias: []
      WeightLearnRateFactor: 1
             WeightL2Factor: 1
        BiasLearnRateFactor: 1
               BiasL2Factor: 0
                  InputSize: 'auto'
                 OutputSize: 10
                       Name: ''
```

The software determines the input size and initializes the weights and bias at training time.

3.4.8 DropoutLayer class

Description

A dropout layer class that contains the probability for dropping input elements and the name of the layer. Dropout layer is used only during training.

Construction

`droplayer = dropoutLayer()` returns a dropout layer, that randomly sets input elements to zero with a probability of 0.5. Dropout might help prevent overfitting.

`droplayer = dropoutLayer(probability)` returns a dropout layer, that randomly sets input elements to zero with a probability specified by the `probability` argument.

`droplayer = dropoutLayer(___, Name,Value)` returns the dropout layer, with the additional option specified by the `Name,Value` pair argument.

Input Arguments

`probability` — Probability for dropping out input elements 0.5 (default) | a scalar value in the range 0 to 1

Properties

`Probability` — Probability for dropping input elements with a scalar value

`Name` — Layer name `''` (default) | character vector

Definitions: Dropout Layer

A dropout layer randomly sets a layer's input elements to zero with a given probability.

This corresponds to temporarily dropping a randomly chosen unit and all of its connections from the network during training. So, for each new input element, the software randomly selects a subset of neurons, hence forms a different layer architecture. These architectures use common weights, but because the learning does not depend on specific neurons and connections, the dropout layer might help prevent overfitting .

Examples: Create a Dropout Layer

Create a dropout layer, which randomly sets about 40% of the input to zero. Name the layer as `dropout1`.

```
droplayer = dropoutLayer(0.4,'Name','dropout1')

droplayer = 

  DropoutLayer with properties:

    Probability: 0.4000
           Name: 'dropout1'
```

3.4.9 SoftmaxLayer class

Description

A softmax layer, which uses the softmax activation function. For a classification problem with more than 2 classes, the softmax function is:

$$P(c_r|x) = \frac{P(x|c_r)P(c_r)}{\sum_{j=1}^{k} P(x|c_j)P(c_j)} = \frac{\exp(a_r)}{\sum_{j=1}^{k} \exp(a_j)},$$

$a_r = \ln(P(x|c_r)P(c_r))$, $P(x|c_r)$

$P(x|c_r)$ is the conditional probability of the sample given class r, and $P(c_r)$ is the class prior probability

Construction

`smlayer = softmaxLayer()` returns a softmax layer for classification problems.

`smlayer = softmaxLayer('Name',layername)` returns a softmax layer, with the additional option specified by the `'Name',layername` name-value pair argument.

Properties

`Name` — Layer name `''` (default) | character vector

Example: Create a Softmax Layer with Specified Name

Create a softmax layer with the name `sml1`.

```
smlayer = softmaxLayer('Name','sml1');
```

3.4.10 ClassificationOutputLayer class

Description

The classification output layer, containing the name of the loss function that is used for training the network, the size of the output, and the class labels.

Construction

`classoutputlayer = classificationLayer()` returns a classification output layer for a neural network.

`classoutputlayer = classificationLayer(Name,Value)` returns the classification output layer, with additional option specified by the `Name,Value` pair argument.

Properties

`OutputSize` — Size of output scalar value

`LossFunction` — Loss function for training `'crossentropyex'`

`ClassNames` — Names of clases empty cell array (before training) | cell array of class names (after training)

`Name` — Layer name `''` (default) | character vector

Examples: Create Classification Output Layer

Create a classification output layer with the name `'coutput'`.

```
coutputlayer = classificationLayer('Name','coutput')

coutputlayer =

  ClassificationOutputLayer with properties:

      OutputSize: 'auto'
    LossFunction: 'crossentropyex'
      ClassNames: {}
            Name: 'coutput'
```

Definitions: Cross Entropy Function for k Mutually Exclusive Classes

For multi-class classification problems the software assigns each input to one of the *k* mutually exclusive classes. The loss (error) function for this case is the cross entropy function for a 1-of-*k* coding scheme :

$$E(\theta) = -\sum_{i=1}^{n}\sum_{j=1}^{k} t_{ij} \ln y_j(x_i, \theta),$$

where θ is the parameter vector, t_{ij} is the indicator that the ith sample belongs to the jth class and $y_j(x_i, \theta)$ is the output for sample *i*. The output $y_j(x_i, \theta)$ can be interpreted as the probability that the network associates the *i*th input with class *j*, i.e., $P(t_j = 1|x_i)$

The output unit activation function is the softmax function:

$$y_r(x, \theta) = \frac{\exp(a_r(x, \theta))}{\sum_{j=1}^{k} \exp(a_j(x, \theta))},$$

where $0 \leq y_r \leq 1$ and $\sum_{j=1}^{k} y_j = 1$.

Chapter 4

IMAGE CATEGORY CLASSIFICATION USING DEEP LEARNING

4.1 OVERVIEW

A Convolutional Neural Network (CNN) is a powerful machine learning technique from the field of deep learning. CNNs are trained using large collections of diverse images. From these large collections, CNNs can learn rich feature representations for a wide range of images. These feature representations often outperform hand-crafted features such as HOG, LBP, or SURF. An easy way to leverage the power of CNNs, without investing time and effort into training, is to use a pre-trained CNN as a feature extractor.

In this example, images from Caltech 101 are classified into categories using a multiclass linear SVM trained with CNN features extracted from the images. This approach to image category classification follows the standard practice of training an off-the-shelf classifier using features extracted from images. For example, the Image Category Classification Using Bag Of Features example uses SURF features within a bag of features framework to train a multiclass SVM. The difference here is that instead of using image features such as HOG or SURF, features are extracted using a CNN. And, as this example will show, the classifier trained using CNN features provides close to 100% accuracy, which is higher than the accuracy achieved using bag of features and SURF.

Note: This example requires Computer Vision System Toolbox™, Image Processing Toolbox™, Neural Network Toolbox (Deep Learning Toolbox from version 18)™, Parallel Computing Toolbox™, Statistics and Machine Learning Toolbox™, and a CUDA-capable NVIDIA™ GPU with compute capability 3.0 or higher.

```
function DeepLearningImageClassificationExample
```

4.2 CHECK SYSTEM REQUIREMENTS

A CUDA-capable NVIDIA™ GPU with compute capability 3.0 or higher is highly recommended to run this example. Query the GPU device to check if it can run this example:

```
% Get GPU device information
deviceInfo = gpuDevice;

% Check the GPU compute capability
computeCapability = str2double(deviceInfo.ComputeCapability);
assert(computeCapability > 3.0, ...
    'This example requires a GPU device with compute capability 3.0
or higher.')
```

4.3 DOWNLOAD IMAGE DATA

The category classifier will be trained on images from Caltech 101. Caltech 101 is one of the most widely cited and used image data sets, collected by Fei-Fei Li, Marco Andreetto, and Marc 'Aurelio Ranzato.

```
% Download the compressed data set from the following location
url =
'http://www.vision.caltech.edu/Image_Datasets/Caltech101/101_Object
Categories.tar.gz';
% Store the output in a temporary folder
outputFolder = fullfile(tempdir, 'caltech101'); % define output
folder
```

Note: Download time of the data depends on your internet connection. The next set of commands use MATLAB to download the data and will block MATLAB. Alternatively, you can use your web browser to first download the dataset to your local disk. To use the file you downloaded from the web, change the 'outputFolder' variable above to the location of the downloaded file.

```
if ~exist(outputFolder, 'dir') % download only once
    disp('Downloading 126MB Caltech101 data set...');
    untar(url, outputFolder);
end
```

4.4 LOAD IMAGES

Instead of operating on all of Caltech 101, which is time consuming, use three of the categories: airplanes, ferry, and laptop. The image category classifier will be trained to distinguish amongst these six categories.

```
rootFolder = fullfile(outputFolder, '101_ObjectCategories');
```

```
categories = {'airplanes', 'ferry', 'laptop'};
```

Create an `ImageDatastore` to help you manage the data.
Because `ImageDatastore` operates on image file locations, images are not loaded into memory until read, making it efficient for use with large image collections.

```
imds = imageDatastore(fullfile(rootFolder, categories),
'LabelSource', 'foldernames');
```

The `imds` variable now contains the images and the category labels associated with each image. The labels are automatically assigned from the folder names of the image files. Use `countEachLabel` to summarize the number of images per category.

```
tbl = countEachLabel(imds)

tbl =

      Label        Count
    _________      _____

    airplanes      800
    ferry           67
    laptop          81
```

Because `imds` above contains an unequal number of images per category, let's first adjust it, so that the number of images in the training set is balanced.

```
minSetCount = min(tbl{:,2}); % determine the smallest amount of
images in a category

% Use splitEachLabel method to trim the set.
imds = splitEachLabel(imds, minSetCount, 'randomize');

% Notice that each set now has exactly the same number of images.
countEachLabel(imds)

ans =

      Label        Count
    _________      _____

    airplanes      67
    ferry          67
    laptop         67
```

Below, you can see example images from three of the categories included in the dataset.

```
% Find the first instance of an image for each category
airplanes = find(imds.Labels == 'airplanes', 1);
ferry = find(imds.Labels == 'ferry', 1);
laptop = find(imds.Labels == 'laptop', 1);

figure
subplot(1,3,1);
imshow(readimage(imds,airplanes))
subplot(1,3,2);
imshow(readimage(imds,ferry))
subplot(1,3,3);
imshow(readimage(imds,laptop))
```

4.5 DOWNLOAD PRE-TRAINED CONVOLUTIONAL NEURAL NETWORK (CNN)

Now that the images are prepared, you will need to download a pre-trained CNN model for this example. There are several pre-trained networks that have gained popularity. Most of these have been trained on the ImageNet dataset, which has 1000 object categories and 1.2 million training images[1]. "AlexNet" is one such model and can be downloaded from MatConvNet[2,3]:

```
% Location of pre-trained "AlexNet"
cnnURL = 'http://www.vlfeat.org/matconvnet/models/beta16/imagenet-caffe-alex.mat';
% Store CNN model in a temporary folder
cnnMatFile = fullfile(tempdir, 'imagenet-caffe-alex.mat');
```

Note: Download time of the data depends on your internet connection. The next set of commands use MATLAB to download the data and will block MATLAB. Alternatively, you can use your web browser to first download the dataset to your local disk. To use the file you downloaded from the web, change the 'cnnMatFile' variable above to the location of the downloaded file.

```
if ~exist(cnnMatFile, 'file') % download only once
    disp('Downloading pre-trained CNN model...');
```

```
    websave(cnnMatFile, cnnURL);
end
```

4.6 LOAD PRE-TRAINED CNN

The CNN model is saved in MatConvNet's format [3]. Load the MatConvNet network data into `convnet`, a `SeriesNetwork`object from Neural Network Toolbox (Deep Learning Toolbox from version 18)™, using the helper function `helperImportMatConvNet`. A SeriesNetwork object can be used to inspect the network architecture, classify new data, and extract network activations from specific layers.

```
% Load MatConvNet network into a SeriesNetwork
convnet = helperImportMatConvNet(cnnMatFile)
```

```
convnet =

  SeriesNetwork with properties:

    Layers: [23×1 nnet.cnn.layer.Layer]
```

`convnet.Layers` defines the architecture of the CNN.

```
% View the CNN architecture
convnet.Layers
```

```
ans =

  23x1 Layer array with layers:

     1   'input'               Image Input                   227x227x3 images with 'zerocenter' normalization
     2   'conv1'               Convolution                   96 11x11x3 convolutions with stride [4  4] and padding [0  0]
     3   'relu1'               ReLU                          ReLU
     4   'norm1'               Cross Channel Normalization   cross channel normalization with 5 channels per element
     5   'pool1'               Max Pooling                   3x3 max pooling with stride [2  2] and padding [0  0]
     6   'conv2'               Convolution                   256 5x5x48 convolutions with stride [1  1] and padding [2  2]
     7   'relu2'               ReLU                          ReLU
     8   'norm2'               Cross Channel Normalization   cross channel normalization with 5 channels per element
     9   'pool2'               Max Pooling                   3x3 max pooling with stride [2  2] and padding [0  0]
    10   'conv3'               Convolution                   384 3x3x256 convolutions with stride [1  1] and padding [1  1]
    11   'relu3'               ReLU                          ReLU
    12   'conv4'               Convolution                   384 3x3x192 convolutions with stride [1  1] and padding [1  1]
    13   'relu4'               ReLU                          ReLU
    14   'conv5'               Convolution                   256 3x3x192 convolutions with stride [1  1] and padding [1  1]
    15   'relu5'               ReLU                          ReLU
    16   'pool5'               Max Pooling                   3x3 max pooling with stride [2  2] and padding [0  0]
    17   'fc6'                 Fully Connected               4096 fully connected layer
    18   'relu6'               ReLU                          ReLU
    19   'fc7'                 Fully Connected               4096 fully connected layer
    20   'relu7'               ReLU                          ReLU
    21   'fc8'                 Fully Connected               1000 fully connected layer
    22   'prob'                Softmax                       softmax
    23   'classificationLayer' Classification Output         cross-entropy with 'n01440764', 'n01443537', and 998 other classes
```

The first layer defines the input dimensions. Each CNN has a different input size requirements. The one used in this example requires image input that is 227-by-227-by-3.

```
% Inspect the first layer
convnet.Layers(1)
```

```
ans =

  ImageInputLayer with properties:

                Name: 'input'
           InputSize: [227 227 3]

   Hyperparameters
    DataAugmentation: 'none'
       Normalization: 'zerocenter'
```

The intermediate layers make up the bulk of the CNN. These are a series of convolutional layers, interspersed with rectified linear units (ReLU) and max-pooling layers [2]. Following the these layers are 3 fully-connected layers.

The final layer is the classification layer and its properties depend on the classification task. In this example, the CNN model that was loaded was trained to solve a 1000-way classification problem. Thus the classification layer has 1000 classes from the ImageNet dataset.

```
% Inspect the last layer
convnet.Layers(end)

% Number of class names for ImageNet classification task
numel(convnet.Layers(end).ClassNames)

ans =

  ClassificationOutputLayer with properties:

            Name: 'classificationLayer'
      ClassNames: {1000×1 cell}
      OutputSize: 1000

   Hyperparameters
    LossFunction: 'crossentropyex'


ans =

        1000
```

Note that the CNN model is not going to be used for the original classification task. It is going to be re-purposed to solve a different classification task on the Caltech 101 dataset.

4.7 PRE-PROCESS IMAGES FOR CNN

As mentioned above, `convnet` can only process RGB images that are 227-by-227. To avoid re-saving all the images in Caltech 101 to this format, setup the `imds` read function, `imds.ReadFcn`, to pre-process images on-the-fly. The `imds.ReadFcn` is called every time an image is read from the `ImageDatastore`.

```
% Set the ImageDatastore ReadFcn
imds.ReadFcn = @(filename)readAndPreprocessImage(filename);
```

Note that other CNN models will have different input size constraints, and may require other pre-processing steps.

```
    function Iout = readAndPreprocessImage(filename)

        I = imread(filename);

        % Some images may be grayscale. Replicate the image 3 times
to
        % create an RGB image.
        if ismatrix(I)
            I = cat(3,I,I,I);
        end

        % Resize the image as required for the CNN.
        Iout = imresize(I, [227 227]);

        % Note that the aspect ratio is not preserved. In Caltech
101, the
        % object of interest is centered in the image and occupies
a
        % majority of the image scene. Therefore, preserving the
aspect
        % ratio is not critical. However, for other data sets, it
may prove
        % beneficial to preserve the aspect ratio of the original
image
        % when resizing.
    end
```

4.8 PREPARE TRAINING AND TEST IMAGE SETS

Split the sets into training and validation data. Pick 30% of images from each set for the training data and the remainder, 70%, for the validation data. Randomize the split to avoid biasing the results. The training and test sets will be processed by the CNN model.

```
[trainingSet, testSet] = splitEachLabel(imds, 0.3, 'randomize');
```

4.9 EXTRACT TRAINING FEATURES USING CNN

Each layer of a CNN produces a response, or activation, to an input image. However, there are only a few layers within a CNN that are suitable for image feature extraction. The layers at the beginning of the network capture basic image features, such as edges and blobs. To see this, visualize the network filter weights from the first convolutional layer. This can help build up an intuition as to why the features extracted from CNNs work so well for image recognition tasks. Note that visualizing deeper layer weights is beyond the scope of this example. You can read more about that in the work of Zeiler and Fergus [4].

```
% Get the network weights for the second convolutional layer
w1 = convnet.Layers(2).Weights;

% Scale and resize the weights for visualization
w1 = mat2gray(w1);
w1 = imresize(w1,5);

% Display a montage of network weights. There are 96 individual
sets of
% weights in the first layer.
figure
montage(w1)
title('First convolutional layer weights')
```

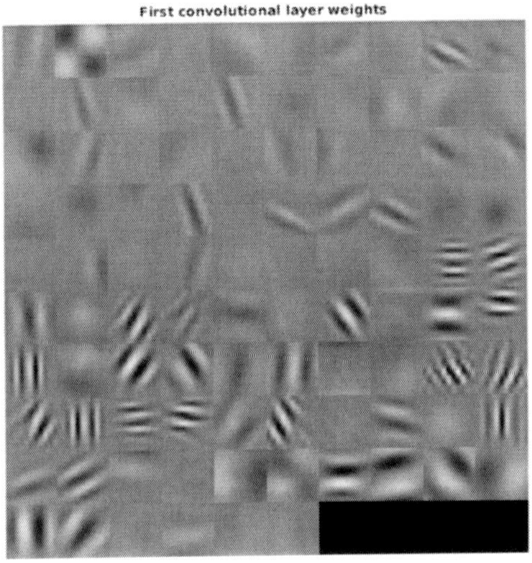

Notice how the first layer of the network has learned filters for capturing blob and edge features. These "primitive" features are then processed by deeper network layers, which combine the early features to form higher level image features. These higher level features are better suited for recognition tasks because they combine all the primitive features into a richer image representation [5].

You can easily extract features from one of the deeper layers using the `activations` method. Selecting which of the deep layers to choose is a design choice, but typically starting with the layer right before the classification layer is a good place to start. In `convnet`, the this layer is named 'fc7'. Let's extract training features using that layer.

```
featureLayer = 'fc7';
trainingFeatures = activations(convnet, trainingSet, featureLayer,
...
    'MiniBatchSize', 32, 'OutputAs', 'columns');
```

Note that the activations function automatically uses a GPU for processing if one is available, otherwise, a CPU is used. Because of the number of layers in AlexNet, using a GPU is highly recommended. Using a the CPU to run the network will greatly increase the time it takes to extract features.

In the code above, the 'MiniBatchSize' is set 32 to ensure that the CNN and image data fit into GPU memory. You may need to lower the 'MiniBatchSize' if your GPU runs out of memory. Also, the activations output is arranged as columns. This helps speed-up the multiclass linear SVM training that follows.

4.10 TRAIN A MULTICLASS SVM CLASSIFIER USING CNN FEATURES

Next, use the CNN image features to train a multiclass SVM classifier. A fast Stochastic Gradient Descent solver is used for training by setting the `fitcecoc` function's 'Learners' parameter to 'Linear'. This helps speed-up the training when working with high-dimensional CNN feature vectors, which each have a length of 4096.

```
% Get training labels from the trainingSet
trainingLabels = trainingSet.Labels;

% Train multiclass SVM classifier using a fast linear solver, and
set
% 'ObservationsIn' to 'columns' to match the arrangement used for
training
% features.
classifier = fitcecoc(trainingFeatures, trainingLabels, ...
    'Learners', 'Linear', 'Coding', 'onevsall', 'ObservationsIn',
'columns');
```

4.11 EVALUATE CLASSIFIER

Repeat the procedure used earlier to extract image features from `testSet`. The test features can then be passed to the classifier to measure the accuracy of the trained classifier.

```
% Extract test features using the CNN
testFeatures = activations(convnet, testSet, featureLayer,
'MiniBatchSize',32);

% Pass CNN image features to trained classifier
predictedLabels = predict(classifier, testFeatures);

% Get the known labels
testLabels = testSet.Labels;

% Tabulate the results using a confusion matrix.
confMat = confusionmat(testLabels, predictedLabels);

% Convert confusion matrix into percentage form
confMat = bsxfun(@rdivide,confMat,sum(confMat,2))

confMat =

     1     0     0
```

```
     0     1     0
     0     0     1


% Display the mean accuracy
mean(diag(confMat))

ans =

     1
```

4.12 TRY THE NEWLY TRAINED CLASSIFIER ON TEST IMAGES

You can now apply the newly trained classifier to categorize new images.

```
newImage = fullfile(rootFolder, 'airplanes', 'image_0690.jpg');

% Pre-process the images as required for the CNN
img = readAndPreprocessImage(newImage);

% Extract image features using the CNN
imageFeatures = activations(convnet, img, featureLayer);

% Make a prediction using the classifier
label = predict(classifier, imageFeatures)

label =

     airplanes
```

4.13 REFERENCES

[1] Deng, Jia, et al. "Imagenet: A large-scale hierarchical image database." Computer Vision and Pattern Recognition, 2009. CVPR 2009. IEEE Conference on. IEEE, 2009.

[2] Krizhevsky, Alex, Ilya Sutskever, and Geoffrey E. Hinton. "Imagenet classification with deep convolutional neural networks." Advances in neural information processing systems. 2012.

[3] Vedaldi, Andrea, and Karel Lenc. "MatConvNet-convolutional neural networks for MATLAB." arXiv preprint arXiv:1412.4564 (2014).

[4] Zeiler, Matthew D., and Rob Fergus. "Visualizing and understanding convolutional networks." Computer Vision-ECCV 2014. Springer International Publishing, 2014. 818-833.

[5] Donahue, Jeff, et al. "Decaf: A deep convolutional activation feature for generic visual recognition." arXiv preprint arXiv:1310.1531 (2013).

Chapter 5

TRANSFER LEARNING USING CONVOLUTIONAL NEURAL NETWORKS AND PRETRAINED CONVOLUTIONAL NEURAL NETWORKS

5.1 TRANSFER LEARNING USING CONVOLUTIONAL NEURAL NETWORKS

Fine-tune a convolutional neural network pretrained on digit images to learn the features of letter images. Transfer learning is considered as the transfer of knowledge from one learned task to a new task in machine learning [1]. In the context of neural networks, it is transferring learned features of a pretrained network to a new problem. Training a convolutional neural network from the beginning in each case usually is not effective when there is not sufficient amount of training data. The common practice in deep learning for such cases is to use a network that is trained on a large data set for a new problem. While the initial layers of the pretrained network can be fixed, the last few layers must be fine-tuned to learn the specific features of the new data set. Transfer learning usually results in faster training times than training a new convolutional neural network because you do not need to estimate all the parameters in the new network.

NOTE: Training a convolutional neural network requires Parallel Computing Toolbox™ and a CUDA®-enabled NVIDIA® GPU with compute capability 3.0 or higher.

Load the sample data as an `ImageDatastore`.

```
digitDatasetPath =
fullfile(matlabroot,'toolbox','nnet','nndemos',...
    'nndatasets','DigitDataset');
digitData = imageDatastore(digitDatasetPath,...
        'IncludeSubfolders',true,'LabelSource','foldernames');
```

The data store contains 10000 synthetic images of digits 0–9. The images are generated by applying random transformations to digit images created using different fonts. Each digit image is 28-by-28 pixels.

Display some of the images in the datastore.

```
for i = 1:20
    subplot(4,5,i);
    imshow(digitData.Files{i});
end
```

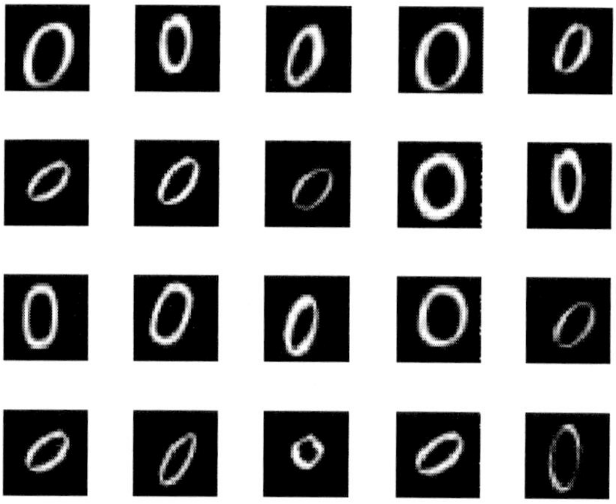

Check the number of images in each digit category.

```
digitData.countEachLabel

ans =

    Label    Count
    _____    _____

    0         988
    1        1026
    2        1003
```

```
    3         993
    4         991
    5        1017
    6         992
    7         999
    8        1003
    9         988
```

The data contains an unequal number of images per category.

To balance the number of images for each digit in the training set, first find the minimum number of images in a category.

```
minSetCount = min(digitData.countEachLabel{:,2})

minSetCount =

   988
```

Divide the dataset so that each category in the training set has 494 images and the testing set has the remaining images from each label.

```
trainingNumFiles = round(minSetCount/2);
rng(1) % For reproducibility
[trainDigitData,testDigitData] = splitEachLabel(digitData,...
                                 trainingNumFiles,'randomize');
```

`splitEachLabel` splits the image files in `digitData` into two new datastores, `trainDigitData` and `testDigitData`.

Create the layers for the convolutional neural network.

```
layers = [imageInputLayer([28 28 1])
          convolution2dLayer(5,20)
          reluLayer()
          maxPooling2dLayer(2,'Stride',2)
          fullyConnectedLayer(10)
          softmaxLayer()
          classificationLayer()];
```

Create the training options. Set the maximum number of epochs at 20, and start the training with an initial learning rate of 0.001.

```
options = trainingOptions('sgdm','MaxEpochs',20,...
        'InitialLearnRate',0.001);
```

Train the network using the training set and the options you defined in the previous step.

```
convnet = trainNetwork(trainDigitData,layers,options);
```

```
|=========================================================================================|
|     Epoch     |   Iteration   | Time Elapsed |  Mini-batch  |  Mini-batch  | Base Learning|
|               |               |  (seconds)   |     Loss     |   Accuracy   |     Rate     |
|=========================================================================================|
|             2 |            50 |         0.71 |       0.2233 |       92.97% |     0.001000 |
|             3 |           100 |         1.37 |       0.0182 |       99.22% |     0.001000 |
|             4 |           150 |         2.02 |       0.0395 |       99.22% |     0.001000 |
|             6 |           200 |         2.70 |       0.0105 |       99.22% |     0.001000 |
|             7 |           250 |         3.35 |       0.0026 |      100.00% |     0.001000 |
|             8 |           300 |         4.00 |       0.0004 |      100.00% |     0.001000 |
|            10 |           350 |         4.67 |       0.0002 |      100.00% |     0.001000 |
|            11 |           400 |         5.32 |       0.0001 |      100.00% |     0.001000 |
|            12 |           450 |         5.95 |       0.0001 |      100.00% |     0.001000 |
|            14 |           500 |         6.60 |       0.0002 |      100.00% |     0.001000 |
|            15 |           550 |         7.23 |       0.0001 |      100.00% |     0.001000 |
|            16 |           600 |         7.87 |       0.0001 |      100.00% |     0.001000 |
|            18 |           650 |         8.52 |       0.0001 |      100.00% |     0.001000 |
|            19 |           700 |         9.15 |       0.0001 |      100.00% |     0.001000 |
|            20 |           750 |         9.79 |       0.0000 |      100.00% |     0.001000 |
|=========================================================================================|
```

Test the network using the testing set and compute the accuracy.

```
YTest = classify(convnet,testDigitData);
TTest = testDigitData.Labels;
accuracy = sum(YTest == TTest)/numel(YTest)

accuracy =

    0.9976
```

Accuracy is the ratio of the number of true labels in the test data matching the classifications from `classify`, to the number of images in the test data. In this case 99.78% of the digit estimations match the true digit values in the test set.

Now, suppose you would like to use the trained network `net` to predict classes on a new set of data. Load the letters training data.

```
load lettersTrainSet.mat
```

`XTrain` contains 1500 28-by-28 grayscale images of the letters A, B, and C in a 4-D array. `TTrain` contains the categorical array of the letter labels.

Display some of the letter images.

```
figure;
for j = 1:20
    subplot(4,5,j);
    selectImage = datasample(XTrain,1,4);
    imshow(selectImage,[]);
end
```

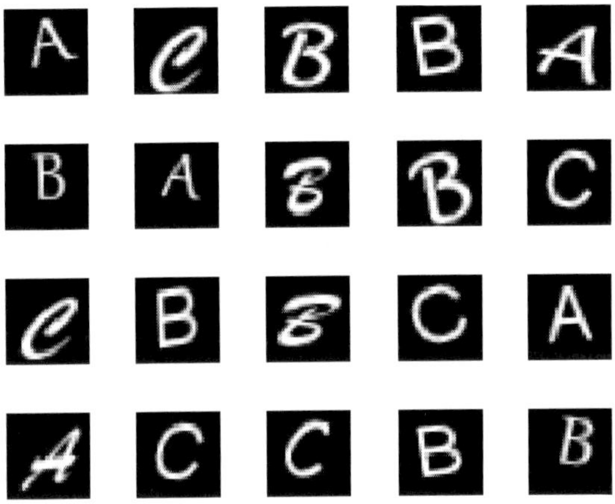

The pixel values in `XTrain` are in the range [0 1]. The digit data used in training the network `net` were in [0 255]; scale the letters data between [0 255].

```
XTrain = XTrain*255;
```

The last three layers of the trained network `net` are tuned for the digit dataset, which has 10 classes. The properties of these layers depend on the classification task. Display the fully connected layer (`fullyConnectedLayer`).

```
convnet.Layers(end-2)

ans =

  FullyConnectedLayer with properties:

          Name: 'fc'

   Hyperparameters
     InputSize: 2880
    OutputSize: 10

   Learnable Parameters
       Weights: [10×2880 single]
          Bias: [10×1 single]

Use properties method to see a list of all properties.
```

Display the last layer (`classificationLayer`).

```
convnet.Layers(end)

ans =

  ClassificationOutputLayer with properties:

            Name: 'classoutput'
      ClassNames: {10×1 cell}
      OutputSize: 10

   Hyperparameters
    LossFunction: 'crossentropyex'
```

These three layers must be fine-tuned for the new classification problem. Extract all the layers but the last three from the trained network, `net`.

```
layersTransfer = convnet.Layers(1:end-3);
```

The letters data set has three classes. Add a new fully connected layer for three classes, and increase the learning rate for this layer.

```
layersTransfer(end+1) = fullyConnectedLayer(3,...
              'WeightLearnRateFactor',10,...
                  'BiasLearnRateFactor',20);
```

`WeightLearnRateFactor` and `BiasLearnRateFactor` are multipliers of the global learning rate for the fully connected layer.

Add a softmax layer and a classification output layer.

```
layersTransfer(end+1) = softmaxLayer();
layersTransfer(end+1) = classificationLayer();
```

Create the options for transfer learning. You do not have to train for many epochs (`MaxEpochs` can be lower than before). Set the `InitialLearnRate` at a lower rate than used for training `net` to improve convergence by taking smaller steps.

```
optionsTransfer = trainingOptions('sgdm',...
        'MaxEpochs',5,...
        'InitialLearnRate',0.000005,...
        'Verbose',true);
```

Perform transfer learning.

```
convnetTransfer = trainNetwork(XTrain,TTrain,...
                   layersTransfer,optionsTransfer);
```

```
|=========================================================================================|
|     Epoch     |   Iteration   | Time Elapsed |  Mini-batch  |  Mini-batch  | Base Learning|
|               |               |  (seconds)   |     Loss     |   Accuracy   |     Rate     |
|=========================================================================================|
|             5 |            50 |         0.43 |       0.0011 |      100.00% |     0.000005 |
|=========================================================================================|
```

Load the letters test data. Similar to the letters training data, scale the testing data between [0 255], because the training data were between that range.

```
load lettersTestSet.mat
XTest = XTest*255;
```

Test the accuracy.

```
YTest = classify(convnetTransfer,XTest);
accuracy = sum(YTest == TTest)/numel(TTest)

accuracy =

    0.9587
```

5.2 PRETRAINED CONVOLUTIONAL NEURAL NETWORK

Training Convolutional Neural Networks (ConvNets) can be difficult and time consuming. In some cases, it makes sense to start with a ConvNet already trained on a large data set and then adapt it to the current problem. You can use a previously trained network for two purposes:

- Feature extraction — Use the ConvNet to extract features from data (images) and then use those features to train a different classifier, e.g., a support vector machine (SVM).
- Transfer learning — Take a network trained on a large dataset and retrain the last few layers on a smaller data set.

The Caffe version of AlexNet (*https://github.com/BVLC/caffe/tree/master/ models/ bvlc_alexnet*), is available to download and use for your problems. The network is trained on a subset of the images from ImageNet database, which are used in ImageNet Large-Scale Visual Recognition Challenge (ILSVRC). There are 1000 categories and about 1000 training images in each category.

You can install the trained network from the Add-Ons gallery. Select **Get Add-Ons** from the **Add-Ons** drop-down menu of the MATLAB® desktop. The add-on files are in the "MathWorks Features" section. Choose Neural Network Toolbox (Deep Learning Toolbox from version 18) Model for AlexNet Network..

After you download the support package, you can access it by typing `alexnet` in the command line.

```
net = alexnet

net =

  SeriesNetwork with properties:

    Layers: [25×1 nnet.cnn.layer.Layer]
```

The trained network is a `SeriesNetwork` object. You can see the details of the architecture by using dot notation.

```
net.Layers

ans =

  25x1 Layer array with layers:

     1   'data'     Image Input                   227x227x3 images with 'zerocenter' normalization
     2   'conv1'    Convolution                   96 11x11x3 convolutions with stride [4  4] and padding [0  0]
     3   'relu1'    ReLU                          ReLU
     4   'norm1'    Cross Channel Normalization   cross channel normalization with 5 channels per element
     5   'pool1'    Max Pooling                   3x3 max pooling with stride [2  2] and padding [0  0]
     6   'conv2'    Convolution                   256 5x5x48 convolutions with stride [1  1] and padding [2  2]
     7   'relu2'    ReLU                          ReLU
     8   'norm2'    Cross Channel Normalization   cross channel normalization with 5 channels per element
     9   'pool2'    Max Pooling                   3x3 max pooling with stride [2  2] and padding [0  0]
    10   'conv3'    Convolution                   384 3x3x256 convolutions with stride [1  1] and padding [1  1]
    11   'relu3'    ReLU                          ReLU
    12   'conv4'    Convolution                   384 3x3x192 convolutions with stride [1  1] and padding [1  1]
    13   'relu4'    ReLU                          ReLU
    14   'conv5'    Convolution                   256 3x3x192 convolutions with stride [1  1] and padding [1  1]
    15   'relu5'    ReLU                          ReLU
    16   'pool5'    Max Pooling                   3x3 max pooling with stride [2  2] and padding [0  0]
    17   'fc6'      Fully Connected               4096 fully connected layer
    18   'relu6'    ReLU                          ReLU
    19   'drop6'    Dropout                       50% dropout
    20   'fc7'      Fully Connected               4096 fully connected layer
    21   'relu7'    ReLU                          ReLU
    22   'drop7'    Dropout                       50% dropout
    23   'fc8'      Fully Connected               1000 fully connected layer
    24   'prob'     Softmax                       softmax
    25   'output'   Classification Output         cross-entropy with 'tench', 'goldfish', and 998 other classes
```

Suppose you want to classify an image using this trained network. First, read the image to classify.

```
I = imread('peppers.png');
```

This image is of size 384-by-512-by-3. You must adjust it to the size of the images the network was trained on. Extract the input size of the network.

```
sz = net.Layers(1).InputSize

sz =

   227   227     3
```

Crop image to the input size of the network.

```
I = I(1:sz(1),1:sz(2),1:sz(3));
```

Classify (predict the label of) the image using AlexNet.

```
label = classify(net, I)
```

```
label =

     bell pepper
```

`classify` is a method of `SeriesNetwork`. Show the image and the classification results.

```
figure
imshow(I)
text(10,20,char(label),'Color','white')
```

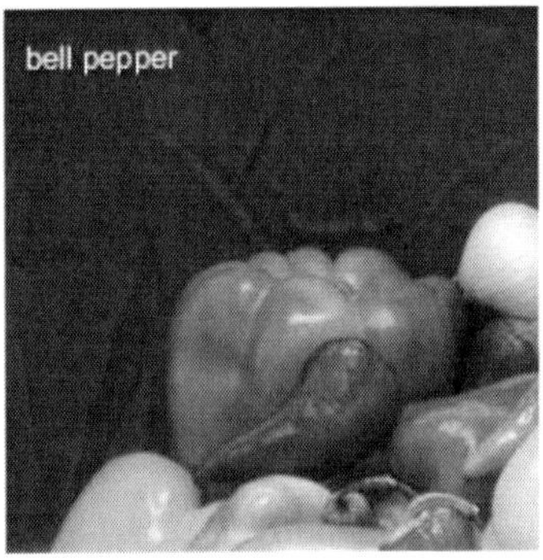

References

[1] https://github.com/BVLC/caffe/tree/master/models/bvlc_alexnet

[2] Krizhevsky, A., I. Sutskever, and G. E. Hinton. "ImageNet Classification with Deep Convolutional Neural Networks. " *Advances in Neural Information Processing Systems*. Vol 25, 2012.

[3] http://www.image-net.org/

Chapter 6

FUNCTIONS FOR PATTERN RECOGNITION AND CLASSIFICATION. AUTOENCODER

6.1 INTRODUCTION

The more important functions for pattern recognition and classification are de following:

`Autoencoder`	Autoencoder class
`nnstart`	Neural network getting started GUI
`view`	View neural network
`trainAutoencoder`	Train an autoencoder
`trainSoftmaxLayer`	Train a softmax layer for classification
`decode`	Decode encoded data
`encode`	Encode input data
`predict`	Reconstruct the inputs using trained autoencoder
`stack`	Stack encoders from several autoencoders together
`network`	Convert Autoencoder object into network object
`patternnet`	Pattern recognition network
`lvqnet`	Learning vector quantization neural network
`train`	Train neural network
`trainlm`	Levenberg-Marquardt backpropagation
`trainbr`	Bayesian regularization backpropagation
`trainscg`	Scaled conjugate gradient backpropagation
`trainrp`	Resilient backpropagation
`mse`	Mean squared normalized error performance function
`regression`	Linear regression
`roc`	Receiver operating characteristic

`plotconfusion`	Plot classification confusion matrix
`ploterrhist`	Plot error histogram
`plotperform`	Plot network performance
`plotregression`	Plot linear regression
`plotroc`	Plot receiver operating characteristic
`plottrainstate`	Plot training state values
`crossentropy`	Neural network performance
`genFunction`	Generate MATLAB function for simulating neural network

6.2 VIEW NEURAL NETWORK

`view(net)` opens a window that shows your neural network (specified in `net`) as a graphical diagram.

This example shows how to view the diagram of a pattern recognition network.

```
[x,t] = iris_dataset;
net = patternnet;
net = configure(net,x,t);
view(net)
```

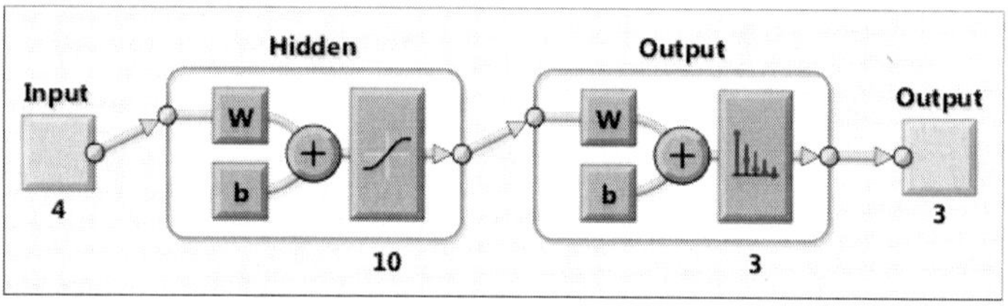

6.3 PATTERN RECOGNITION AND LEARNING VECTOR QUANTIZATION

6.3.1 Pattern recognition network: patternnet

Syntax

```
patternnet(hiddenSizes,trainFcn,performFcn)
```

Description

Pattern recognition networks are feedforward networks that can be trained to classify inputs according to target classes. The target data for pattern recognition networks should consist of vectors of all zero values except for a 1 in element `i`, where `i` is the class they are to represent.

`patternnet(hiddenSizes,trainFcn,performFcn)` takes these arguments,

`hiddenSizes`	Row vector of one or more hidden layer sizes (default = 10)
`trainFcn`	Training function (default = `'trainscg'`)
`performFcn`	Performance function (default = `'crossentropy'`)

and returns a pattern recognition neural network.

Example of Pattern Recognition

This example shows how to design a pattern recognition network to classify iris flowers.

```
[x,t] = iris_dataset;
net = patternnet(10);
net = train(net,x,t);
view(net)
y = net(x);
perf = perform(net,t,y);
classes = vec2ind(y);
```

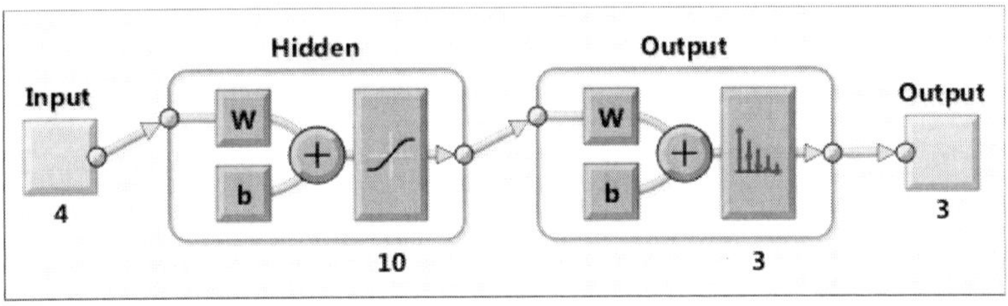


```
net = fitnet(hiddenSizes)
net = fitnet(hiddenSizes,trainFcn)
```

`net = fitnet(hiddenSizes)` returns a function fitting neural network with a hidden layer size of `hiddenSizes (default=10)`.

The argument `hiddenSizes` represents the size of the hidden layers in the network, specified as a row vector. The length of the vector determines the number of hidden layers in the network. For example, you can specify a network with 3 hidden layers, where the first hidden layer size is 10, the second is 8, and the third is 5 as follows: `[10,8,5]`

`net = fitnet(hiddenSizes,trainFcn)` returns a function fitting neural network with a hidden layer size of `hiddenSizes` and training function, specified by `trainFcn (deafut='trainlm')`. The training functions are the following:

Training Function	Algorithm
'trainlm'	Levenberg-Marquardt
'trainbr'	Bayesian Regularization
'trainbfg'	BFGS Quasi-Newton
'trainrp'	Resilient Backpropagation
'trainscg'	Scaled Conjugate Gradient
'traincgb'	Conjugate Gradient with Powell/Beale Restarts
'traincgf'	Fletcher-Powell Conjugate Gradient
'traincgp'	Polak-Ribiére Conjugate Gradient
'trainoss'	One Step Secant
'traingdx'	Variable Learning Rate Gradient Descent
'traingdm'	Gradient Descent with Momentum
'traingd'	Gradient Descent

6.3.2 Learning vector quantization neural network: lvqnet

Syntax

```
lvqnet(hiddenSize,lvqLR,lvqLF)
```

Description

LVQ (learning vector quantization) neural networks consist of two layers. The first layer maps input vectors into clusters that are found by the network during training. The second layer merges groups of first layer clusters into the classes defined by the target data.

The total number of first layer clusters is determined by the number of hidden neurons. The larger the hidden layer the more clusters the first layer can learn, and the more complex mapping of input to target classes can be made. The relative number of first layer clusters assigned to each target class are determined according to the distribution of target classes at the time of network initialization. This occurs when the network is automatically configured the first time `train` is called, or manually configured with the function `configure`, or manually initialized with the function `init` is called.

`lvqnet(hiddenSize,lvqLR,lvqLF)` takes these arguments,

hiddenSize	Size of hidden layer (default = 10)

lvqLR	LVQ learning rate (default = 0.01)
lvqLF	LVQ learning function (default = 'learnlv1')

and returns an LVQ neural network.

The other option for the lvq learning function is learnlv2.

Example: Train a Learning Vector Quantization Network

Here, an LVQ network is trained to classify iris flowers.

```
[x,t] = iris_dataset;
net = lvqnet(10);
net.trainParam.epochs = 50;
net = train(net,x,t);
view(net)
y = net(x);
perf = perform(net,y,t)
classes = vec2ind(y);
perf =

    0.0489
```

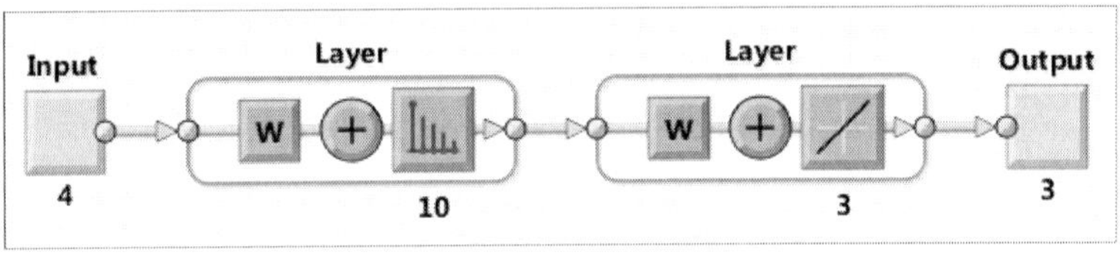

6.4 TRAINING OPTIONS AND NETWORK PERFORMANCE

The following functions are used to training and network performance.

train	Train neural network
trainlm	Levenberg-Marquardt backpropagation
trainbr	Bayesian regularization backpropagation
trainscg	Scaled conjugate gradient backpropagation
trainrp	Resilient backpropagation
mse	Mean squared normalized error performance function
regression	Linear regression
roc	Receiver operating characteristic
plotconfusion	Plot classification confusion matrix

`ploterrhist`	Plot error histogram
`plotperform`	Plot network performance
`plotregression`	Plot linear regression
`plotroc`	Plot receiver operating characteristic
`plottrainstate`	Plot training state values
`crossentropy`	Neural network performance
`genFunction`	Generate MATLAB function for simulating neural network

6.4.1 Receiver operating characteristic: roc

Syntax

```
[tpr,fpr,thresholds] = roc(targets,outputs)
```

Description

The *receiver operating characteristic* is a metric used to check the quality of classifiers. For each class of a classifier, `roc`applies threshold values across the interval `[0,1]` to outputs. For each threshold, two values are calculated, the True Positive Ratio (TPR) and the False Positive Ratio (FPR). For a particular class *i*, TPR is the number of outputs whose actual and predicted class is class *i*, divided by the number of outputs whose predicted class is class *i*. FPR is the number of outputs whose actual class is not class *i*, but predicted class is class *i*, divided by the number of outputs whose predicted class is not class *i*.

You can visualize the results of this function with `plotroc`.

`[tpr,fpr,thresholds] = roc(targets,outputs)` takes these arguments:

`targets`	`S`-by-`Q` matrix, where each column vector contains a single `1` value, with all other elements `0`. The index of the `1` indicates which of `S` categories that vector represents.
`outputs`	`S`-by-`Q` matrix, where each column contains values in the range `[0,1]`. The index of the largest element in the column indicates which of `S` categories that vector presents. Alternately, `1`-by-`Q`vector, where values greater or equal to `0.5` indicate class membership, and values below `0.5`, nonmembership.

and returns these values:

`tpr`	`1`-by-`S` cell array of `1`-by-`N` true-positive/positive ratios.
`fpr`	`1`-by-`S` cell array of `1`-by-`N` false-positive/negative ratios.
`thresholds`	`1`-by-`S` cell array of `1`-by-`N` thresholds over interval `[0,1]`.

`roc(targets,outputs)` takes these arguments:

`targets`	`1`-by-`Q` matrix of Boolean values indicating class membership.

`outputs`	`S`-by-`Q` matrix, of values in `[0,1]` interval, where values greater than or equal to `0.5` indicate class membership.

and returns these values:

`tpr`	`1`-by-`N` vector of true-positive/positive ratios.
`fpr`	`1`-by-`N` vector of false-positive/negative ratios.
`thresholds`	`1`-by-`N` vector of thresholds over interval `[0,1]`.

Examples

```
load iris_dataset

net = patternnet(20);

net = train(net,irisInputs,irisTargets);

irisOutputs = sim(net,irisInputs);

[tpr,fpr,thresholds] = roc(irisTargets,irisOutputs)
```

6.4.2 Plot receiver operating characteristic: plotroc

Syntax

```
plotroc(targets,outputs)
plotroc(targets1,outputs2,'name1',...)
```

Description

`plotroc(targets,outputs)` plots the receiver operating characteristic for each output class. The more each curve hugs the left and top edges of the plot, the better the classification.

`plotroc(targets1,outputs2,'name1',...)` generates multiple plots.

Examples: Plot Receiver Operating Characteristic

```
load simplecluster_dataset
net = patternnet(20);
net = train(net,simpleclusterInputs,simpleclusterTargets);
simpleclusterOutputs = sim(net,simpleclusterInputs);
plotroc(simpleclusterTargets,simpleclusterOutputs)
```

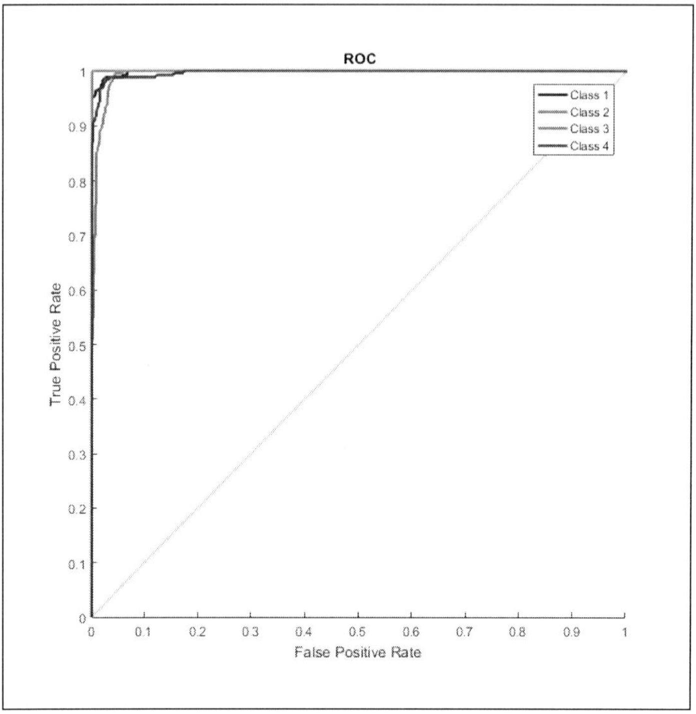

6.4.3 Plot classification confusion matrix: plotconfusion

Syntax

- `plotconfusion(targets,outputs)`
- example
- `plotconfusion(targets,outputs,name)`
- `plotconfusion(targets1,outputs1,name1,targets2,outputs2,name2,...,targetsn,outputsn,namen)`

Description

`plotconfusion(targets,outputs)` returns a confusion matrix plot for the target and output data in `targets` and `outputs`, respectively.

On the confusion matrix plot, the rows correspond to the predicted class (`Output Class`), and the columns show the true class (`Target Class`). The diagonal cells show for how many (and what percentage) of the examples the trained network correctly estimates the classes of observations. That is, it shows what percentage of the true and predicted classes match. The off diagonal cells show where the classifier has made mistakes. The column on the far right of the plot shows the accuracy for each predicted class, while the row at the bottom of the plot shows the accuracy for each true class. The cell in the bottom right of the plot shows the overall accuracy.

`plotconfusion(targets,outputs,name)` returns a confusion matrix plot with the title starting with `name`.

`plotconfusion(targets1,outputs1,name1,targets2,outputs2,name2,...,targetsn,outputsn,namen)`returns several confusion plots in one figure, and prefixes the `name` arguments to the titles of the appropriate plots.

Examples: Plot Confusion Matrix

This example shows how to train a pattern recognition network and plot its accuracy.

Load the sample data.

```
[x,t] = cancer_dataset;
```

`cancerInputs` is a 9x699 matrix defining nine attributes of 699 biopsies. `cancerTargets` is a 2x966 matrix where each column indicates a correct category with a one in either element 1 (benign) or element 2 (malignant). For more information on this dataset, type `help cancer_dataset` in the command line.
Create a pattern recognition network and train it using the sample data.

```
net = patternnet(10);
net = train(net,x,t);
```

Estimate the cancer status using the trained network, `net` .

```
y = net(x);
```

Plot the confusion matrix.

```
plotconfusion(t,y)
```

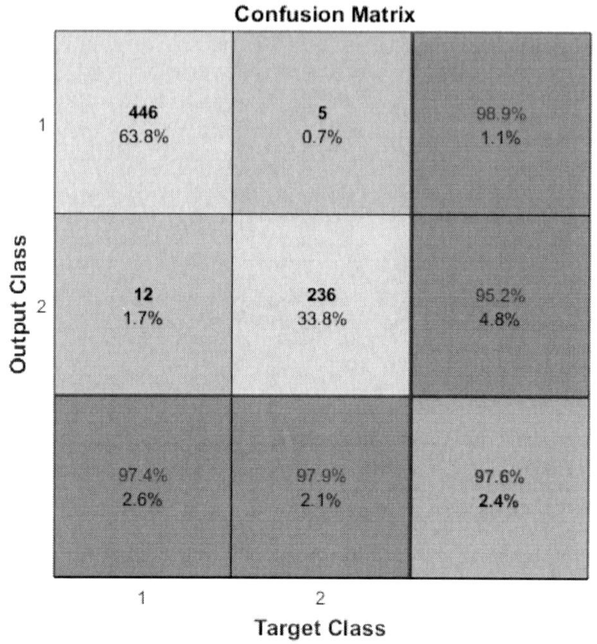

In this figure, the first two diagonal cells show the number and percentage of correct classifications by the trained network. For example 446 biopsies are correctly classifed as benign. This corresponds to 63.8% of all 699 biopsies. Similarly, 236 cases are correctly classified as malignant. This corresponds to 33.8% of all biopsies.

5 of the malignant biopsies are incorrectly classified as benign and this corresponds to 0.7% of all 699 biopsies in the data. Similarly, 12 of the benign biopsies are incorrectly classified as malignant and this corresponds to 1.7% of all data.

Out of 451 benign predictions, 98.9% are correct and 1.1% are wrong. Out of 248 malignant predictions, 95.2% are correct and 4.8% are wrong. Out of 458 benign cases, 97.4% are correctly predicted as benign and 2.6% are predicted as malignant. Out of 241 malignant cases, 97.9% are correctly classified as malignant and 2.1% are classified as benign.

Overall, 97.6% of the predictions are correct and 2.4% are wrong classifications.

6.4.4 Neural network performance: crossentropy

Syntax

- `perf = crossentropy(net,targets,outputs,perfWeights)`
- `perf = crossentropy(__,Name,Value)`

Description

`perf = crossentropy(net,targets,outputs,perfWeights)` calculates a network performance given targets and outputs, with optional performance weights and other parameters. The function returns a result that heavily penalizes outputs that are extremely inaccurate (y near `1-t`), with very little penalty for fairly correct classifications (y near `t`). Minimizing cross-entropy leads to good classifiers.

The cross-entropy for each pair of output-target elements is calculated as: `ce = -t .* log(y)`.

The aggregate cross-entropy performance is the mean of the individual values: `perf = sum(ce(:))/numel(ce)`.

Special case (N = 1): If an output consists of only one element, then the outputs and targets are interpreted as binary encoding. That is, there are two classes with targets of 0 and 1, whereas in 1-of-N encoding, there are two or more classes. The binary cross-entropy expression is: `ce = -t .* log(y) - (1-t) .* log(1-y)` .

`perf = crossentropy(__,Name,Value)` supports customization according to the specified name-value pair arguments.

Examples: Calculate Network Performance

This example shows how to design a classification network with cross-entropy and 0.1 regularization, then calculation performance on the whole dataset.

```
[x,t] = iris_dataset;
net = patternnet(10);
net.performParam.regularization = 0.1;
net = train(net,x,t);
y = net(x);
perf = crossentropy(net,t,y,{1},'regularization',0.1)
perf =

    0.0278
```

6.4.5 Construct and Train a Function Fitting Network

Load the training data.

```
[x,t] = simplefit_dataset;
```

The 1-by-94 matrix x contains the input values and the 1-by-94 matrix `t` contains the associated target output values.

Construct a function fitting neural network with one hidden layer of size 10.

```
net = fitnet(10);
```

View the network.

```
view(net)
```

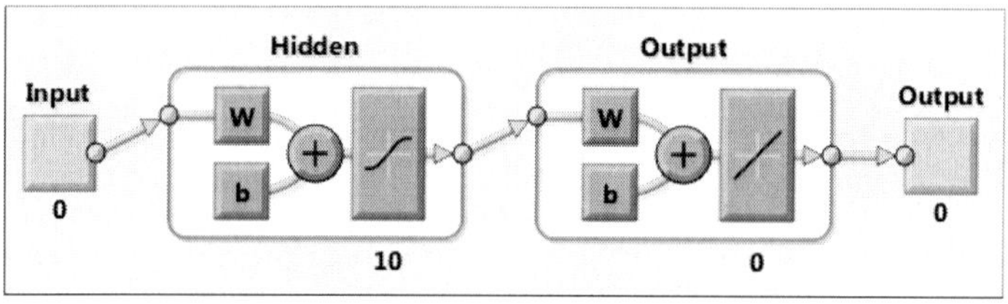

The sizes of the input and output are zero. The software adjusts the sizes of these during training according to the training data.

Train the network `net` using the training data.

```
net = train(net,x,t);
```

View the trained network.

```
view(net)
```

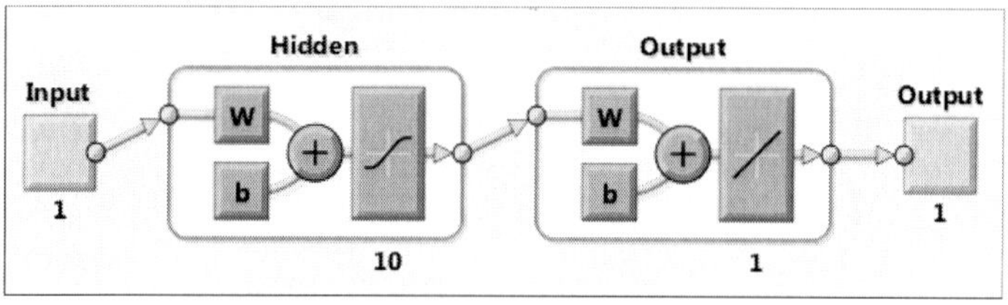

You can see that the sizes of the input and output are 1.

Estimate the targets using the trained network.

```
y = net(x);
```

Assess the performance of the trained network. The default performance function is mean squared error.

```
perf = perform(net,y,t)
perf =

   1.4639e-04
```

The default training algorithm for a function fitting network is Levenberg-Marquardt (`'trainlm'`). Use the Bayesian regularization training algorithm and compare the performance results.

```
net = fitnet(10,'trainbr');
net = train(net,x,t);
y = net(x);
perf = perform(net,y,t)
perf =

   3.3416e-10
```

The Bayesian regularization training algorithm improves the performance of the network in terms of estimating the target values.

6.4.6 Create and train Feedforward Neural Network

`feedforwardnet(hiddenSizes,trainFcn)`

This command construct the feedforward neural network. Feedforward networks consist of a series of layers. The first layer has a connection from the network input. Each subsequent layer has a connection from the previous layer. The final layer produces the network's output.

Feedforward networks can be used for any kind of input to output mapping. A feedforward network with one hidden layer and enough neurons in the hidden layers, can fit any finite input-output mapping problem.

Specialized versions of the feedforward network include fitting (`fitnet`) and pattern recognition (`patternnet`) networks. A variation on the feedforward network is the cascade forward network (`cascadeforwardnet`) which has additional connections from the input to every layer, and from each layer to all following layers.

`feedforwardnet(hiddenSizes,trainFcn)` takes these arguments,

`hiddenSizes`	Row vector of one or more hidden layer sizes (default = 10)
`trainFcn`	Training function (default = `'trainlm'`)

and returns a feedforward neural network.

This example shows how to use feedforward neural network to solve a simple problem.

```
[x,t] = simplefit_dataset;
net = feedforwardnet(10);
net = train(net,x,t);
view(net)
y = net(x);
perf = perform(net,y,t)
perf =

   1.4639e-04
```

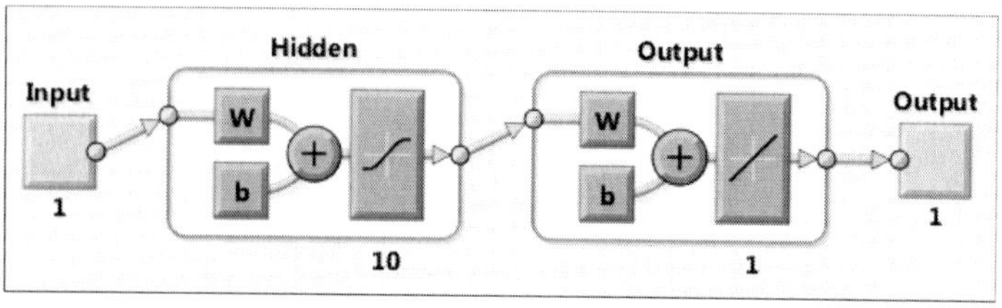

6.4.7 Create and Train a Cascade Network

`cascadeforwardnet(hiddenSizes,trainFcn)`

Cascade-forward networks are similar to feed-forward networks, but include a connection from the input and every previous layer to following layers. As with feed-forward networks, a two-or more layer cascade-network can learn any finite input-output relationship arbitrarily well given enough hidden neurons.

`cascadeforwardnet(hiddenSizes,trainFcn)` takes these arguments,

`hiddenSizes`	Row vector of one or more hidden layer sizes (default = 10)
`trainFcn`	Training function (default = `'trainlm'`)

and returns a new cascade-forward neural network.

Here a cascade network is created and trained on a simple fitting problem.

```
[x,t] = simplefit_dataset;
net = cascadeforwardnet(10);
net = train(net,x,t);
view(net)
y = net(x);
perf = perform(net,y,t)
perf =

   1.9372e-05
```

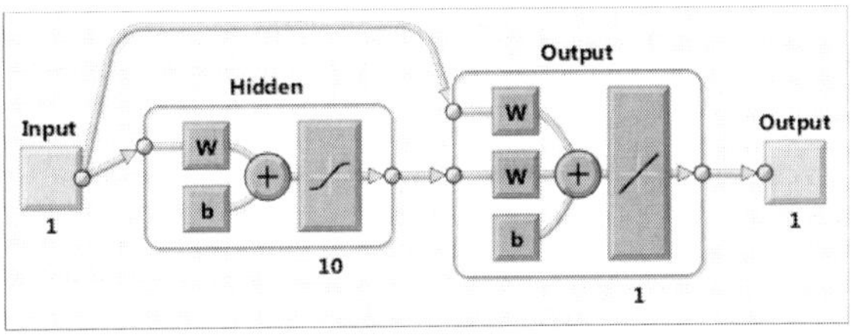

6.5 NETWORK PERFORMANCE

In MATLAB `mse` is a network performance function. It measures the network's performance according to the mean of squared errors.

6.5.1 Description

`perf = mse(net,t,y,ew)` takes these arguments:

`net`	Neural network
`t`	Matrix or cell array of targets
`y`	Matrix or cell array of outputs
`ew`	Error weights (optional)

and returns the mean squared error.

This function has two optional parameters, which are associated with networks whose `net.trainFcn` is set to this function:

- `'regularization'` can be set to any value between 0 and 1. The greater the regularization value, the more squared weights and biases are included in the performance calculation relative to errors. The default is 0, corresponding to no regularization.
- `'normalization'` can be set to `'none'` (the default); `'standard'`, which normalizes errors between -2 and 2, corresponding to normalizing outputs and targets between -1 and 1; and `'percent'`, which normalizes errors between -1 and 1. This feature is useful for networks with multi-element outputs. It ensures that the relative accuracy of output elements with differing target value ranges are treated as equally important, instead of prioritizing the relative accuracy of the output element with the largest target value range.

You can create a standard network that uses `mse` with `feedforwardnet` or `cascadeforwardnet`. To prepare a custom network to be trained with `mse`, set `net.performFcn` to `'mse'`. This automatically sets `net.performParam` to a structure with the default optional parameter values.

6.5.2 Examples

Here a two-layer feedforward network is created and trained to predict median house prices using the `mse` performance function and a regularization value of 0.01, which is the default performance function for `feedforwardnet`.

```
[x,t] = house_dataset;
net = feedforwardnet(10);
net.performFcn = 'mse';  % Redundant, MSE is default
net.performParam.regularization = 0.01;
net = train(net,x,t);
y = net(x);
perf  = perform(net,t,y);
```

Alternately, you can call this function directly.

```
perf = mse(net,x,t,'regularization',0.01);
```

6.6 FIT REGRESSION MODEL AND PLOT FITTED VALUES VERSUS TARGETS

6.6.1 Description

`[r,m,b] = regression(t,y)` takes these arguments,

t	Target matrix or cell array data with a total of N matrix rows
y	Output matrix or cell array data of the same size

and returns these outputs,

r	Regression values for each of the N matrix rows
m	Slope of regression fit for each of the N matrix rows
b	Offset of regression fit for each of the N matrix rows

`[r,m,b] = regression(t,y,'one')` combines all matrix rows before regressing, and returns single scalar regression, slope, and offset values.

`plotregression(targets,outputs)` plots the linear regression of `targets` relative to `outputs`.

`plotregression(targs1,outs1,'name1',targs2,outs2,'name2',...)` generates multiple plots.

6.6.2 Examples

Train a feedforward network, then calculate and plot the regression between its targets and outputs.

```
[x,t] = simplefit_dataset;
net = feedforwardnet(20);
net = train(net,x,t);
y = net(x);
[r,m,b] = regression(t,y)
plotregression(t,y)
r =

    1.0000

m =

    1.0000

b =

   1.0878e-04
```

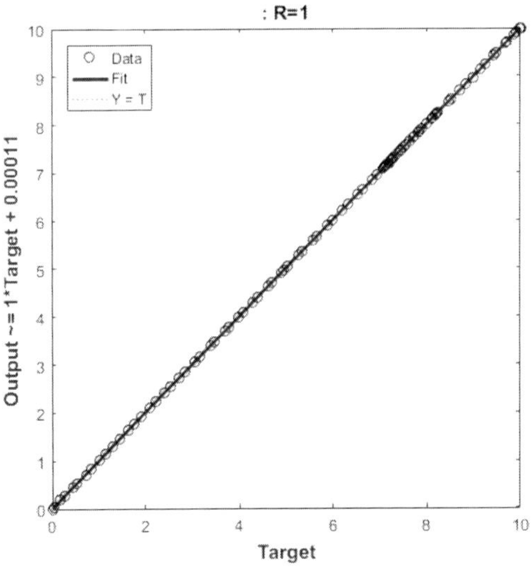

The next example Plot Linear Regression

```
[x,t] = simplefit_dataset;
```

```
net = feedforwardnet(10);
net = train(net,x,t);
y = net(x);
plotregression(t,y,'Regression')
```

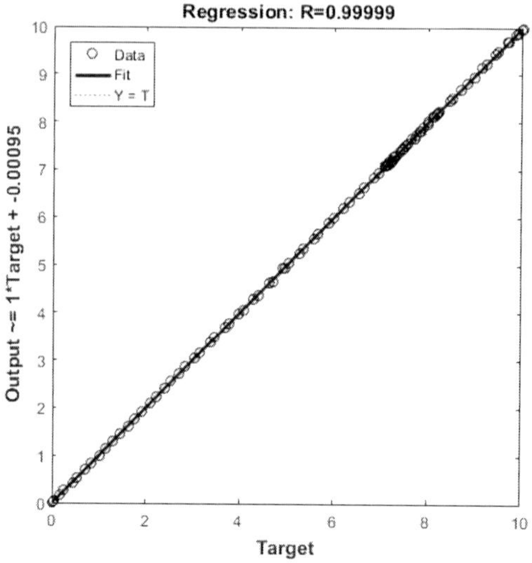

6.7 PLOT OUTPUT AND TARGET VALUES

6.7.1 Description

`plotfit(net,inputs,targets)` plots the output function of a network across the range of the inputs `inputs` and also plots target `targets` and output data points associated with values in `inputs`. Error bars show the difference between outputs and `targets`.

The plot appears only for networks with one input.

Only the first output/targets appear if the network has more than one output.

`plotfit(targets1,inputs1,'name1',...)` displays a series of plots.

6.7.2 Examples

This example shows how to use a feed-forward network to solve a simple fitting problem.

```
[x,t] = simplefit_dataset;
net = feedforwardnet(10);
```

```
net = train(net,x,t);
plotfit(net,x,t)
```

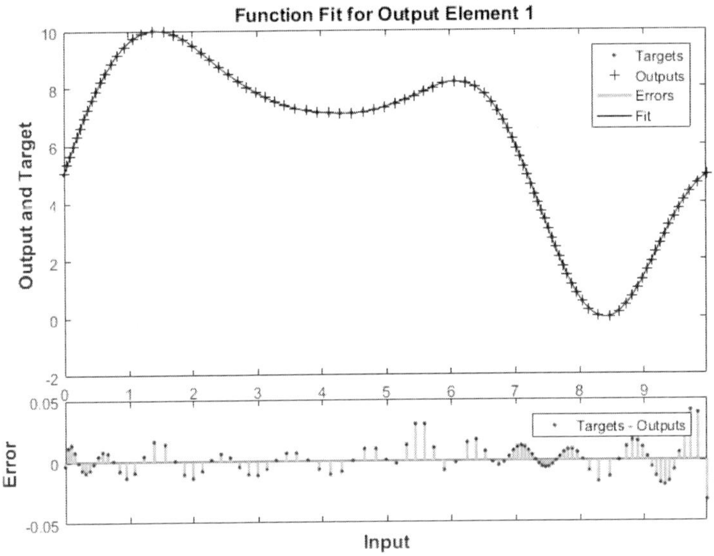

6.8 PLOT TRAINING STATE VALUES

`plottrainstate(tr)` plots the training state from a training record `tr` returned by `train`.

Below is an example:

```
[x,t] = house_dataset;
net = feedforwardnet(10);
[net,tr] = train(net,x,t);
plottrainstate(tr)
```

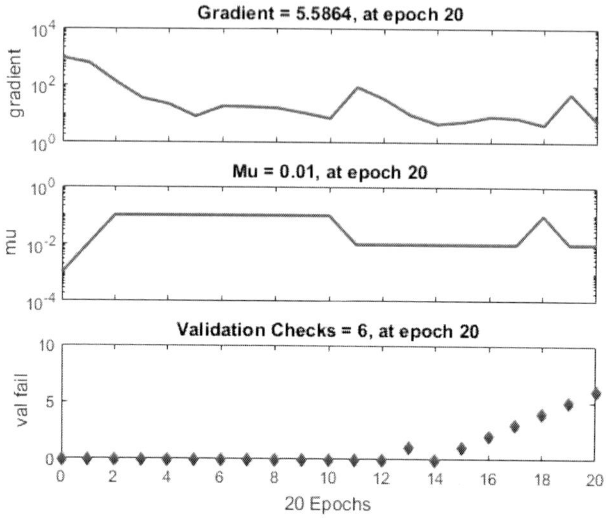

6.9 PLOT PERFORMANCES

`plotperform(TR)` plots error vs. epoch for the training, validation, and test performances of the training record `TR` returned by the function `train`.

This example shows how to use `plotperform` to obtain a plot of training record error values against the number of training epochs.

```
[x,t] = house_dataset;
net = feedforwardnet(10);
[net,tr] = train(net,x,t);
plotperform(tr)
```

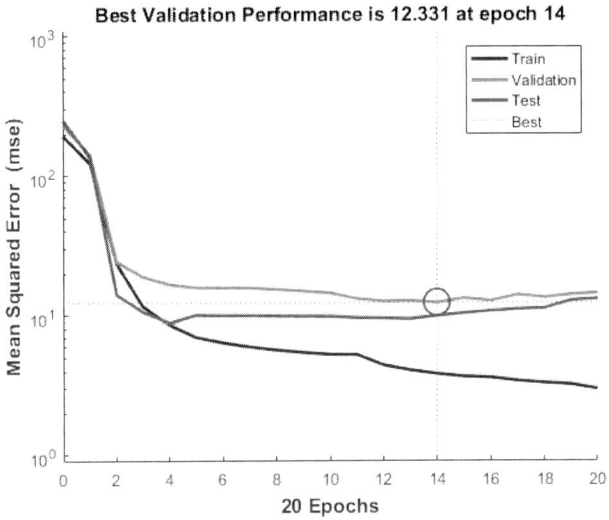

Generally, the error reduces after more epochs of training, but might start to increase on the validation data set as the network starts overfitting the training data. In the default setup, the training stops after six consecutive increases in validation error, and the best performance is taken from the epoch with the lowest validation error.

6.10 PLOT HISTOGRAM OF ERROR VALUES

6.10.1 Syntax

```
ploterrhist(e)
ploterrhist(e1,'name1',e2,'name2',...)
ploterrhist(...,'bins',bins)
```

6.10.2 Description

`ploterrhist(e)` plots a histogram of error values e.

`ploterrhist(e1,'name1',e2,'name2',...)` takes any number of errors and names and plots each pair.

`ploterrhist(...,'bins',bins)` takes an optional property name/value pair which defines the number of bins to use in the histogram plot. The default is 20.

6.10.3 Examples

Here a feedforward network is used to solve a simple fitting problem:

```
[x,t] = simplefit_dataset;
net = feedforwardnet(20);
net = train(net,x,t);
y = net(x);
e = t - y;
ploterrhist(e,'bins',30)
```

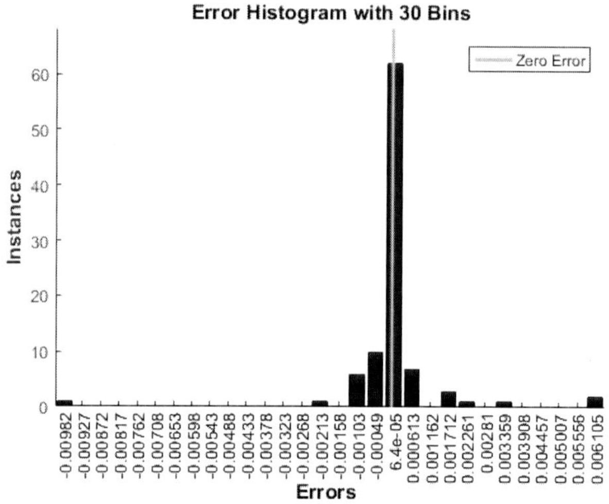

6.11 GENERATE MATLAB FUNCTION FOR SIMULATING NEURAL NETWORK

`genFunction(net,pathname)` generates a complete stand-alone MATLAB function for simulating a neural network including all settings, weight and bias values, module functions, and calculations in one file. The result is a standalone MATLAB function file. You can also use this function with MATLAB Compiler™ and MATLAB Coder™ tools.

`genFunction(__,'MatrixOnly','yes')` overrides the default cell/matrix notation and instead generates a function that uses only matrix arguments compatible with MATLAB Coder tools. For static networks, the matrix columns are interpreted as independent samples. For dynamic networks, the matrix columns are interpreted as a series of time steps. The default value is `'no'`.

`genFunction(__,'ShowLinks','no')` disables the default behavior of displaying links to generated help and source code. The default is `'yes'`.

6.11.1 Create Functions from Static Neural Network

This example shows how to create a MATLAB function and a MEX-function from a static neural network.

First, train a static network and calculate its outputs for the training data.

```
[x,t] = house_dataset;
houseNet = feedforwardnet(10);
houseNet = train(houseNet,x,t);
y = houseNet(x);
```

Next, generate and test a MATLAB function. Then the new function is compiled to a shared/dynamically linked library with `mcc`.

```
genFunction(houseNet,'houseFcn');
y2 = houseFcn(x);
accuracy2 = max(abs(y-y2))
mcc -W lib:libHouse -T link:lib houseFcn
```

Next, generate another version of the MATLAB function that supports only matrix arguments (no cell arrays), and test the function. Use the MATLAB Coder tool `codegen` to generate a MEX-function, which is also tested.

```
genFunction(houseNet,'houseFcn','MatrixOnly','yes');
y3 = houseFcn(x);
accuracy3 = max(abs(y-y3))

x1Type = coder.typeof(double(0),[13 Inf]); % Coder type of input 1
codegen houseFcn.m -config:mex -o houseCodeGen -args {x1Type}
y4 = houseCodeGen(x);
accuracy4 = max(abs(y-y4))
```

6.11.2 Create Functions from Dynamic Neural Network

This example shows how to create a MATLAB function and a MEX-function from a dynamic neural network.

First, train a dynamic network and calculate its outputs for the training data.

```
[x,t] = maglev_dataset;
maglevNet = narxnet(1:2,1:2,10);
[X,Xi,Ai,T] = preparets(maglevNet,x,{},t);
maglevNet = train(maglevNet,X,T,Xi,Ai);
[y,xf,af] = maglevNet(X,Xi,Ai);
```

Next, generate and test a MATLAB function. Use the function to create a shared/dynamically linked library with mcc.

```
genFunction(maglevNet,'maglevFcn');
[y2,xf,af] = maglevFcn(X,Xi,Ai);
accuracy2 = max(abs(cell2mat(y)-cell2mat(y2)))
mcc -W lib:libMaglev -T link:lib maglevFcn
```

Next, generate another version of the MATLAB function that supports only matrix arguments (no cell arrays), and test the function. Use the MATLAB Coder tool codegen to generate a MEX-function, which is also tested.

```
genFunction(maglevNet,'maglevFcn','MatrixOnly','yes');

x1 = cell2mat(X(1,:)); % Convert each input to matrix
x2 = cell2mat(X(2,:));
xi1 = cell2mat(Xi(1,:)); % Convert each input state to matrix
xi2 = cell2mat(Xi(2,:));
[y3,xf1,xf2] = maglevFcn(x1,x2,xi1,xi2);
accuracy3 = max(abs(cell2mat(y)-y3))

x1Type = coder.typeof(double(0),[1 Inf]); % Coder type of input 1
x2Type = coder.typeof(double(0),[1 Inf]); % Coder type of input 2
xi1Type = coder.typeof(double(0),[1 2]); % Coder type of input 1
states
xi2Type = coder.typeof(double(0),[1 2]); % Coder type of input 2
states
codegen maglevFcn.m -config:mex -o maglevNetCodeGen -args {x1Type
x2Type xi1Type xi2Type}
[y4,xf1,xf2] = maglevNetCodeGen(x1,x2,xi1,xi2);
dynamic_codegen_accuracy = max(abs(cell2mat(y)-y4))
```

6.12 A COMPLETE EXAMPLE: HOUSE PRICE ESTIMATION

This example illustrates how a function fitting neural network can estimate median house prices for a neighborhood based on neighborhood demographics.

6.12.1 The Problem: Estimate House Values

In this example we attempt to build a neural network that can estimate the median price of a home in a neighborhood described by thirteen demographic attributes:

- Per capita crime rate per town
- Proportion of residential land zoned for lots over 25,000 sq. ft.

- Proportion of non-retail business acres per town
- 1 if tract bounds Charles river, 0 otherwise
- Nitric oxides concentration (parts per 10 million)
- Average number of rooms per dwelling
- Proportion of owner-occupied units built prior to 1940
- Weighted distances to five Boston employment centres
- Index of accessibility to radial highways
- Full-value property-tax rate per $10,000
- Pupil-teacher ratio by town
- 1000(Bk - 0.63)^2
- Percent lower status of the population

This is an example of a fitting problem, where inputs are matched up to associated target outputs, and we would like to create a neural network which not only estimates the known targets given known inputs, but can generalize to accurately estimate outputs for inputs that were not used to design the solution.

6.12.2 Why Neural Networks?

Neural networks are very good at function fit problems. A neural network with enough elements (called neurons) can fit any data with arbitrary accuracy. They are particularly well suited for addressing non-linear problems. Given the non-linear nature of real world phenomena, like house valuation, neural networks are a good candidate for solving the problem.

The thirteeen neighborhood attributes will act as inputs to a neural network, and the median home price will be the target.

The network will be designed by using the attributes of neighborhoods whose median house value is already known to train it to produce the target valuations.

6.12.3 Preparing the Data

Data for function fitting problems are set up for a neural network by organizing the data into two matrices, the input matrix X and the target matrix T.

Each ith column of the input matrix will have thirteen elements representing a neighborhood whose median house value is already known.

Each corresponding column of the target matrix will have one element, representing the median house price in 1000's of dollars.

Here such a dataset is loaded.

```
[x,t] = house_dataset;
```

We can view the sizes of inputs X and targets T.

Note that both X and T have 506 columns. These represent 506 neighborhood attributes (inputs) and associated median house values (targets).

Input matrix X has thirteen rows, for the thirteen attributes. Target matrix T has only one row, as for each example we only have one desired output, the median house value.

```
size(x)
size(t)
ans =

    13   506

ans =

     1   506
```

6.12.4 Fitting a Function with a Neural Network

The next step is to create a neural network that will learn to estimate median house values.

Since the neural network starts with random initial weights, the results of this example will differ slightly every time it is run. The random seed is set to avoid this randomness. However this is not necessary for your own applications.

```
setdemorandstream(491218382)
```

Two-layer (i.e. one-hidden-layer) feed forward neural networks can fit any input-output relationship given enough neurons in the hidden layer. Layers which are not output layers are called hidden layers.

We will try a single hidden layer of 10 neurons for this example. In general, more difficult problems require more neurons, and perhaps more layers. Simpler problems require fewer neurons.

The input and output have sizes of 0 because the network has not yet been configured to match our input and target data. This will happen when the network is trained.

```
net = fitnet(10);
view(net)
```

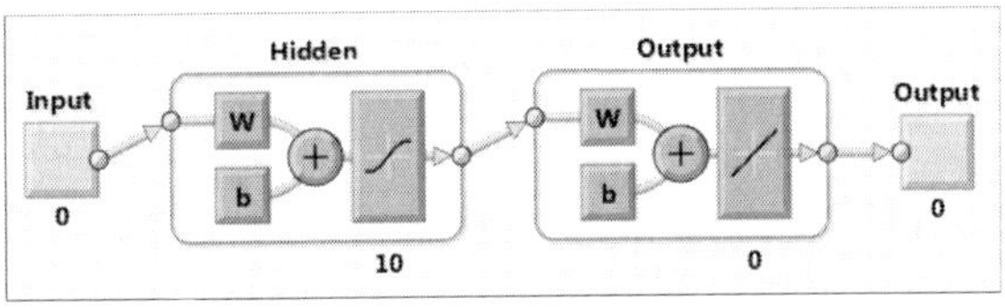

Now the network is ready to be trained. The samples are automatically divided into training, validation and test sets. The training set is used to teach the network. Training continues as long as the network continues improving on the validation set. The test set provides a completely independent measure of network accuracy.

The NN Training Tool shows the network being trained and the algorithms used to train it. It also displays the training state during training and the criteria which stopped training will be highlighted in green.

The buttons at the bottom open useful plots which can be opened during and after training. Links next to the algorithm names and plot buttons open documentation on those subjects.

```
[net,tr] = train(net,x,t);
nntraintool
```

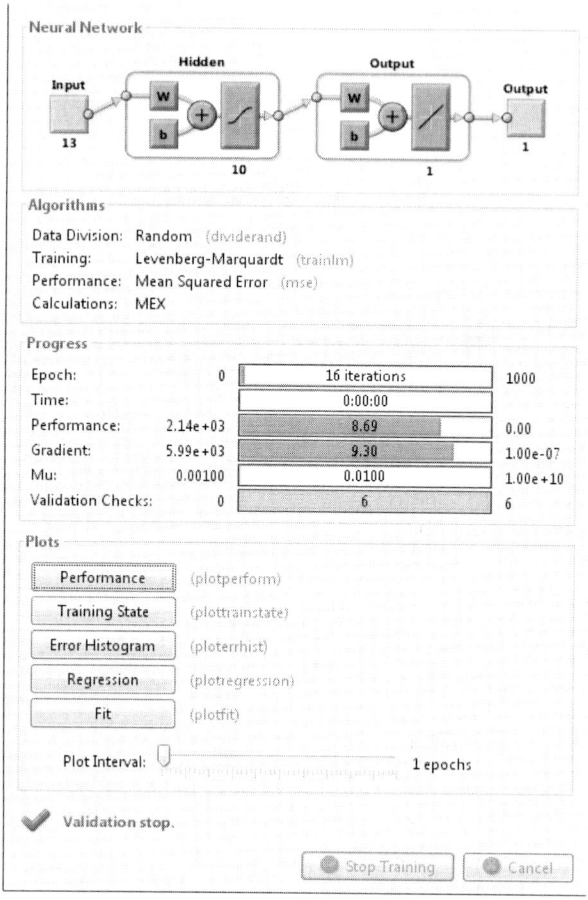

To see how the network's performance improved during training, either click the "Performance" button in the training tool, or call PLOTPERFORM.

Performance is measured in terms of mean squared error, and shown in log scale. It rapidly decreased as the network was trained.

Performance is shown for each of the training, validation and test sets. The version of the network that did best on the validation set is was after training.

```
plotperform(tr)
```

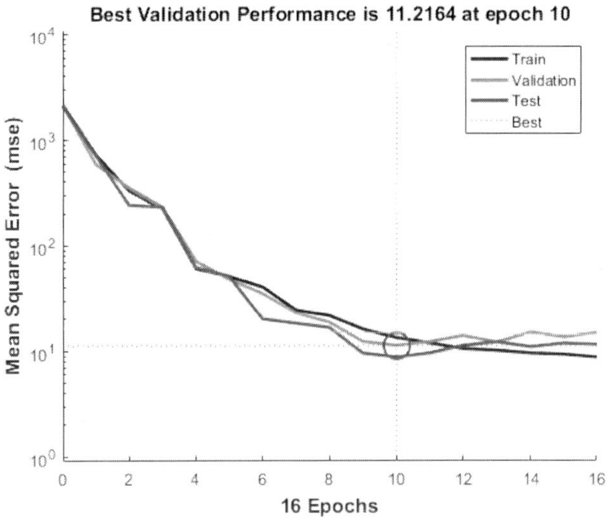

6.12.5 Testing the Neural Network

The mean squared error of the trained neural network can now be measured with respect to the testing samples. This will give us a sense of how well the network will do when applied to data from the real world.

```
testX = x(:,tr.testInd);
testT = t(:,tr.testInd);

testY = net(testX);

perf = mse(net,testT,testY)
perf =

    8.6959
```

Another measure of how well the neural network has fit the data is the regression plot. Here the regression is plotted across all samples.

The regression plot shows the actual network outputs plotted in terms of the associated target values. If the network has learned to fit the data well, the linear fit to this output-target relationship should closely intersect the bottom-left and top-right corners of the plot.

If this is not the case then further training, or training a network with more hidden neurons, would be advisable.

```
y = net(x);
```

```
plotregression(t,y)
```

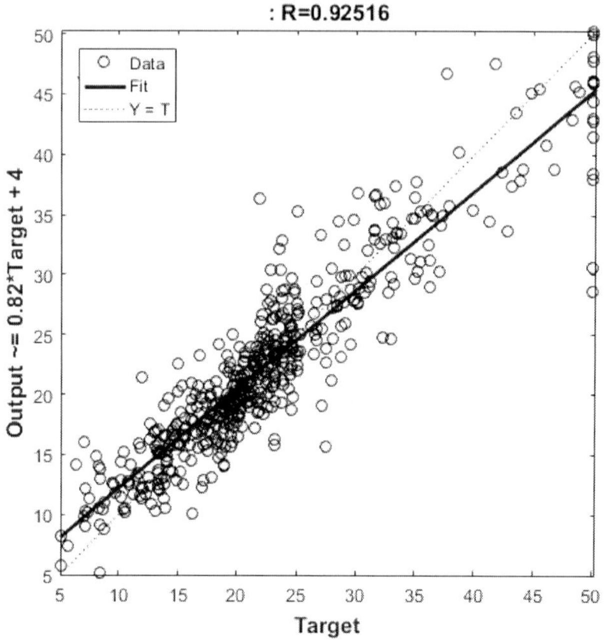

Another third measure of how well the neural network has fit data is the error histogram. This shows how the error sizes are distributed. Typically most errors are near zero, with very few errors far from that.

```
e = t - y;

ploterrhist(e)
```

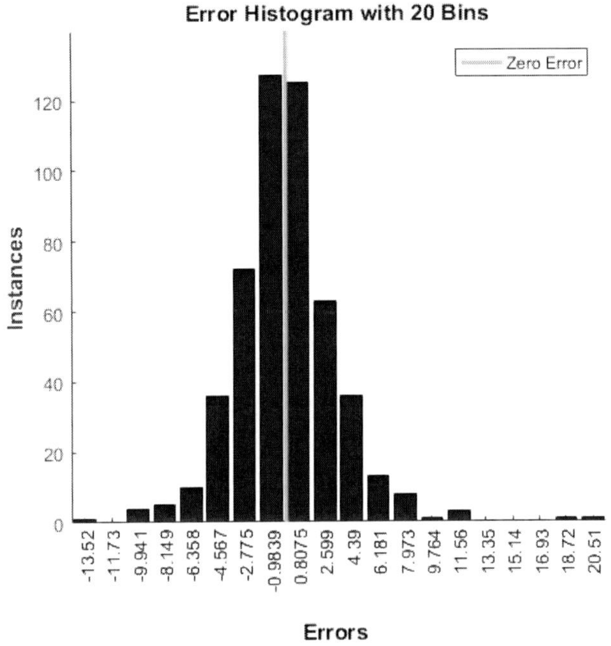

This example illustrated how to design a neural network that estimates the median house value from neighborhood characteristics.

6.13 AUTOENCODER CLASS

Description

An `Autoencoder` object contains an autoencoder network, which consists of an encoder and a decoder. The encoder maps the input to a hidden representation. The decoder attempts to map this representation back to the original input.

Construction

`autoenc = trainAutoencoder(X)` returns an autoencoder trained using the training data in `X`.

`autoenc = trainAutoencoder(X,hiddenSize)` returns an autoencoder with the hidden representation size of `hiddenSize`.

`autoenc = trainAutoencoder(__,Name,Value)` for any of the above input arguments with additional options specified by one or more `Name,Value` pair arguments.

Input Arguments

`X` — training data
matrix | cell array of image data

`Hiddensize` — size of hidden representation of the autoencoder
10 (default) | positive integer value

Methods

decode	Decode encoded data
encode	Encode input data
generateFunction	Generate a MATLAB function to run the autoencoder
generateSimulink	Generate a Simulink model for the autoencoder
network	Convert `Autoencoder` object into `network` object
plotWeights	Plot a visualization of the weights for the encoder of an autoencoder
predict	Reconstruct the inputs using trained autoencoder
stack	Stack encoders from several autoencoders together
view	View autoencoder

6.14 AUTOENCODER FUNCTIONS

6.14.1 Functions

`trainAutoencoder`	Train an autoencoder
`trainSoftmaxLayer`	Train a softmax layer for classification
`decode`	Decode encoded data
`encode`	Encode input data
`generateFunction`	Generate a MATLAB function to run the autoencoder
`generateSimulink`	Generate a Simulink model for the autoencoder
`network`	Convert Autoencoder object into network object
`plotWeights`	Plot a visualization of the weights for the encoder of an autoencoder
`predict`	Reconstruct the inputs using trained autoencoder
`stack`	Stack encoders from several autoencoders together
`view`	View autoencoder

6.14.2 trainAutoencoder

Train an autoencoder

Syntax

- `autoenc = trainAutoencoder(X)`
- `autoenc = trainAutoencoder(X,hiddenSize)`
- `autoenc = trainAutoencoder(__,Name,Value)`

Description

`autoenc = trainAutoencoder(X)` returns an autoencoder, `autoenc`, trained using the training data in `X`.

`autoenc = trainAutoencoder(X,hiddenSize)` returns an autoencoder `autoenc`, with the hidden representation size of `hiddenSize`.

`autoenc = trainAutoencoder(__,Name,Value)` returns an autoencoder `autoenc`, for any of the above input arguments with additional options specified by one or more `Name,Value` pair arguments.

For example, you can specify the sparsity proportion or the maximum number of training iterations.

Examples. Train Sparse Autoencoder

Load the sample data.

```
X = abalone_dataset;
```

X is an 8-by-4177 matrix defining eight attributes for 4177 different abalone shells: sex (M, F, and I (for infant)), length, diameter, height, whole weight, shucked weight, viscera weight, shell weight. For more information on the dataset, type `help abalone_dataset` in the command line.

Train a sparse autoencoder with default settings.

```
autoenc = trainAutoencoder(X);
```

Reconstruct the abalone shell ring data using the trained autoencoder.

```
XReconstructed = predict(autoenc,X);
```

Compute the mean squared reconstruction error.

```
mseError = mse(X-XReconstructed)
mseError =

    0.0167
```

Train Autoencoder with Specified Options

Load the sample data.

```
X = abalone_dataset;
```

X is an 8-by-4177 matrix defining eight attributes for 4177 different abalone shells: sex (M, F, and I (for infant)), length, diameter, height, whole weight, shucked weight, viscera weight, shell weight. For more information on the dataset, type `help abalone_dataset` in the command line.

Train a sparse autoencoder with hidden size 4, 400 maximum epochs, and linear transfer function for the decoder.

```
autoenc = trainAutoencoder(X,4,'MaxEpochs',400,...
'DecoderTransferFunction','purelin');
```

Reconstruct the abalone shell ring data using the trained autoencoder.

```
XReconstructed = predict(autoenc,X);
```

Compute the mean squared reconstruction error.

```
mseError = mse(X-XReconstructed)
mseError =

    0.0056
```

Reconstruct Observations Using Sparse Autoencoder

Generate the training data.

```
rng(0,'twister'); % For reproducibility
n = 1000;
r = linspace(-10,10,n)';
x = 1 + r*5e-2 + sin(r)./r + 0.2*randn(n,1);
```

Train autoencoder using the training data.

```
hiddenSize = 25;
autoenc = trainAutoencoder(x',hiddenSize,...
        'EncoderTransferFunction','satlin',...
        'DecoderTransferFunction','purelin',...
        'L2WeightRegularization',0.01,...
        'SparsityRegularization',4,...
        'SparsityProportion',0.10);
```

Generate the test data.

```
n = 1000;
r = sort(-10 + 20*rand(n,1));
xtest = 1 + r*5e-2 + sin(r)./r + 0.4*randn(n,1);
```

Predict the test data using the trained autoencoder, `autoenc` .

```
xReconstructed = predict(autoenc,xtest');
```
Plot the actual test data and the predictions.

```
figure;
plot(xtest,'r.');
hold on
plot(xReconstructed,'go');
```

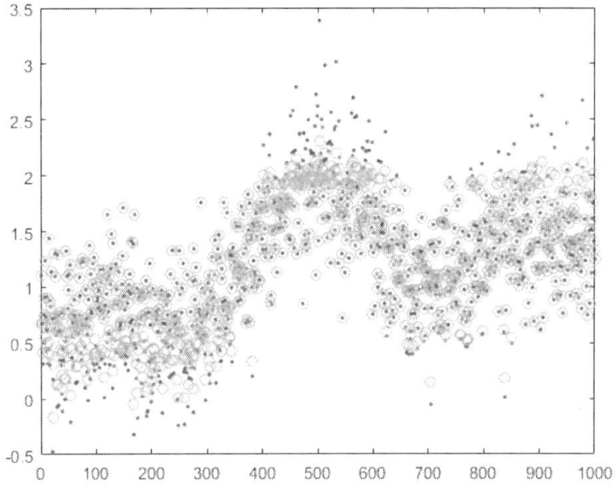

Reconstruct Handwritten Digit Images Using Sparse Autoencoder

Load the training data.

```
X = digittrain_dataset;
```

The training data is a 1-by-5000 cell array, where each cell containing a 28-by-28 matrix representing a synthetic image of a handwritten digit.

Train an autoencoder with a hidden layer containing 25 neurons.

```
hiddenSize = 25;
autoenc = trainAutoencoder(X,hiddenSize,...
        'L2WeightRegularization',0.004,...
        'SparsityRegularization',4,...
        'SparsityProportion',0.15);
```

Load the test data.

```
x = digittest_dataset;
```

The test data is a 1-by-5000 cell array, with each cell containing a 28-by-28 matrix representing a synthetic image of a handwritten digit.

Reconstruct the test image data using the trained autoencoder, `autoenc`.

```
xReconstructed = predict(autoenc,x);
```

View the actual test data.

```
figure;
for i = 1:20
    subplot(4,5,i);
    imshow(X{i});
end
```

View the reconstructed test data.

```
figure;
for i = 1:20
    subplot(4,5,i);
    imshow(xReconstructed{i});
end
```

6.14.3 decode

Decode encoded data

Syntax

- `Y = decode(autoenc,Z)`

Description

`Y = decode(autoenc,Z)`returns the decoded data `Y`, using the autoencoder object `autoenc`.

Trained autoencoder, returned by the `trainAutoencoder` function as an object of the `Autoencoder` class.

Data encoded by `autoenc`, specified as a matrix. Each column of `Z` represents an encoded sample (observation).

Decoded data, returned as a matrix or a cell array of image data.

If the autoencoder `autoenc` was trained on a cell array of image data, then `Y` is also a cell array of images.

If the autoencoder `autoenc` was trained on a matrix, then `Y` is also a matrix, where each column of `Y` corresponds to one sample or observation.

Example: Decode Encoded Data For New Images

Load the training data.

```
X = digitTrainCellArrayData;
```

X is a 1-by-5003 cell array, where each cell contains a 28-by-28 matrix representing a synthetic image of a handwritten digit.
Train an autoencoder using the training data with a hidden size of 15.

```
hiddenSize = 15;
autoenc = trainAutoencoder(X,hiddenSize);
```

Extract the encoded data for new images using the autoencoder.

```
Xnew = digitTestCellArrayData;
features = encode(autoenc,Xnew);
```

Decode the encoded data from the autoencoder.

```
Y = decode(autoenc,features);
```
Y is a 1-by-4997 cell array, where each cell contains a 28-by-28 matrix representing a synthetic image of a handwritten digit.

6.14.4 encode

Encode input data

Syntax

```
Z = encode(autoenc,Xnew)
```

Description

`Z = encode(autoenc,Xnew)` returns the encoded data, `Z`, for the input data `Xnew`, using the autoencoder, `autoenc`.

Example. Encode Decoded Data for New Images

Load the sample data.

```
X = digitTrainCellArrayData;
```

X is a 1-by-5003 cell array, where each cell contains a 28-by-28 matrix representing a synthetic image of a handwritten digit.
Train an autoencoder with a hidden size of 50 using the training data.

```
autoenc = trainAutoencoder(X,50);
```

Encode decoded data for new image data.

```
Xnew = digitTestCellArrayData;
Z = encode(autoenc,Xnew);
```

`Xnew` is a 1-by-4997 cell array. `Z` is a 50-by-4997 matrix, where each column represents the image data of one handwritten digit in the new data `Xnew`.

6.14.5 predict

Reconstruct the inputs using trained autoencoder

Syntax

- `Y = predict(autoenc,X)`

Description

`Y = predict(autoenc,X)` returns the predictions `Y` for the input data `X`, using the autoencoder `autoenc`. The result `Y` is a reconstruction of `X`.

Examples: Predict Continuous Measurements Using Trained Autoencoder

Load the training data.

```
X = iris_dataset;
```

The training data contains measurements on four attributes of iris flowers: Sepal length, sepal width, petal length, petal width.

Train an autoencoder on the training data using the positive saturating linear transfer function in the encoder and linear transfer function in the decoder.

```
autoenc = trainAutoencoder(X,'EncoderTransferFunction',...
'satlin','DecoderTransferFunction','purelin');
```

Reconstruct the measurements using the trained network, `autoenc`.

```
xReconstructed = predict(autoenc,X);
```

Plot the predicted measurement values along with the actual values in the training dataset.

```
for i = 1:4
h(i) = subplot(1,4,i);
```

```
plot(X(i,:),'r.');
hold on
plot(xReconstructed(i,:),'go');
hold off;
end
title(h(1),{'Sepal';'Length'});
title(h(2),{'Sepal';'Width'});
title(h(3),{'Petal';'Length'});
title(h(4),{'Petal';'Width'});
```

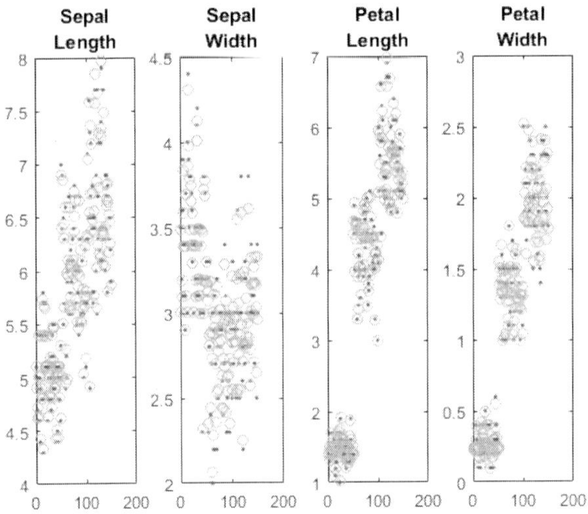

The red dots represent the training data and the green circles represent the reconstructed data.

6.14.6 stack

Stack encoders from several autoencoders together

Syntax

- `stackednet = stack(autoenc1,autoenc2,...)`
- `stackednet = stack(autoenc1,autoenc2,...,net1)`

Description

`stackednet = stack(autoenc1,autoenc2,...)` returns a network object created by stacking the encoders of the autoencoders, `autoenc1`, `autoenc2`, and so on.

`stackednet = stack(autoenc1,autoenc2,...,net1)` returns a network object created by stacking the encoders of the autoencoders and the network object `net1`.

The autoencoders and the network object can be stacked only if their dimensions match.

Tips

- The size of the hidden representation of one autoencoder must match the input size of the next autoencoder or network in the stack.
- The first input argument of the stacked network is the input argument of the first autoencoder. The output argument from the encoder of the first autoencoder is the input of the second autoencoder in the stacked network. The output argument from the encoder of the second autoencoder is the input argument to the third autoencoder in the stacked network, and so on.
- The stacked network object `stacknet` inherits its training parameters from the final input argument `net1`.

Examples. Create a Stacked Network

Load the training data.

```
[X,T] = iris_dataset;
```

Train an autoencoder with a hidden layer of size 5 and a linear transfer function for the decoder. Set the L2 weight regularizer to 0.001, sparsity regularizer to 4 and sparsity proportion to 0.05.

```
hiddenSize = 5;
autoenc = trainAutoencoder(X, hiddenSize, ...
    'L2WeightRegularization', 0.001, ...
    'SparsityRegularization', 4, ...
    'SparsityProportion', 0.05, ...
    'DecoderTransferFunction','purelin');
```

Extract the features in the hidden layer.

```
features = encode(autoenc,X);
```

Train a softmax layer for classification using the `features` .

```
softnet = trainSoftmaxLayer(features,T);
```

Stack the encoder and the softmax layer to form a deep network.

```
stackednet = stack(autoenc,softnet);
```

View the stacked network.

```
view(stackednet);
```

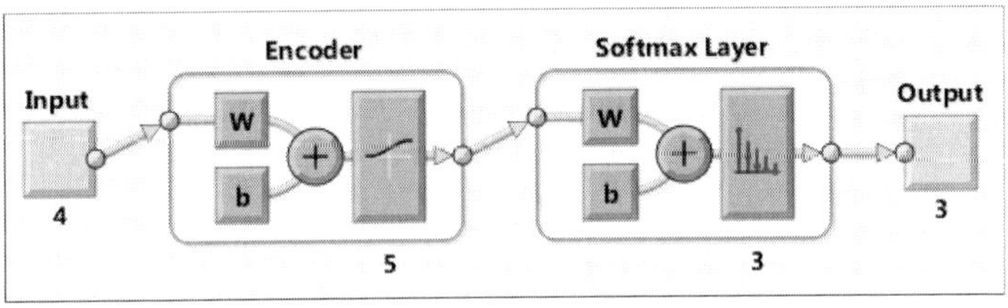

6.14.7 generateFunction

Generate a MATLAB function to run the autoencoder

Syntax

- `generateFunction(autoenc)`
- `generateFunction(autoenc,pathname)`
- `generateFunction(autoenc,pathname,Name,Value)`

Description

`generateFunction(autoenc)` generates a complete stand-alone function in the current directory, to run the autoencoder `autoenc` on input data.

`generateFunction(autoenc,pathname)` generates a complete stand-alone function to run the autoencoder `autoenc` on input data in the location specified by `pathname`.

`generateFunction(autoenc,pathname,Name,Value)` generates a complete stand-alone function with additional options specified by the `Name,Value` pair argument.

Tips

- If you do not specify the path and the file name, `generateFunction`, by default, creates the code in an m-file with the name `neural_function.m`. You can change the file name after `generateFunction` generates it. Or you can specify the path and file name using the `pathname` input argument in the call to `generateFunction`.

Input Arguments

`autoenc` — Trained autoencoder `Autoencoder` object

`pathname` — Location for generated function string

Examples: Generate MATLAB Function for Running Autoencoder

Load the sample data.

```
X = iris_dataset;
```

Train an autoencoder with 4 neurons in the hidden layer.

```
autoenc = trainAutoencoder(X,4);
```

Generate the code for running the autoencoder. Show the links to the MATLAB® function.

```
generateFunction(autoenc)
```

```
MATLAB function generated: neural_function.m
To view generated function code: edit neural_function
For examples of using function: help neural_function
```

Generate the code for the autoencoder in a specific path.

```
generateFunction(autoenc,'H:\Documents\Autoencoder')
```

```
MATLAB function generated: H:\Documents\Autoencoder.m
To view generated function code: edit Autoencoder
For examples of using function: help Autoencoder
```

6.14.8 generateSimulink

Generate a Simulink model for the autoencoder

Syntax

- `generateSimulink(autoenc)`

Description

`generateSimulink(autoenc)` creates a Simulink® model for the autoencoder, `autoenc`.

Input Arguments

`autoenc — Trained autoencoder Autoencoder object`

Examples: Generate Simulink Model for Autoencoder

Load the training data.

```
X = digitsmall_dataset;
```

The training data is a 1-by-500 cell array, where each cell containing a 28-by-28 matrix representing a synthetic image of a handwritten digit.

Train an autoencoder with a hidden layer containing 25 neurons.

```
hiddenSize = 25;
autoenc = trainAutoencoder(X,hiddenSize,...
        'L2WeightRegularization',0.004,...
        'SparsityRegularization',4,...
        'SparsityProportion',0.15);
```

Create a Simulink model for the autoencoder, `autoenc`.

```
generateSimulink(autoenc)
```

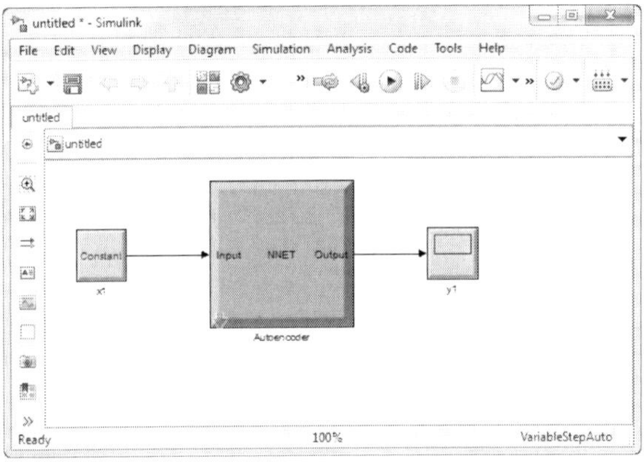

6.14.9 plotWeights

Plot a visualization of the weights for the encoder of an autoencoder

Syntax

- `plotWeights(autoenc)`

- `h = plotWeights(autoenc)`

Description

`plotWeights(autoenc)` visualizes the weights for the autoencoder, `autoenc`.

`h = plotWeights(autoenc)` returns a function handle `h`, for the visualization of the encoder weights for the autoencoder, `autoenc`.

Tips

- `plotWeights` allows the visualization of the features that the autoencoder learns. Use it when the autoencoder is trained on image data. The visualization of the weights has the same dimensions as the images used for training.

Input Arguments

`autoenc` — Trained autoencoder `Autoencoder` object

Output Arguments

h — Image object handle

Examples: Visualize Learned Features

Load the training data.

```
X = digitTrainCellArrayData;
```

The training data is a 1-by-5003 cell array, where each cell contains a 28-by-28 matrix representing a synthetic image of a handwritten digit.

Train an autoencoder with a hidden layer of 25 neurons.

```
hiddenSize = 25;
autoenc = trainAutoencoder(X,hiddenSize, ...
  'L2WeightRegularization',0.004, ...
  'SparsityRegularization',4, ...
  'SparsityProportion',0.2);
```

Visualize the learned features.

```
plotWeights(autoenc);
```

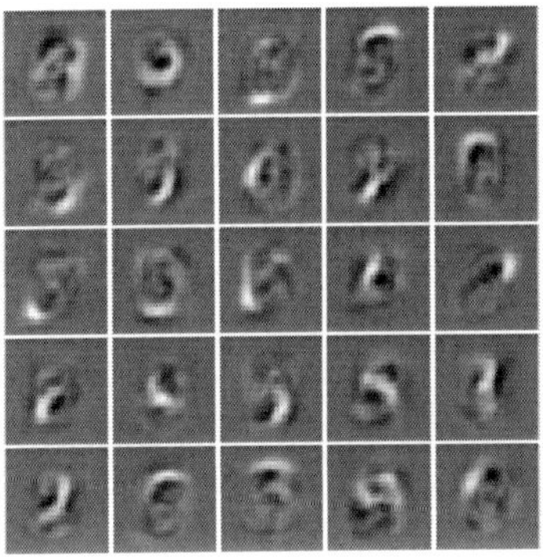

6.14.10 view

View autoencoder

Syntax

- `view(autoenc)`

Description

`view(autoenc)` returns a diagram of the autoencoder, `autoenc`.

Input Arguments

`autoenc` — Trained autoencoder
`Autoencoder` object

Examples: View Autoencoder

Load the training data.

```
X = iris_dataset;
```

Train an autoencoder with a hidden layer of size 5 and a linear transfer function for the decoder. Set the L2 weight regularizer to 0.001, sparsity regularizer to 4 and sparsity proportion to 0.05.

```
hiddenSize = 5;
autoenc = trainAutoencoder(X, hiddenSize, ...
    'L2WeightRegularization',0.001, ...
    'SparsityRegularization',4, ...
    'SparsityProportion',0.05, ...
    'DecoderTransferFunction','purelin');
```

View the autoencoder.

```
view(autoenc)
```

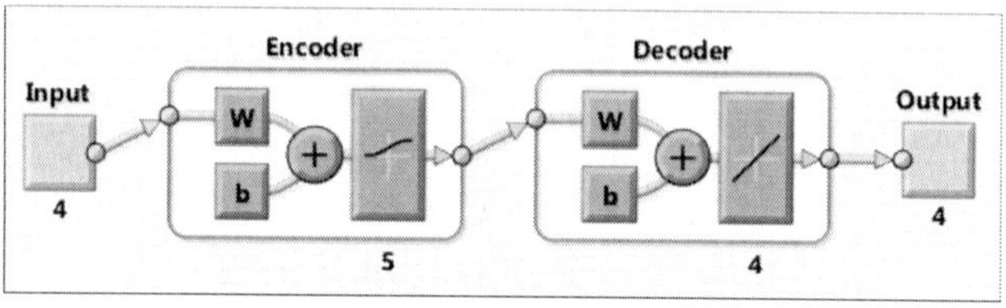

6.15 CONSTRUCT DEEP NETWORK USING AUTOENCODERS

Load the sample data.

```
[X,T] = wine_dataset;
```

Train an autoencoder with a hidden layer of size 10 and a linear transfer function for the decoder. Set the L2 weight regularizer to 0.001, sparsity regularizer to 4 and sparsity proportion to 0.05.

```
hiddenSize = 10;
autoenc1 = trainAutoencoder(X,hiddenSize,...
    'L2WeightRegularization',0.001,...
    'SparsityRegularization',4,...
    'SparsityProportion',0.05,...
    'DecoderTransferFunction','purelin');
```

Extract the features in the hidden layer.

```
features1 = encode(autoenc1,X);
```

Train a second autoencoder using the features from the first autoencoder. Do not scale the data.

```
hiddenSize = 10;
autoenc2 = trainAutoencoder(features1,hiddenSize,...
    'L2WeightRegularization',0.001,...
    'SparsityRegularization',4,...
    'SparsityProportion',0.05,...
    'DecoderTransferFunction','purelin',...
    'ScaleData',false);
```

Extract the features in the hidden layer.

```
features2 = encode(autoenc2,features1);
```

Train a softmax layer for classification using the features, `features2`, from the second autoencoder, `autoenc2`.

```
softnet =
trainSoftmaxLayer(features2,T,'LossFunction','crossentropy');
```

Stack the encoders and the softmax layer to form a deep network.

```
deepnet = stack(autoenc1,autoenc2,softnet);
```

Train the deep network on the wine data.

```
deepnet = train(deepnet,X,T);
```

Estimate the wine types using the deep network, `deepnet`.

```
wine_type = deepnet(X);
```

Plot the confusion matrix.

```
plotconfusion(T,wine_type);
```

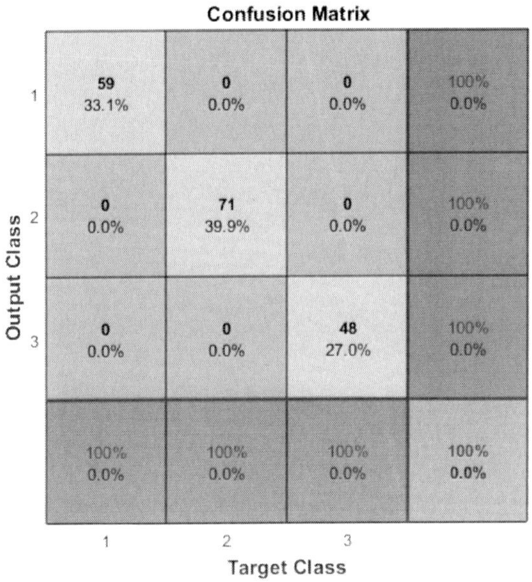

Chapter 7

MULTILAYER NEURAL NETWORK

7.1 CREATE, CONFIGURE, AND INITIALIZE MULTILAYER NEURAL NETWORKS

After the data has been collected, the next step in training a network is to create the network object. The function feedforwardnet creates a multilayer feedforward network. If this function is invoked with no input arguments, then a default network object is created that has not been configured. The resulting network can then be configured with the configure command.

As an example, the file housing.mat contains a predefined set of input and target vectors. The input vectors define data regarding real-estate properties and the target values define relative values of the properties. Load the data using the following command:

```
load house_dataset
```

Loading this file creates two variables. The input matrix houseInputs consists of 506 column vectors of 13 real estate variables for 506 different houses. The target matrix houseTargets consists of the corresponding 506 relative valuations.

The next step is to create the network. The following call to feedforwardnet creates a two-layer network with 10 neurons in the hidden layer. (During the configuration step, the number of neurons in the output layer is set to one, which is the number of elements in each vector of targets.)

```
net = feedforwardnet;
```

```
net = configure(net,houseInputs,houseTargets);
```

Optional arguments can be provided to feedforwardnet. For instance, the first argument is an array containing the number of neurons in each hidden layer. (The default setting is 10, which means one hidden layer with 10 neurons. One hidden layer generally produces excellent results, but you may want to try two hidden layers, if the results with one are not adequate. Increasing the number of neurons in the hidden layer increases the power of the network, but requires more computation and is more likely to produce overfitting.) The second argument contains the name of the training function to be used. If no arguments are supplied, the default number of layers is 2, the default number of neurons in the hidden layer is 10, and the default training function is trainlm. The default transfer function for hidden layers is tansig and the default for the output layer is purelin.

The configure command configures the network object and also initializes the weights and biases of the network; therefore the network is ready for training. There are times when you might want to reinitialize the weights, or to perform a custom initialization. Initializing Weights (init) explains the details of the initialization process. You can also skip the configuration step and go directly to training the network. The train command will automatically configure the network and initialize the weights.

7.1.1 Other Related Architectures

While two-layer feedforward networks can potentially learn virtually any input-output relationship, feedforward networks with more layers might learn complex relationships more quickly. For most problems, it is best to start with two layers, and then increase to three layers, if the performance with two layers is not satisfactory.

The function cascadeforwardnet creates cascade-forward networks. These are similar to feedforward networks, but include a weight connection from the input to each layer, and from each layer to the successive layers. For example, a three-layer network has connections from layer 1 to layer 2, layer 2 to layer 3, and layer 1 to layer 3. The three-layer network also has connections from the input to all three layers. The additional connections might improve the speed at which the network learns the desired relationship.

The function patternnet creates a network that is very similar to feedforwardnet, except that it uses the tansig transfer function in the last layer. This network is generally used for pattern recognition. Other networks can learn dynamic or time-series relationships.

7.2 FUNCTIONS FOR CREATE, CONFIGURE, AND INITIALIZE MULTILAYER NEURAL NETWORKS

7.2.1 Initializing Weights (init)

Before training a feedforward network, you must initialize the weights and biases. The configure command automatically initializes the weights, but you might want to reinitialize them. You do this with the init command. This function takes a network object as input and returns a network object with all weights and biases initialized. Here is how a network is initialized (or reinitialized):

```
net = init(net);
```

7.2.2 feedforwardnet

Feedforward neural network

Syntax

```
feedforwardnet(hiddenSizes,trainFcn)
```

Description

Feedforward networks consist of a series of layers. The first layer has a connection from the network input. Each subsequent layer has a connection from the previous layer. The final layer produces the network's output.

Feedforward networks can be used for any kind of input to output mapping. A feedforward network with one hidden layer and enough neurons in the hidden layers, can fit any finite input-output mapping problem.

Specialized versions of the feedforward network include fitting (`fitnet`) and pattern recognition (`patternnet`) networks. A variation on the feedforward network is the cascade forward network (`cascadeforwardnet`) which has additional connections from the input to every layer, and from each layer to all following layers.

`feedforwardnet(hiddenSizes,trainFcn)` takes these arguments,

`hiddenSizes`	Row vector of one or more hidden layer sizes (default = 10)
`trainFcn`	Training function (default = `'trainlm'`)

and returns a feedforward neural network.

Examples

Feedforward Neural Network

This example shows how to use feedforward neural network to solve a simple problem.

```
[x,t] = simplefit_dataset;
net = feedforwardnet(10);
net = train(net,x,t);
view(net)
y = net(x);
perf = perform(net,y,t)
perf =

   1.4639e-04
```

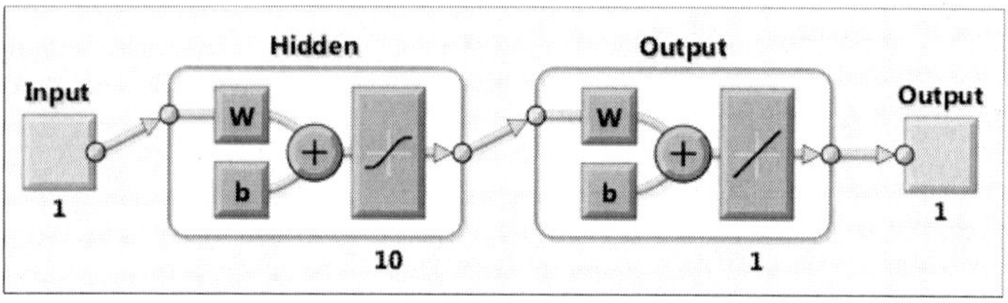

7.2.3 configure

Configure network inputs and outputs to best match input and target data

Syntax

```
net = configure(net,x,t)
net = configure(net,x)
net = configure(net,'inputs',x,i)
net = configure(net,'outputs',t,i)
```

Description

Configuration is the process of setting network input and output sizes and ranges, input preprocessing settings and output postprocessing settings, and weight initialization settings to match input and target data.

Configuration must happen before a network's weights and biases can be initialized. Unconfigured networks are automatically configured and initialized the first time train is called. Alternately, a network can be configured manually either by calling this function or by setting a network's input and output sizes, ranges, processing settings, and initialization settings properties manually.

`net = configure(net,x,t)` takes input data x and target data t, and configures the network's inputs and outputs to match.

`net = configure(net,x)` configures only inputs.

`net = configure(net,'inputs',x,i)` configures the inputs specified with the index vector i. If i is not specified all inputs are configured.

`net = configure(net,'outputs',t,i)` configures the outputs specified with the index vector i. If i is not specified all targets are configured.

Examples

Here a feedforward network is created and manually configured for a simple fitting problem (as opposed to allowing train to configure it).

```
[x,t] = simplefit_dataset;

net = feedforwardnet(20); view(net)

net = configure(net,x,t); view(net)
```

7.2.4 init

Initialize neural network

Syntax

```
net = init(net)
```

To Get Help

Type `help network/init`.

Description

`net = init(net)` returns neural network net with weight and bias values updated according to the network initialization function, indicated by `net.initFcn`, and the parameter values, indicated by `net.initParam`.

Examples

Here a perceptron is created, and then configured so that its input, output, weight, and bias dimensions match the input and target data.

```
x = [0 1 0 1; 0 0 1 1];
t = [0 0 0 1];
net = perceptron;
net = configure(net,x,t);
net.iw{1,1}
net.b{1}
```

Training the perceptron alters its weight and bias values.

```
net = train(net,x,t);
net.iw{1,1}
net.b{1}
```

init reinitializes those weight and bias values.

```
net = init(net);
net.iw{1,1}
net.b{1}
```

The weights and biases are zeros again, which are the initial values used by perceptron networks.

Algorithms

`init` calls `net.initFcn` to initialize the weight and bias values according to the parameter values `net.initParam`.

Typically, `net.initFcn` is set to `'initlay'`, which initializes each layer's weights and biases according to its `net.layers{i}.initFcn`.

Backpropagation networks have `net.layers{i}.initFcn` set to `'initnw'`, which calculates the weight and bias values for layer `i` using the Nguyen-Widrow initialization method.

Other networks have `net.layers{i}.initFcn` set to `'initwb'`, which initializes each weight and bias with its own initialization function. The most common weight and bias initialization function is `rands`, which generates random values between –1 and 1.

7.2.5 train

Train neural network

Syntax

```
[net,tr] = train(net,X,T,Xi,Ai,EW)
[net,__] = train(__,'useParallel',__)
[net,__] = train(__,'useGPU',__)
[net,__] = train(__,'showResources',__)
[net,__] = train(Xcomposite,Tcomposite,__)
[net,__] = train(Xgpu,Tgpu,__)
net =
train(__,'CheckpointFile','path/name','CheckpointDelay',numDel
ays)
```

Description

`train` trains a network `net` according to `net.trainFcn` and `net.trainParam`.

`[net,tr] = train(net,X,T,Xi,Ai,EW)` takes

`net`	Network
`X`	Network inputs
`T`	Network targets (default = zeros)
`Xi`	Initial input delay conditions (default = zeros)
`Ai`	Initial layer delay conditions (default = zeros)
`EW`	Error weights

and returns

`net`	Newly trained network
`tr`	Training record (`epoch` and `perf`)

Note that `T` is optional and need only be used for networks that require targets. `Xi` is also optional and need only be used for networks that have input or layer delays.

`train` arguments can have two formats: matrices, for static problems and networks with single inputs and outputs, and cell arrays for multiple timesteps and networks with multiple inputs and outputs.

The matrix format is as follows:

`X`	R-by-Q matrix
`T`	U-by-Q matrix

The cell array format is more general, and more convenient for networks with multiple inputs and outputs, allowing sequences of inputs to be presented.

X	Ni-by-TS cell array	Each element X{i,ts} is an Ri-by-Q matrix.
T	No-by-TS cell array	Each element T{i,ts} is a Ui-by-Q matrix.
Xi	Ni-by-ID cell array	Each element Xi{i,k} is an Ri-by-Q matrix.
Ai	Nl-by-LD cell array	Each element Ai{i,k} is an Si-by-Q matrix.
EW	No-by-TS cell array	Each element EW{i,ts} is a Ui-by-Q matrix

where

Ni	=	net.numInputs
Nl	=	net.numLayers
No	=	net.numOutputs
ID	=	net.numInputDelays
LD	=	net.numLayerDelays
TS	=	Number of time steps
Q	=	Batch size
Ri	=	net.inputs{i}.size
Si	=	net.layers{i}.size
Ui	=	net.outptus{i}.size

The columns of Xi and Ai are ordered from the oldest delay condition to the most recent:

Xi{i,k}	=	Input i at time ts = k - ID
Ai{i,k}	=	Layer output i at time ts = k - LD

The error weights EW can also have a size of 1 in place of all or any of No, TS, Ui or Q. In that case, EW is automatically dimension extended to match the targets T. This allows for conveniently weighting the importance in any dimension (such as per sample) while having equal importance across another (such as time, with TS=1). If all dimensions are 1, for instance if EW = {1}, then all target values are treated with the same importance. That is the default value of EW.

The matrix format can be used if only one time step is to be simulated (TS = 1). It is convenient for networks with only one input and output, but can be used with networks that have more.

Each matrix argument is found by storing the elements of the corresponding cell array argument in a single matrix:

X	(sum of Ri)-by-Q matrix
T	(sum of Ui)-by-Q matrix
Xi	(sum of Ri)-by-(ID*Q) matrix
Ai	(sum of Si)-by-(LD*Q) matrix
EW	(sum of Ui)-by-Q matrix

As noted above, the error weights `EW` can be of the same dimensions as the targets `T`, or have some dimensions set to 1. For instance if `EW` is `1`-by-`Q`, then target samples will have different importances, but each element in a sample will have the same importance. If `EW` is (`sum` of `Ui`)-by-`Q`, then each output element has a different importance, with all samples treated with the same importance.

The training record `TR` is a structure whose fields depend on the network training function (`net.NET.trainFcn`). It can include fields such as:

- Training, data division, and performance functions and parameters
- Data division indices for training, validation and test sets
- Data division masks for training validation and test sets
- Number of epochs (`num_epochs`) and the best epoch (`best_epoch`).
- A list of training state names (`states`).
- Fields for each state name recording its value throughout training
- Performances of the best network (`best_perf`, `best_vperf`, `best_tperf`)

`[net,__] = train(__,'useParallel',__)`, `[net,__] = train(__,'useGPU',__)`, or `[net,__] = train(__,'showResources',__)` accepts optional name/value pair arguments to control how calculations are performed. Two of these options allow training to happen faster or on larger datasets using parallel workers or GPU devices if Parallel Computing Toolbox is available. These are the optional name/value pairs:

`'useParallel','no'`	Calculations occur on normal MATLAB thread. This is the default `'useParallel'` setting.
`'useParallel','yes'`	Calculations occur on parallel workers if a parallel pool is open. Otherwise calculations occur on the normal MATLAB thread.
`'useGPU','no'`	Calculations occur on the CPU. This is the default 'useGPU' setting.
`'useGPU','yes'`	Calculations occur on the current gpuDevice if it is a supported GPU (See Parallel Computing Toolbox for GPU requirements.) If the current gpuDevice is not supported, calculations remain on the CPU. If `'useParallel'` is also `'yes'` and a parallel pool is open, then each worker with a unique GPU uses that GPU, other workers run calculations on their respective CPU cores.
`'useGPU','only'`	If no parallel pool is open, then this setting is the same as `'yes'`. If a parallel pool is open then only workers with unique GPUs are used. However, if a parallel pool is open, but no supported GPUs are available, then calculations revert to performing on all worker CPUs.
`'showResources','no'`	Do not display computing resources used at the command line. This is the default setting.
`'showResources','yes'`	Show at the command line a summary of the computing resources actually used. The actual resources may differ from the requested

	resources, if parallel or GPU computing is requested but a parallel pool is not open or a supported GPU is not available. When parallel workers are used, each worker's computation mode is described, including workers in the pool that are not used.
'reduction',N	For most neural networks, the default CPU training computation mode is a compiled MEX algorithm. However, for large networks the calculations might occur with a MATLAB calculation mode. This can be confirmed using 'showResources'. If MATLAB is being used and memory is an issue, setting the reduction option to a value N greater than 1, reduces much of the temporary storage required to train by a factor of N, in exchange for longer training times.

[net,__] = train(Xcomposite,Tcomposite,__) takes Composite data and returns Composite results. If Composite data is used, then 'useParallel' is automatically set to 'yes'.

[net,__] = train(Xgpu,Tgpu,__) takes gpuArray data and returns gpuArray results. If gpuArray data is used, then 'useGPU' is automatically set to 'yes'.

net = train(__,'CheckpointFile','path/name','CheckpointDelay',numDelays) periodically saves intermediate values of the neural network and training record during training to the specified file. This protects training results from power failures, computer lock ups, Ctrl+C, or any other event that halts the training process before train returns normally.

The value for 'CheckpointFile' can be set to a filename to save in the current working folder, to a file path in another folder, or to an empty string to disable checkpoint saves (the default value).

The optional parameter 'CheckpointDelay' limits how often saves happen. Limiting the frequency of checkpoints can improve efficiency by keeping the amount of time saving checkpoints low compared to the time spent in calculations. It has a default value of 60, which means that checkpoint saves do not happen more than once per minute. Set the value of 'CheckpointDelay' to 0 if you want checkpoint saves to occur only once every epoch.

Note Any NaN values in the inputs X or the targets T, are treated as missing data. If a column of X or T contains at least one NaN, that column is not used for training, testing, or validation.

Examples

Train and Plot Networks

Here input x and targets t define a simple function that you can plot:

```
x = [0 1 2 3 4 5 6 7 8];
t = [0 0.84 0.91 0.14 -0.77 -0.96 -0.28 0.66 0.99];
plot(x,t,'o')
```

Here `feedforwardnet` creates a two-layer feed-forward network. The network has one hidden layer with ten neurons.

```
net = feedforwardnet(10);
net = configure(net,x,t);
y1 = net(x)
plot(x,t,'o',x,y1,'x')
```

The network is trained and then resimulated.

```
net = train(net,x,t);
y2 = net(x)
plot(x,t,'o',x,y1,'x',x,y2,'*')
```

Train NARX Time Series Network

This example trains an open-loop nonlinear-autoregressive network with external input, to model a levitated magnet system defined by a control current x and the magnet's vertical position response `t`, then simulates the network. The function `preparets` prepares the data before training and simulation. It creates the open-loop network's combined inputs xo, which contains both the external input x and previous values of position `t`. It also prepares the delay states `xi`.

```
[x,t] = maglev_dataset;
net = narxnet(10);
[xo,xi,~,to] = preparets(net,x,{},t);
net = train(net,xo,to,xi);
y = net(xo,xi)
```

This same system can also be simulated in closed-loop form.

```
netc = closeloop(net);
view(netc)
[xc,xi,ai,tc] = preparets(netc,x,{},t);
yc = netc(xc,xi,ai);
```

Train a Network in Parallel on a Parallel Pool

Parallel Computing Toolbox™ allows Neural Network Toolbox (Deep Learning Toolbox from version 18)™ to simulate and train networks faster and on larger datasets than can fit on one PC. Parallel training is currently supported for backpropagation training only, not for self-organizing maps.

Here training and simulation happens across parallel MATLAB workers.

```
parpool
```

```
[X,T] = vinyl_dataset;
net = feedforwardnet(10);
net = train(net,X,T,'useParallel','yes','showResources','yes');
Y = net(X);
```

Use Composite values to distribute the data manually, and get back the results as a Composite value. If the data is loaded as it is distributed then while each piece of the dataset must fit in RAM, the entire dataset is limited only by the total RAM of all the workers.

```
[X,T] = vinyl_dataset;
Q = size(X,2);
Xc = Composite;
Tc = Composite;
numWorkers = numel(Xc);
ind = [0 ceil((1:4)*(Q/4))];
for i=1:numWorkers
    indi = (ind(i)+1):ind(i+1);
    Xc{i} = X(:,indi);
    Tc{i} = T(:,indi);
end
net = feedforwardnet;
net = configure(net,X,T);
net = train(net,Xc,Tc);
Yc = net(Xc);
```

Note in the example above the function configure was used to set the dimensions and processing settings of the network's inputs. This normally happens automatically when train is called, but when providing composite data this step must be done manually with non-Composite data.

Train a Network on GPUs

Networks can be trained using the current GPU device, if it is supported by Parallel Computing Toolbox. GPU training is currently supported for backpropagation training only, not for self-organizing maps.

```
[X,T] = vinyl_dataset;
net = feedforwardnet(10);
net = train(net,X,T,'useGPU','yes');
y = net(X);
```

To put the data on a GPU manually:

```
[X,T] = vinyl_dataset;
Xgpu = gpuArray(X);
Tgpu = gpuArray(T);
net = configure(net,X,T);
net = train(net,Xgpu,Tgpu);
```

```
Ygpu = net(Xgpu);
Y = gather(Ygpu);
```

Note in the example above the function configure was used to set the dimensions and processing settings of the network's inputs. This normally happens automatically when train is called, but when providing gpuArray data this step must be done manually with non-gpuArray data.

To run in parallel, with workers each assigned to a different unique GPU, with extra workers running on CPU:

```
net = train(net,X,T,'useParallel','yes','useGPU','yes');
y = net(X);
```

Using only workers with unique GPUs might result in higher speed, as CPU workers might not keep up.

```
net = train(net,X,T,'useParallel','yes','useGPU','only');
Y = net(X);
```

Train Network Using Checkpoint Saves

Here a network is trained with checkpoints saved at a rate no greater than once every two minutes.

```
[x,t] = vinyl_dataset;
net = fitnet([60 30]);
net =
train(net,x,t,'CheckpointFile','MyCheckpoint','CheckpointDelay',120
);
```

After a computer failure, the latest network can be recovered and used to continue training from the point of failure. The checkpoint file includes a structure variable `checkpoint`, which includes the network, training record, filename, time, and number.

```
[x,t] = vinyl_dataset;
load MyCheckpoint
net = checkpoint.net;
net = train(net,x,t,'CheckpointFile','MyCheckpoint');
```

Another use for the checkpoint feature is when you stop a parallel training session (started with the `'UseParallel'` parameter) even though the Neural Network Training Tool is not available during parallel training. In this case, set a `'CheckpointFile'`, use Ctrl+C to stop training any time, then load your checkpoint file to get the network and training record.

Algorithms

`train` calls the function indicated by `net.trainFcn`, using the training parameter values indicated by `net.trainParam`.

Typically one epoch of training is defined as a single presentation of all input vectors to the network. The network is then updated according to the results of all those presentations.

Training occurs until a maximum number of epochs occurs, the performance goal is met, or any other stopping condition of the function `net.trainFcn` occurs.

Some training functions depart from this norm by presenting only one input vector (or sequence) each epoch. An input vector (or sequence) is chosen randomly for each epoch from concurrent input vectors (or sequences). `competlayer` returns networks that use `trainru`, a training function that does this.

7.2.6 trainlm

Levenberg-Marquardt backpropagation

Syntax

```
net.trainFcn = 'trainlm'
[net,tr] = train(net,...)
```

Description

`trainlm` is a network training function that updates weight and bias values according to Levenberg-Marquardt optimization.

`trainlm` is often the fastest backpropagation algorithm in the toolbox, and is highly recommended as a first-choice supervised algorithm, although it does require more memory than other algorithms.

`net.trainFcn = 'trainlm'` sets the network `trainFcn` property.

`[net,tr] = train(net,...)` trains the network with `trainlm`.

Training occurs according to `trainlm` training parameters, shown here with their default values:

`net.trainParam.epochs`	`1000`	Maximum number of epochs to train
`net.trainParam.goal`	`0`	Performance goal
`net.trainParam.max_fail`	`6`	Maximum validation failures
`net.trainParam.min_grad`	`1e-7`	Minimum performance gradient
`net.trainParam.mu`	`0.001`	Initial `mu`
`net.trainParam.mu_dec`	`0.1`	`mu` decrease factor
`net.trainParam.mu_inc`	`10`	`mu` increase factor

`net.trainParam.mu_max`	`1e10`	Maximum `mu`
`net.trainParam.show`	`25`	Epochs between displays (`NaN` for no displays)
`net.trainParam.showCommandLine`	`false`	Generate command-line output
`net.trainParam.showWindow`	`true`	Show training GUI
`net.trainParam.time`	`inf`	Maximum time to train in seconds

Validation vectors are used to stop training early if the network performance on the validation vectors fails to improve or remains the same for `max_fail` epochs in a row. Test vectors are used as a further check that the network is generalizing well, but do not have any effect on training.

`trainlm` is the default training function for several network creation functions including `newcf`, `newdtdnn`, `newff`, and `newnarx`.

Network Use

You can create a standard network that uses `trainlm` with `feedforwardnet` or `cascadeforwardnet`.

To prepare a custom network to be trained with `trainlm`,

1. Set `net.trainFcn` to `'trainlm'`. This sets `net.trainParam` to `trainlm`'s default parameters.
2. Set `net.trainParam` properties to desired values.

In either case, calling `train` with the resulting network trains the network with `trainlm`.

See `help feedforwardnet` and `help cascadeforwardnet` for examples.

Examples

Here a neural network is trained to predict median house prices.

```
[x,t] = house_dataset;

net = feedforwardnet(10,'trainlm');

net = train(net,x,t);

y = net(x)
```

Definitions

Like the quasi-Newton methods, the Levenberg-Marquardt algorithm was designed to approach second-order training speed without having to compute the Hessian matrix. When the performance function has the form of a sum of squares (as is typical in training feedforward networks), then the Hessian matrix can be approximated as

$$\mathbf{H} = \mathbf{J}^T\mathbf{J}$$

and the gradient can be computed as

$$\mathbf{g} = \mathbf{J}^T\mathbf{e}$$

where **J** is the Jacobian matrix that contains first derivatives of the network errors with respect to the weights and biases, and **e** is a vector of network errors. The Jacobian matrix can be computed through a standard backpropagation technique (see [HaMe94]) that is much less complex than computing the Hessian matrix.

The Levenberg-Marquardt algorithm uses this approximation to the Hessian matrix in the following Newton-like update:

$$\mathbf{x}_{k+1} = \mathbf{x}_k - [\mathbf{J}^T\mathbf{J} + \mu\mathbf{I}]^{-1}\mathbf{J}^T\mathbf{e}$$

When the scalar μ is zero, this is just Newton's method, using the approximate Hessian matrix. When μ is large, this becomes gradient descent with a small step size. Newton's method is faster and more accurate near an error minimum, so the aim is to shift toward Newton's method as quickly as possible. Thus, μ is decreased after each successful step (reduction in performance function) and is increased only when a tentative step would increase the performance function. In this way, the performance function is always reduced at each iteration of the algorithm.

The original description of the Levenberg-Marquardt algorithm is given in [Marq63]. The application of Levenberg-Marquardt to neural network training is described in [HaMe94] and starting on page 12-19 of [HDB96]. This algorithm appears to be the fastest method for training moderate-sized feedforward neural networks (up to several hundred weights). It also has an efficient implementation in MATLAB® software, because the solution of the matrix equation is a built-in function, so its attributes become even more pronounced in a MATLAB environment.

Try the *Neural Network Design* demonstration `nnd12m` [HDB96] for an illustration of the performance of the batch Levenberg-Marquardt algorithm.

Limitations

This function uses the Jacobian for calculations, which assumes that performance is a mean or sum of squared errors. Therefore, networks trained with this function must use either the `mse` or `sse` performance function.

Algorithms

`trainlm` supports training with validation and test vectors if the network's `NET.divideFcn` property is set to a data division function. Validation vectors are used to stop training early if the network performance on the validation vectors fails to improve or remains the same for `max_fail` epochs in a row. Test vectors are used as a further check that the network is generalizing well, but do not have any effect on training.

`trainlm` can train any network as long as its weight, net input, and transfer functions have derivative functions.

Backpropagation is used to calculate the Jacobian `jX` of performance `perf` with respect to the weight and bias variables `X`. Each variable is adjusted according to Levenberg-Marquardt,

```
jj = jX * jX
je = jX * E
dX = -(jj+I*mu) \ je
```

where `E` is all errors and `I` is the identity matrix.

The adaptive value `mu` is increased by `mu_inc` until the change above results in a reduced performance value. The change is then made to the network and `mu` is decreased by `mu_dec`.

Training stops when any of these conditions occurs:

- The maximum number of `epochs` (repetitions) is reached.
- The maximum amount of `time` is exceeded.
- Performance is minimized to the `goal`.
- The performance gradient falls below `min_grad`.
- `mu` exceeds `mu_max`.
- Validation performance has increased more than `max_fail` times since the last time it decreased (when using validation).

7.2.7 tansig

Hyperbolic tangent sigmoid transfer function

Graph and Symbol

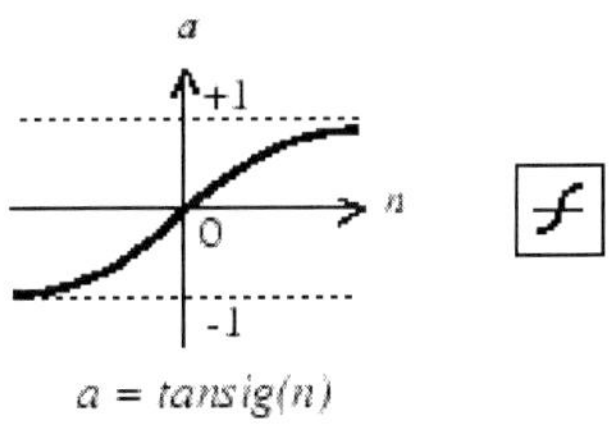

Tan-Sigmoid Transfer Function

Syntax

```
A = tansig(N,FP)
```

Description

`tansig` is a neural transfer function. Transfer functions calculate a layer's output from its net input.

`A = tansig(N,FP)` takes `N` and optional function parameters,

`N`	S-by-Q matrix of net input (column) vectors
`FP`	Struct of function parameters (ignored)

and returns `A`, the `S`-by-`Q` matrix of `N`'s elements squashed into `[-1 1]`.

Examples

Here is the code to create a plot of the `tansig` transfer function.

```
n = -5:0.1:5;

a = tansig(n);

plot(n,a)
```

Assign this transfer function to layer `i` of a network.

```
net.layers{i}.transferFcn = 'tansig';
```

Algorithms

```
a = tansig(n) = 2/(1+exp(-2*n))-1
```

This is mathematically equivalent to `tanh(N)`. It differs in that it runs faster than the MATLAB implementation of `tanh`, but the results can have very small numerical differences. This function is a good tradeoff for neural networks, where speed is important and the exact shape of the transfer function is not.

7.2.8 purelin

Linear transfer function

Graph and Symbol

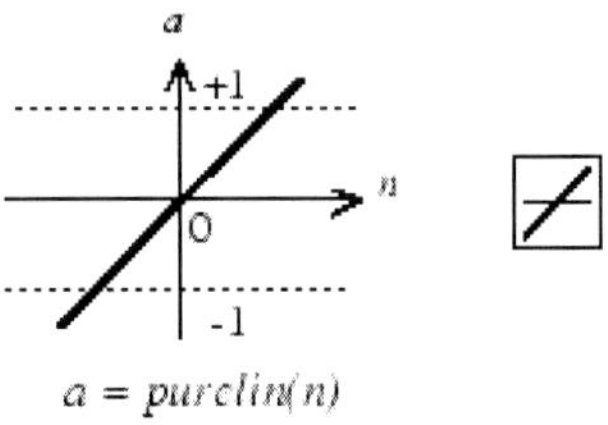

Linear Transfer Function

Syntax

```
A = purelin(N,FP)
info = purelin('code')
```

Description

`purelin` is a neural transfer function. Transfer functions calculate a layer's output from its net input.

`A = purelin(N,FP)` takes `N` and optional function parameters,

`N`	`S`-by-`Q` matrix of net input (column) vectors
`FP`	Struct of function parameters (ignored)

and returns `A`, an `S`-by-`Q` matrix equal to `N`.

`info = purelin('code')` returns useful information for each supported *code* string:

`purelin('name')` returns the name of this function.

`purelin('output',FP)` returns the `[min max]` output range.

`purelin('active',FP)` returns the `[min max]` active input range.

`purelin('fullderiv')` returns 1 or 0, depending on whether `dA_dN` is `S`-by-`S`-by-`Q` or `S`-by-`Q`.

`purelin('fpnames')` returns the names of the function parameters.

`purelin('fpdefaults')` returns the default function parameters.

Examples

Here is the code to create a plot of the `purelin` transfer function.

```
n = -5:0.1:5;

a = purelin(n);
```

```
plot(n,a)
```

Assign this transfer function to layer i of a network.

```
net.layers{i}.transferFcn = 'purelin';
```

Algorithms

```
a = purelin(n) = n
```

7.2.9 cascadeforwardnet

Cascade-forward neural network

Syntax

```
cascadeforwardnet(hiddenSizes,trainFcn)
```

Description

Cascade-forward networks are similar to feed-forward networks, but include a connection from the input and every previous layer to following layers.

As with feed-forward networks, a two-or more layer cascade-network can learn any finite input-output relationship arbitrarily well given enough hidden neurons.

`cascadeforwardnet(hiddenSizes,trainFcn)` takes these arguments,

`hiddenSizes`	Row vector of one or more hidden layer sizes (default = 10)
`trainFcn`	Training function (default = `'trainlm'`)

and returns a new cascade-forward neural network.

Examples

Create and Train a Cascade Network

Here a cascade network is created and trained on a simple fitting problem.

```
[x,t] = simplefit_dataset;
net = cascadeforwardnet(10);
net = train(net,x,t);
view(net)
y = net(x);
perf = perform(net,y,t)
perf =

   1.9372e-05
```

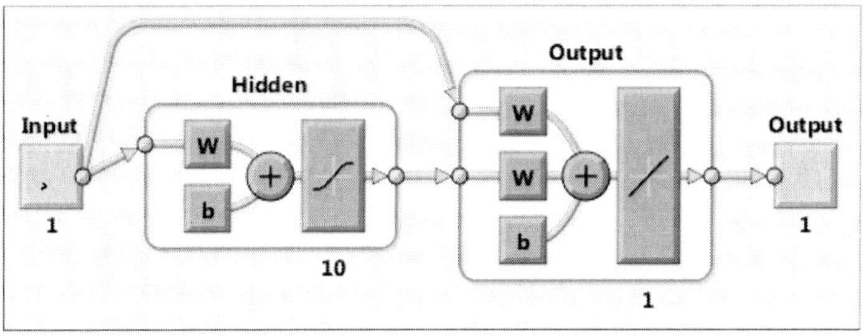

7.2.10 patternnet

Pattern recognition network

Syntax

```
patternnet(hiddenSizes,trainFcn,performFcn)
```

Description

Pattern recognition networks are feedforward networks that can be trained to classify inputs according to target classes. The target data for pattern recognition networks should consist of vectors of all zero values except for a 1 in element `i`, where `i` is the class they are to represent.

`patternnet(hiddenSizes,trainFcn,performFcn)` takes these arguments,

`hiddenSizes`	Row vector of one or more hidden layer sizes (default = 10)
`trainFcn`	Training function (default = `'trainscg'`)
`performFcn`	Performance function (default = `'crossentropy'`)

and returns a pattern recognition neural network.

Examples

Pattern Recognition

This example shows how to design a pattern recognition network to classify iris flowers.

```
[x,t] = iris_dataset;
net = patternnet(10);
net = train(net,x,t);
view(net)
y = net(x);
perf = perform(net,t,y);
classes = vec2ind(y);
```

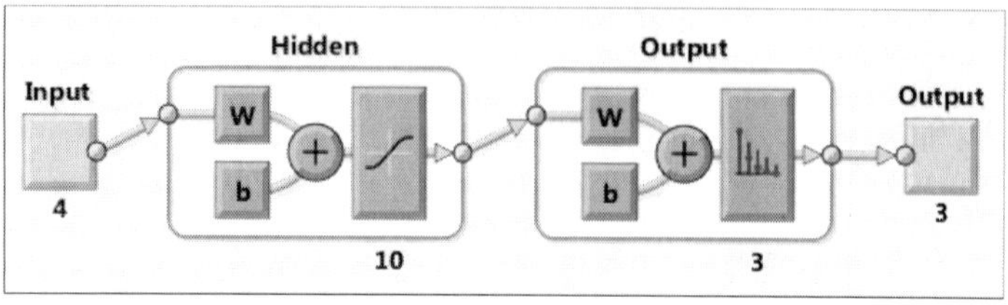

7.3 TRAIN AND APPLY MULTILAYER NEURAL NETWORKS

This topic presents part of a typical multilayer network workflow.

When the network weights and biases are initialized, the network is ready for training. The multilayer feedforward network can be trained for function approximation (nonlinear regression) or pattern recognition. The training process requires a set of examples of proper network behavior—network inputs p and target outputs `t`.

The process of training a neural network involves tuning the values of the weights and biases of the network to optimize network performance, as defined by the network performance function `net.performFcn`. The default performance function for feedforward networks is mean square error `mse`—the average squared error between the network outputs a and the target outputs `t`. It is defined as follows:

$$F = mse = \frac{1}{N}\sum_{i=1}^{N}(e_i)^2 = \frac{1}{N}\sum_{i=1}^{N}(t_i - a_i)^2$$

(Individual squared errors can also be weighted. There are two different ways in which training can be implemented: incremental mode and batch mode. In incremental mode, the gradient is computed and the weights are updated after each input is applied to the network. In batch mode, all the inputs in the training set are applied to the network before the weights are updated. This topic describes batch mode training with the `train` command. Incremental training with the `adapt`command is discussed in Incremental Training with adapt. For most problems, when using the Neural Network Toolbox (Deep Learning Toolbox from version 18)™ software, batch training is significantly faster and produces smaller errors than incremental training.

For training multilayer feedforward networks, any standard numerical optimization algorithm can be used to optimize the performance function, but there are a few key ones that have shown excellent performance for neural network training. These optimization methods use either the gradient of the network performance with respect to the network weights, or the Jacobian of the network errors with respect to the weights.

The gradient and the Jacobian are calculated using a technique called the *backpropagation* algorithm, which involves performing computations backward through the network. The backpropagation computation is derived using the chain rule of calculus and is described in Chapters 11 (for the gradient) and 12 (for the Jacobian) of [HDB96].

7.3.1 Training Algorithms

As an illustration of how the training works, consider the simplest optimization algorithm — gradient descent. It updates the network weights and biases in the direction in which the performance function decreases most rapidly, the negative of the gradient. One iteration of this algorithm can be written as

$$\mathbf{x}_{k+1}=\mathbf{x}_k-\alpha_k\mathbf{g}_k$$

where $\mathbf{x}_k$ is a vector of current weights and biases, $\mathbf{g}_k$ is the current gradient, and α_k is the learning rate. This equation is iterated until the network converges.

A list of the training algorithms that are available in the Neural Network Toolbox (Deep Learning Toolbox from version 18) software and that use gradient- or Jacobian-based methods, is shown in the following table.

For a detailed description of several of these techniques, see also Hagan, M.T., H.B. Demuth, and M.H. Beale, *Neural Network Design*, Boston, MA: PWS Publishing, 1996, Chapters 11 and 12.

Function	Algorithm
`trainlm`	Levenberg-Marquardt
`trainbr`	Bayesian Regularization
`trainbfg`	BFGS Quasi-Newton
`trainrp`	Resilient Backpropagation
`trainscg`	Scaled Conjugate Gradient
`traincgb`	Conjugate Gradient with Powell/Beale Restarts
`traincgf`	Fletcher-Powell Conjugate Gradient
`traincgp`	Polak-Ribiére Conjugate Gradient
`trainoss`	One Step Secant
`traingdx`	Variable Learning Rate Gradient Descent
`traingdm`	Gradient Descent with Momentum
`traingd`	Gradient Descent

The fastest training function is generally `trainlm`, and it is the default training function for `feedforwardnet`. The quasi-Newton method, `trainbfg`, is also quite fast. Both of these methods tend to be less efficient for large networks (with thousands of weights), since they require more memory and more computation time for these cases. Also, `trainlm` performs better on function fitting (nonlinear regression) problems than on pattern recognition problems.

When training large networks, and when training pattern recognition networks, `trainscg` and `trainrp` are good choices. Their memory requirements are relatively small, and yet they are much faster than standard gradient descent algorithms.

See Choose a Multilayer Neural Network Training Function for a full comparison of the performances of the training algorithms shown in the table above.

As a note on terminology, the term "backpropagation" is sometimes used to refer specifically to the gradient descent algorithm, when applied to neural network training. That terminology is not used here, since the process of computing the gradient and Jacobian by performing calculations backward through the network is applied in all of the training functions listed above. It is clearer to use the name of the specific optimization algorithm that is being used, rather than to use the term backpropagation alone.

Also, the multilayer network is sometimes referred to as a backpropagation network. However, the backpropagation technique that is used to compute gradients and Jacobians in a multilayer network can also be applied to many different network architectures. In fact, the gradients and Jacobians for any network that has differentiable transfer functions, weight functions and net input functions can be computed using the Neural Network Toolbox (Deep Learning Toolbox from version 18) software through a backpropagation process. You can even create your own custom networks and then train them using any of the training functions in the table above. The gradients and Jacobians will be automatically computed for you.

7.3.2 Training Example

To illustrate the training process, execute the following commands:

```
load house_dataset
net = feedforwardnet(20);
[net,tr] = train(net,houseInputs,houseTargets);
```

Notice that you did not need to issue the `configure` command, because the configuration is done automatically by the `train` function. The training window will appear during training, as shown in the following figure. If you do not want to have this window displayed during training, you can set the parameter `net.trainParam.showWindow` to `false`. If you want training information displayed in the command line, you can set the next parameter

`net.trainParam.showCommandLine` to `true`

This window shows that the data has been divided using the `dividerand` function, and the Levenberg-Marquardt (`trainlm`) training method has been used with the mean square error performance function. Recall that these are the default settings for `feedforwardnet`.

During training, the progress is constantly updated in the training window. Of most interest are the performance, the magnitude of the gradient of performance and the number of validation checks. The magnitude of the gradient and the number of validation checks are used to terminate the training. The gradient will become very small as the training reaches a minimum of the performance. If the magnitude of the gradient is less than 1e-5, the training will stop. This limit can be adjusted by setting the parameter `net.trainParam.min_grad`. The number of validation checks represents the number of successive iterations that the validation performance fails to decrease. If this number reaches 6 (the default value), the training will stop. In this run, you can see that the training did stop because of the number of validation checks. You can change this criterion by setting the parameter `net.trainParam.max_fail`. (Note that your results may be different than those shown in the following figure, because of the random setting of the initial weights and biases.)

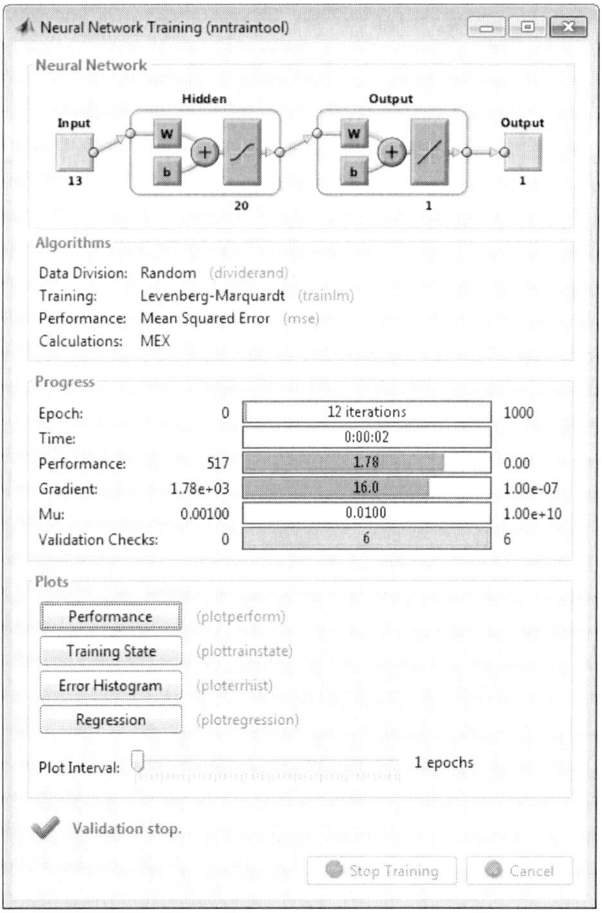

There are other criteria that can be used to stop network training. They are listed in the following table.

Parameter	Stopping Criteria
`min_grad`	Minimum Gradient Magnitude
`max_fail`	Maximum Number of Validation Increases
`time`	Maximum Training Time
`goal`	Minimum Performance Value
`epochs`	Maximum Number of Training Epochs (Iterations)

The training will also stop if you click the **Stop Training** button in the training window. You might want to do this if the performance function fails to decrease significantly over many iterations. It is always possible to continue the training by reissuing the `train` command shown above. It will continue to train the network from the completion of the previous run.

From the training window, you can access four plots: performance, training state, error histogram, and regression. The performance plot shows the value of the performance function versus the iteration number. It plots training, validation, and test performances. The training state plot shows the progress of other training variables, such as the gradient magnitude, the number of validation checks, etc. The error histogram plot shows the distribution of the network errors. The regression plot shows a regression between network outputs and network targets. You can use the histogram and regression plots to validate network performance.

7.3.3 Use the Network

After the network is trained and validated, the network object can be used to calculate the network response to any input. For example, if you want to find the network response to the fifth input vector in the building data set, you can use the following

```
a = net(houseInputs(:,5))
a =
  34.3922
```

If you try this command, your output might be different, depending on the state of your random number generator when the network was initialized. Below, the network object is called to calculate the outputs for a concurrent set of all the input vectors in the housing data set. This is the batch mode form of simulation, in which all the input vectors are placed in one matrix. This is much more efficient than presenting the vectors one at a time.

```
a = net(houseInputs);
```

Each time a neural network is trained, can result in a different solution due to different initial weight and bias values and different divisions of data into training, validation, and test sets. As a result, different neural networks trained on the same problem can give different outputs for the same input. To ensure that a neural network of good accuracy has been found, retrain several times.

7.4 TRAIN ALGORITMS IN MULTILAYER NEURAL NETWORKS

The next table resume the MATLAB training algoritms for multilayer neural networks

Function	Algorithm
trainlm	Levenberg-Marquardt
trainbr	Bayesian Regularization
trainbfg	BFGS Quasi-Newton
trainrp	Resilient Backpropagation
trainscg	Scaled Conjugate Gradient
traincgb	Conjugate Gradient with Powell/Beale Restarts
traincgf	Fletcher-Powell Conjugate Gradient
traincgp	Polak-Ribiére Conjugate Gradient
trainoss	One Step Secant
traingdx	Variable Learning Rate Gradient Descent
traingdm	Gradient Descent with Momentum
traingd	Gradient Descent

7.4.1 trainbr:Bayesian Regularization

Syntax

```
net.trainFcn = 'trainbr'
[net,tr] = train(net,...)
```

Description

`trainbr` is a network training function that updates the weight and bias values according to Levenberg-Marquardt optimization. It minimizes a combination of squared errors and weights, and then determines the correct combination so as to produce a network that generalizes well. The process is called Bayesian regularization.

`net.trainFcn = 'trainbr'` sets the network `trainFcn` property.

`[net,tr] = train(net,...)` trains the network with `trainbr`.

Training occurs according to `trainbr` training parameters, shown here with their default values:

net.trainParam.epochs	1000	Maximum number of epochs to train
net.trainParam.goal	0	Performance goal
net.trainParam.mu	0.005	Marquardt adjustment parameter
net.trainParam.mu_dec	0.1	Decrease factor for mu
net.trainParam.mu_inc	10	Increase factor for mu
net.trainParam.mu_max	1e10	Maximum value for mu
net.trainParam.max_fail	0	Maximum validation failures
net.trainParam.min_grad	1e-7	Minimum performance gradient
net.trainParam.show	25	Epochs between displays (NaN for no displays)
net.trainParam.showCommandLine	false	Generate command-line output
net.trainParam.showWindow	true	Show training GUI
net.trainParam.time	inf	Maximum time to train in seconds

Validation stops are disabled by default (`max_fail = 0`) so that training can continue until an optimal combination of errors and weights is found. However, some weight/bias minimization can still be achieved with shorter training times if validation is enabled by setting `max_fail` to 6 or some other strictly positive value.

Network Use

You can create a standard network that uses `trainbr` with `feedforwardnet` or `cascadeforwardnet`. To prepare a custom network to be trained with `trainbr`,

- Set `NET.trainFcn` to `'trainbr'`. This sets `NET.trainParam` to `trainbr`'s default parameters.
- Set `NET.trainParam` properties to desired values.

In either case, calling `train` with the resulting network trains the network with `trainbr`. See `feedforwardnet` and `cascadeforwardnet` for examples.

Examples

Here is a problem consisting of inputs p and targets `t` to be solved with a network. It involves fitting a noisy sine wave.

```
p = [-1:.05:1];
t = sin(2*pi*p)+0.1*randn(size(p));
```

A feed-forward network is created with a hidden layer of 2 neurons.

```
net = feedforwardnet(2,'trainbr');
```

Here the network is trained and tested.

```
net = train(net,p,t);
```

```
a = net(p)
```

Limitations

This function uses the Jacobian for calculations, which assumes that performance is a mean or sum of squared errors. Therefore networks trained with this function must use either the `mse` or `sse` performance function.

Algorithms

`trainbr` can train any network as long as its weight, net input, and transfer functions have derivative functions.

Bayesian regularization minimizes a linear combination of squared errors and weights. It also modifies the linear combination so that at the end of training the resulting network has good generalization qualities. See MacKay (*Neural Computation*, Vol. 4, No. 3, 1992, pp. 415 to 447) and Foresee and Hagan (*Proceedings of the International Joint Conference on Neural Networks*, June, 1997) for more detailed discussions of Bayesian regularization.

This Bayesian regularization takes place within the Levenberg-Marquardt algorithm. Backpropagation is used to calculate the Jacobian `jX` of performance `perf` with respect to the weight and bias variables `X`. Each variable is adjusted according to Levenberg-Marquardt,

```
jj = jX * jX

je = jX * E

dX = -(jj+I*mu) \ je
```

where `E` is all errors and `I` is the identity matrix.

The adaptive value `mu` is increased by `mu_inc` until the change shown above results in a reduced performance value. The change is then made to the network, and `mu` is decreased by `mu_dec`.

Training stops when any of these conditions occurs:

- The maximum number of `epochs` (repetitions) is reached.
- The maximum amount of `time` is exceeded.
- Performance is minimized to the `goal`.
- The performance gradient falls below `min_grad`.
- `mu` exceeds `mu_max`.

7.4.2 trainscg: Scaled conjugate gradient backpropagation

Syntax

```
net.trainFcn = 'trainscg'
[net,tr] = train(net,...)
```

Description

`trainscg` is a network training function that updates weight and bias values according to the scaled conjugate gradient method.

`net.trainFcn = 'trainscg'` sets the network `trainFcn` property.

`[net,tr] = train(net,...)` trains the network with `trainscg`.

Training occurs according to `trainscg` training parameters, shown here with their default values:

`net.trainParam.epochs`	`1000`	Maximum number of epochs to train
`net.trainParam.show`	`25`	Epochs between displays (NaN for no displays)
`net.trainParam.showCommandLine`	`false`	Generate command-line output
`net.trainParam.showWindow`	`true`	Show training GUI
`net.trainParam.goal`	`0`	Performance goal
`net.trainParam.time`	`inf`	Maximum time to train in seconds
`net.trainParam.min_grad`	`1e-6`	Minimum performance gradient
`net.trainParam.max_fail`	`6`	Maximum validation failures
`net.trainParam.sigma`	`5.0e-5`	Determine change in weight for second derivative approximation
`net.trainParam.lambda`	`5.0e-7`	Parameter for regulating the indefiniteness of the Hessian

Network Use

You can create a standard network that uses `trainscg` with `feedforwardnet` or `cascadeforwardnet`. To prepare a custom network to be trained with `trainscg`,

- Set `net.trainFcn` to `'trainscg'`. This sets `net.trainParam` to `trainscg`'s default parameters.
- Set `net.trainParam` properties to desired values.
- In either case, calling `train` with the resulting network trains the network with `trainscg`.

Examples

Here is a problem consisting of inputs p and targets `t` to be solved with a network.

```
p = [0 1 2 3 4 5];
t = [0 0 0 1 1 1];
```

A two-layer feed-forward network with two hidden neurons and this training function is created.

```
net = feedforwardnet(2,'trainscg');
```

Here the network is trained and retested.

```
net = train(net,p,t);
a = net(p)
```

See `help feedforwardnet` and `help cascadeforwardnet` for other examples.

Algorithms

`trainscg` can train any network as long as its weight, net input, and transfer functions have derivative functions. Backpropagation is used to calculate derivatives of performance `perf` with respect to the weight and bias variables X.

The scaled conjugate gradient algorithm is based on conjugate directions, as in `traincgp`, `traincgf`, and `traincgb`, but this algorithm does not perform a line search at each iteration. See Moller (*Neural Networks*, Vol. 6, 1993, pp. 525–533) for a more detailed discussion of the scaled conjugate gradient algorithm.

Training stops when any of these conditions occurs:

- The maximum number of `epochs` (repetitions) is reached.
- The maximum amount of `time` is exceeded.
- Performance is minimized to the `goal`.
- The performance gradient falls below `min_grad`.
- Validation performance has increased more than `max_fail` times since the last time it decreased (when using validation).

7.4.3 trainrp: Resilient backpropagation

Syntax

```
net.trainFcn = 'trainrp'
[net,tr] = train(net,...)
```

Description

`trainrp` is a network training function that updates weight and bias values according to the resilient backpropagation algorithm (Rprop).

`net.trainFcn = 'trainrp'` sets the network `trainFcn` property.

`[net,tr] = train(net,...)` trains the network with `trainrp`.

Training occurs according to `trainrp` training parameters, shown here with their default values:

`net.trainParam.epochs`	`1000`	Maximum number of epochs to train
`net.trainParam.show`	`25`	Epochs between displays (`NaN` for no displays)
`net.trainParam.showCommandLine`	`false`	Generate command-line output
`net.trainParam.showWindow`	`true`	Show training GUI
`net.trainParam.goal`	`0`	Performance goal
`net.trainParam.time`	`inf`	Maximum time to train in seconds
`net.trainParam.min_grad`	`1e-5`	Minimum performance gradient
`net.trainParam.max_fail`	`6`	Maximum validation failures
`net.trainParam.lr`	`0.01`	Learning rate
`net.trainParam.delt_inc`	`1.2`	Increment to weight change
`net.trainParam.delt_dec`	`0.5`	Decrement to weight change
`net.trainParam.delta0`	`0.07`	Initial weight change
`net.trainParam.deltamax`	`50.0`	Maximum weight change

Network Use

You can create a standard network that uses `trainrp` with `feedforwardnet` or `cascadeforwardnet`.

To prepare a custom network to be trained with `trainrp`,

- Set `net.trainFcn` to `'trainrp'`. This sets `net.trainParam` to `trainrp`'s default parameters.
- Set `net.trainParam` properties to desired values.

In either case, calling `train` with the resulting network trains the network with `trainrp`.

Examples

Here is a problem consisting of inputs p and targets `t` to be solved with a network.

```
p = [0 1 2 3 4 5];

t = [0 0 0 1 1 1];
```

A two-layer feed-forward network with two hidden neurons and this training function is created.

Create and test a network.

```
net = feedforwardnet(2,'trainrp');
```

Here the network is trained and retested.

```
net.trainParam.epochs = 50;

net.trainParam.show = 10;

net.trainParam.goal = 0.1;

net = train(net,p,t);

a = net(p)
```

See `help feedforwardnet` and `help cascadeforwardnet` for other examples.

Definitions

Multilayer networks typically use sigmoid transfer functions in the hidden layers. These functions are often called "squashing" functions, because they compress an infinite input range into a finite output range. Sigmoid functions are characterized by the fact that their slopes must approach zero as the input gets large. This causes a problem when you use steepest descent to train a multilayer network with sigmoid functions, because the gradient can have a very small magnitude and, therefore, cause small changes in the weights and biases, even though the weights and biases are far from their optimal values.

The purpose of the resilient backpropagation (Rprop) training algorithm is to eliminate these harmful effects of the magnitudes of the partial derivatives. Only the sign of the derivative can determine the direction of the weight update; the magnitude of the derivative has no effect on the weight update. The size of the weight change is determined by a separate update value. The update value for each weight and bias is increased by a factor `delt_inc` whenever the derivative of the performance function with respect to that weight has the same sign for two successive iterations. The update value is decreased by a factor `delt_dec` whenever the derivative with respect to that weight changes sign from the previous iteration. If the derivative is zero, the update value remains the same. Whenever the weights are oscillating, the weight change is reduced. If the weight continues to change in the same direction for several iterations, the magnitude of the weight change increases. A complete description of the Rprop algorithm is given in [RiBr93].

The following code recreates the previous network and trains it using the Rprop algorithm. The training parameters for `trainrp` are `epochs`, `show`, `goal`, `time`, `min_grad`, `max_fail`, `delt_inc`, `delt_dec`, `delta0`, and `deltamax`. The first eight parameters have been previously discussed. The last two are the initial step size and the maximum step size, respectively. The performance of Rprop is not very sensitive to the settings of the training parameters. For the example below, the training parameters are left at the default values:

```
p = [-1 -1 2 2;0 5 0 5];

t = [-1 -1 1 1];

net = feedforwardnet(3,'trainrp');

net = train(net,p,t);

y = net(p)
```

`rprop` is generally much faster than the standard steepest descent algorithm. It also has the nice property that it requires only a modest increase in memory requirements. You do need to store the update values for each weight and bias, which is equivalent to storage of the gradient.

Algorithms

`trainrp` can train any network as long as its weight, net input, and transfer functions have derivative functions.

Backpropagation is used to calculate derivatives of performance `perf` with respect to the weight and bias variables `X`. Each variable is adjusted according to the following:

```
dX = deltaX.*sign(gX);
```

where the elements of `deltaX` are all initialized to `delta0`, and `gX` is the gradient. At each iteration the elements of `deltaX` are modified. If an element of `gX` changes sign from one iteration to the next, then the corresponding element of `deltaX` is decreased by `delta_dec`. If an element of `gX` maintains the same sign from one iteration to the next, then the corresponding element of `deltaX` is increased by `delta_inc`. See Riedmiller, M., and H. Braun, "A direct adaptive method for faster backpropagation learning: The RPROP algorithm," *Proceedings of the IEEE International Conference on Neural Networks*,1993, pp. 586–591.

Training stops when any of these conditions occurs:

- The maximum number of `epochs` (repetitions) is reached.
- The maximum amount of `time` is exceeded.
- Performance is minimized to the `goal`.
- The performance gradient falls below `min_grad`.
- Validation performance has increased more than `max_fail` times since the last time it decreased (when using validation).

7.4.4 trainbfg: BFGS quasi-Newton backpropagation

Syntax

```
net.trainFcn = 'trainbfg'
[net,tr] = train(net,...)
```

Description

`trainbfg` is a network training function that updates weight and bias values according to the BFGS quasi-Newton method.

`net.trainFcn = 'trainbfg'` sets the network `trainFcn` property.

`[net,tr] = train(net,...)` trains the network with `trainbfg`.

Training occurs according to `trainbfg` training parameters, shown here with their default values:

`net.trainParam.epochs`	`1000`	Maximum number of epochs to train
`net.trainParam.showWindow`	`true`	Show training window
`net.trainParam.show`	`25`	Epochs between displays (`NaN` for no displays)
`net.trainParam.showCommandLine`	`false`	Generate command-line output
`net.trainParam.goal`	`0`	Performance goal
`net.trainParam.time`	`inf`	Maximum time to train in seconds
`net.trainParam.min_grad`	`1e-6`	Minimum performance gradient
`net.trainParam.max_fail`	`6`	Maximum validation failures
`net.trainParam.searchFcn`	`'srchbac'`	Name of line search routine to use

Parameters related to line search methods (not all used for all methods):

`net.trainParam.scal_tol`	`20`	Divide into `delta` to determine tolerance for linear search.
`net.trainParam.alpha`	`0.001`	Scale factor that determines sufficient reduction in `perf`
`net.trainParam.beta`	`0.1`	Scale factor that determines sufficiently large step size
`net.trainParam.delta`	`0.01`	Initial step size in interval location step
`net.trainParam.gama`	`0.1`	Parameter to avoid small reductions in performance, usually set to 0.1 (see `srch_cha`)
`net.trainParam.low_lim`	`0.1`	Lower limit on change in step size
`net.trainParam.up_lim`	`0.5`	Upper limit on change in step size
`net.trainParam.maxstep`	`100`	Maximum step length
`net.trainParam.minstep`	`1.0e-`	Minimum step length

	6	
net.trainParam.bmax	26	Maximum step size
net.trainParam.batch_frag	0	In case of multiple batches, they are considered independent. Any nonzero value implies a fragmented batch, so the final layer's conditions of a previous trained epoch are used as initial conditions for the next epoch.

Network Use

You can create a standard network that uses `trainbfg` with `feedfowardnet` or `cascadeforwardnet`. To prepare a custom network to be trained with `trainbfg`:

- Set `NET.trainFcn` to `'trainbfg'`. This sets `NET.trainParam` to `trainbfg`'s default parameters.
- Set `NET.trainParam` properties to desired values.

In either case, calling `train` with the resulting network trains the network with `trainbfg`.

Examples

Here a neural network is trained to predict median house prices.

```
[x,t] = house_dataset;

net = feedforwardnet(10,'trainbfg');

net = train(net,x,t);

y = net(x)
```

Definitions

Newton's method is an alternative to the conjugate gradient methods for fast optimization. The basic step of Newton's method is

$$\mathbf{x}_{k+1}=\mathbf{x}_k-\mathbf{A}_{-1k}\mathbf{g}_k$$

where $\mathbf{A}_{-1k}$ is the Hessian matrix (second derivatives) of the performance index at the current values of the weights and biases. Newton's method often converges faster than conjugate gradient methods. Unfortunately, it is complex and expensive to compute the Hessian matrix for feedforward neural networks. There is a class of algorithms that is based on Newton's method, but which does not require calculation of second derivatives. These are called quasi-Newton (or secant) methods. They update an approximate Hessian matrix at each iteration of the algorithm. The update is computed as a function of the gradient. The quasi-Newton method that has been most successful in published studies is the Broyden, Fletcher, Goldfarb, and Shanno (BFGS) update. This algorithm is implemented in the `trainbfg` routine.

The BFGS algorithm is described in [DeSc83]. This algorithm requires more computation in each iteration and more storage than the conjugate gradient methods, although it generally converges in fewer iterations. The approximate Hessian must be stored, and its dimension is *n* x *n*, where *n* is equal to the number of weights and biases in the network. For very large networks it might be better to use Rprop or one of the conjugate gradient algorithms. For smaller networks, however, `trainbfg` can be an efficient training function.

Algorithms

`trainbfg` can train any network as long as its weight, net input, and transfer functions have derivative functions.

Backpropagation is used to calculate derivatives of performance `perf` with respect to the weight and bias variables `X`. Each variable is adjusted according to the following:

```
X = X + a*dX;
```

where `dX` is the search direction. The parameter `a` is selected to minimize the performance along the search direction. The line search function `searchFcn` is used to locate the minimum point. The first search direction is the negative of the gradient of performance. In succeeding iterations the search direction is computed according to the following formula:

```
dX = -H\gX;
```

where `gX` is the gradient and `H` is a approximate Hessian matrix. See page 119 of Gill, Murray, and Wright (*Practical Optimization*, 1981) for a more detailed discussion of the BFGS quasi-Newton method.

Training stops when any of these conditions occurs:

- The maximum number of `epochs` (repetitions) is reached.
- The maximum amount of `time` is exceeded.
- Performance is minimized to the `goal`.
- The performance gradient falls below `min_grad`.
- Validation performance has increased more than `max_fail` times since the last time it decreased (when using validation).

7.4.5 traincgb: Conjugate gradient backpropagation with Powell-Beale restarts

Syntax

```
net.trainFcn = 'traincgb'
[net,tr] = train(net,...)
```

Description

`traincgb` is a network training function that updates weight and bias values according to the conjugate gradient backpropagation with Powell-Beale restarts.

`net.trainFcn = 'traincgb'` sets the network `trainFcn` property.

`[net,tr] = train(net,...)` trains the network with `traincgb`.

Training occurs according to `traincgb` training parameters, shown here with their default values:

`net.trainParam.epochs`	`1000`	Maximum number of epochs to train
`net.trainParam.show`	`25`	Epochs between displays (`NaN` for no displays)
`net.trainParam.showCommandLine`	`false`	Generate command-line output
`net.trainParam.showWindow`	`true`	Show training GUI
`net.trainParam.goal`	`0`	Performance goal
`net.trainParam.time`	`inf`	Maximum time to train in seconds
`net.trainParam.min_grad`	`1e-10`	Minimum performance gradient
`net.trainParam.max_fail`	`6`	Maximum validation failures
`net.trainParam.searchFcn`	`'srchcha'`	Name of line search routine to use

Parameters related to line search methods (not all used for all methods):

`net.trainParam.scal_tol`	`20`	Divide into `delta` to determine tolerance for linear search.
`net.trainParam.alpha`	`0.001`	Scale factor that determines sufficient reduction in `perf`
`net.trainParam.beta`	`0.1`	Scale factor that determines sufficiently large step size
`net.trainParam.delta`	`0.01`	Initial step size in interval location step
`net.trainParam.gama`	`0.1`	Parameter to avoid small reductions in performance, usually set to `0.1`(see `srch_cha`)
`net.trainParam.low_lim`	`0.1`	Lower limit on change in step size
`net.trainParam.up_lim`	`0.5`	Upper limit on change in step size
`net.trainParam.maxstep`	`100`	Maximum step length

net.trainParam.minstep	1.0e-6	Minimum step length
net.trainParam.bmax	26	Maximum step size

Network Use

You can create a standard network that uses traincgb with feedforwardnet or cascadeforwardnet.

To prepare a custom network to be trained with traincgb,

- Set net.trainFcn to 'traincgb'. This sets net.trainParam to traincgb's default parameters.
- Set net.trainParam properties to desired values.

In either case, calling train with the resulting network trains the network with traincgb.

Examples

Here a neural network is trained to predict median house prices.

```
[x,t] = house_dataset;

net = feedforwardnet(10,'traincgb');

net = train(net,x,t);

y = net(x)
```

Definitions

For all conjugate gradient algorithms, the search direction is periodically reset to the negative of the gradient. The standard reset point occurs when the number of iterations is equal to the number of network parameters (weights and biases), but there are other reset methods that can improve the efficiency of training. One such reset method was proposed by Powell [Powe77], based on an earlier version proposed by Beale [Beal72]. This technique restarts if there is very little orthogonality left between the current gradient and the previous gradient. This is tested with the following inequality:

If this condition is satisfied, the search direction is reset to the negative of the gradient.

The traincgb routine has somewhat better performance than traincgp for some problems, although performance on any given problem is difficult to predict. The storage requirements for the Powell-Beale algorithm (six vectors) are slightly larger than for Polak-Ribiére (four vectors).

Algorithms

`traincgb` can train any network as long as its weight, net input, and transfer functions have derivative functions.

Backpropagation is used to calculate derivatives of performance `perf` with respect to the weight and bias variables `X`. Each variable is adjusted according to the following:

```
X = X + a*dX;
```

where `dX` is the search direction. The parameter `a` is selected to minimize the performance along the search direction. The line search function `searchFcn` is used to locate the minimum point. The first search direction is the negative of the gradient of performance. In succeeding iterations the search direction is computed from the new gradient and the previous search direction according to the formula

```
dX = -gX + dX_old*Z;
```

where `gX` is the gradient. The parameter `Z` can be computed in several different ways. The Powell-Beale variation of conjugate gradient is distinguished by two features. First, the algorithm uses a test to determine when to reset the search direction to the negative of the gradient. Second, the search direction is computed from the negative gradient, the previous search direction, and the last search direction before the previous reset. See Powell, *Mathematical Programming,* Vol. 12, 1977, pp. 241 to 254, for a more detailed discussion of the algorithm.

Training stops when any of these conditions occurs:

- The maximum number of `epochs` (repetitions) is reached.
- The maximum amount of `time` is exceeded.
- Performance is minimized to the `goal`.
- The performance gradient falls below `min_grad`.
- Validation performance has increased more than `max_fail` times since the last time it decreased (when using validation).

7.4.6 traincgf: Conjugate gradient backpropagation with Fletcher-Reeves updates

Syntax

```
net.trainFcn = 'traincgf'
[net,tr] = train(net,...)
```

Description

`traincgf` is a network training function that updates weight and bias values according to conjugate gradient backpropagation with Fletcher-Reeves updates.

`net.trainFcn = 'traincgf'` sets the network `trainFcn` property.

`[net,tr] = train(net,...)` trains the network with `traincgf`.

Training occurs according to `traincgf` training parameters, shown here with their default values:

`net.trainParam.epochs`	`1000`	Maximum number of epochs to train
`net.trainParam.show`	`25`	Epochs between displays (`NaN` for no displays)
`net.trainParam.showCommandLine`	`false`	Generate command-line output
`net.trainParam.showWindow`	`true`	Show training GUI
`net.trainParam.goal`	`0`	Performance goal
`net.trainParam.time`	`inf`	Maximum time to train in seconds
`net.trainParam.min_grad`	`1e-10`	Minimum performance gradient
`net.trainParam.max_fail`	`6`	Maximum validation failures
`net.trainParam.searchFcn`	`'srchcha'`	Name of line search routine to use

Parameters related to line search methods (not all used for all methods):

`net.trainParam.scal_tol`	`20`	Divide into `delta` to determine tolerance for linear search.
`net.trainParam.alpha`	`0.001`	Scale factor that determines sufficient reduction in `perf`
`net.trainParam.beta`	`0.1`	Scale factor that determines sufficiently large step size
`net.trainParam.delta`	`0.01`	Initial step size in interval location step
`net.trainParam.gama`	`0.1`	Parameter to avoid small reductions in performance, usually set to `0.1`(see `srch_cha`)
`net.trainParam.low_lim`	`0.1`	Lower limit on change in step size
`net.trainParam.up_lim`	`0.5`	Upper limit on change in step size
`net.trainParam.maxstep`	`100`	Maximum step length
`net.trainParam.minstep`	`1.0e-6`	Minimum step length
`net.trainParam.bmax`	`26`	Maximum step size

Network Use

You can create a standard network that uses `traincgf` with `feedforwardnet` or `cascadeforwardnet`.

To prepare a custom network to be trained with `traincgf`,

- Set `net.trainFcn` to `'traincgf'`. This sets `net.trainParam` to `traincgf`'s default parameters.
- Set `net.trainParam` properties to desired values.

In either case, calling `train` with the resulting network trains the network with `traincgf`.

Examples

Here a neural network is trained to predict median house prices.

```
[x,t] = house_dataset;
net = feedforwardnet(10,'traincgf');
net = train(net,x,t);
y = net(x)
```

Definitions

All the conjugate gradient algorithms start out by searching in the steepest descent direction (negative of the gradient) on the first iteration.

$$\mathbf{p}_0=-\mathbf{g}_0$$

A line search is then performed to determine the optimal distance to move along the current search direction:

$$\mathbf{x}_{k+1}=\mathbf{x}_k\alpha_k\mathbf{p}_k$$

Then the next search direction is determined so that it is conjugate to previous search directions. The general procedure for determining the new search direction is to combine the new steepest descent direction with the previous search direction:

$$\mathbf{p}_k=-\mathbf{g}_k+\beta_k\mathbf{p}_{k-1}$$

The various versions of the conjugate gradient algorithm are distinguished by the manner in which the constant β_k is computed. For the Fletcher-Reeves update the procedure is

$$\beta_k = \frac{\mathbf{g}_k^T\mathbf{g}_k}{\mathbf{g}_{k-1}^T\mathbf{g}_{k-1}}$$

This is the ratio of the norm squared of the current gradient to the norm squared of the previous gradient.

See [FlRe64] or [HDB96] for a discussion of the Fletcher-Reeves conjugate gradient algorithm.

The conjugate gradient algorithms are usually much faster than variable learning rate backpropagation, and are sometimes faster than `trainrp`, although the results vary from one problem to another. The conjugate gradient algorithms require only a little more storage than the simpler algorithms. Therefore, these algorithms are good for networks with a large number of weights.

Try the *Neural Network Design* demonstration `nnd12cg` [HDB96] for an illustration of the performance of a conjugate gradient algorithm.

Algorithms

`traincgf` can train any network as long as its weight, net input, and transfer functions have derivative functions.

Backpropagation is used to calculate derivatives of performance `perf` with respect to the weight and bias variables `X`. Each variable is adjusted according to the following:

```
X = X + a*dX;
```

where `dX` is the search direction. The parameter `a` is selected to minimize the performance along the search direction. The line search function `searchFcn` is used to locate the minimum point. The first search direction is the negative of the gradient of performance. In succeeding iterations the search direction is computed from the new gradient and the previous search direction, according to the formula

```
dX = -gX + dX_old*Z;
```

where `gX` is the gradient. The parameter `Z` can be computed in several different ways. For the Fletcher-Reeves variation of conjugate gradient it is computed according to

```
Z = normnew_sqr/norm_sqr;
```

where `norm_sqr` is the norm square of the previous gradient and `normnew_sqr` is the norm square of the current gradient. See page 78 of Scales (*Introduction to Non-Linear Optimization*) for a more detailed discussion of the algorithm.

Training stops when any of these conditions occurs:

- The maximum number of `epochs` (repetitions) is reached.
- The maximum amount of `time` is exceeded.
- Performance is minimized to the `goal`.
- The performance gradient falls below `min_grad`.

- Validation performance has increased more than `max_fail` times since the last time it decreased (when using validation).

7.4.7 traincgp: Conjugate gradient backpropagation with Polak-Ribiére updates

Syntax

```
net.trainFcn = 'traincgp'
[net,tr] = train(net,...)
```

Description

`traincgp` is a network training function that updates weight and bias values according to conjugate gradient backpropagation with Polak-Ribiére updates.

`net.trainFcn = 'traincgp'` sets the network `trainFcn` property.

`[net,tr] = train(net,...)` trains the network with `traincgp`.

Training occurs according to `traincgp` training parameters, shown here with their default values:

`net.trainParam.epochs`	`1000`	Maximum number of epochs to train
`net.trainParam.show`	`25`	Epochs between displays (`NaN` for no displays)
`net.trainParam.showCommandLine`	`false`	Generate command-line output
`net.trainParam.showWindow`	`true`	Show training GUI
`net.trainParam.goal`	`0`	Performance goal
`net.trainParam.time`	`inf`	Maximum time to train in seconds
`net.trainParam.min_grad`	`1e-10`	Minimum performance gradient
`net.trainParam.max_fail`	`6`	Maximum validation failures
`net.trainParam.searchFcn`	`'srchcha'`	Name of line search routine to use

Parameters related to line search methods (not all used for all methods):

`net.trainParam.scal_tol`	`20`	Divide into `delta` to determine tolerance for linear search.
`net.trainParam.alpha`	`0.001`	Scale factor that determines sufficient reduction in `perf`
`net.trainParam.beta`	`0.1`	Scale factor that determines sufficiently large step size
`net.trainParam.delta`	`0.01`	Initial step size in interval location step
`net.trainParam.gama`	`0.1`	Parameter to avoid small reductions in performance, usually set to `0.1`(see `srch_cha`)

`net.trainParam.low_lim`	`0.1`	Lower limit on change in step size
`net.trainParam.up_lim`	`0.5`	Upper limit on change in step size
`net.trainParam.maxstep`	`100`	Maximum step length
`net.trainParam.minstep`	`1.0e-6`	Minimum step length
`net.trainParam.bmax`	`26`	Maximum step size

Network Use

You can create a standard network that uses `traincgp` with `feedforwardnet` or `cascadeforwardnet`. To prepare a custom network to be trained with `traincgp`,

- Set `net.trainFcn` to `'traincgp'`.This sets `net.trainParam` to `traincgp`'s default parameters.
- Set `net.trainParam` properties to desired values.

In either case, calling `train` with the resulting network trains the network with `traincgp`.

Examples

Here a neural network is trained to predict median house prices.

```
[x,t] = house_dataset;

net = feedforwardnet(10,'traincgp');

net = train(net,x,t);

y = net(x)
```

Definitions

Another version of the conjugate gradient algorithm was proposed by Polak and Ribiére. As with the Fletcher-Reeves algorithm, `traincgf`, the search direction at each iteration is determined by

$$\mathbf{p}_k = -\mathbf{g}_k + \beta_k \mathbf{p}_{k-1}$$

For the Polak-Ribiére update, the constant β_k is computed by

$$\beta_k = \frac{\Delta \mathbf{g}_{k-1}^T \mathbf{g}_k}{\mathbf{g}_{k-1}^T \mathbf{g}_{k-1}}$$

This is the inner product of the previous change in the gradient with the current gradient divided by the norm squared of the previous gradient. See [FlRe64] or [HDB96] for a discussion of the Polak-Ribiére conjugate gradient algorithm.

The `traincgp` routine has performance similar to `traincgf`. It is difficult to predict which algorithm will perform best on a given problem. The storage requirements for Polak-Ribiére (four vectors) are slightly larger than for Fletcher-Reeves (three vectors).

Algorithms

`traincgp` can train any network as long as its weight, net input, and transfer functions have derivative functions.

Backpropagation is used to calculate derivatives of performance `perf` with respect to the weight and bias variables `X`. Each variable is adjusted according to the following:

```
X = X + a*dX;
```

where `dX` is the search direction. The parameter `a` is selected to minimize the performance along the search direction. The line search function `searchFcn` is used to locate the minimum point. The first search direction is the negative of the gradient of performance. In succeeding iterations the search direction is computed from the new gradient and the previous search direction according to the formula

```
dX = -gX + dX_old*Z;
```

where `gX` is the gradient. The parameter `Z` can be computed in several different ways. For the Polak-Ribiére variation of conjugate gradient, it is computed according to

```
Z = ((gX - gX_old)'*gX)/norm_sqr;
```

where `norm_sqr` is the norm square of the previous gradient, and `gX_old` is the gradient on the previous iteration. See page 78 of Scales (*Introduction to Non-Linear Optimization*, 1985) for a more detailed discussion of the algorithm.

Training stops when any of these conditions occurs:

- The maximum number of `epochs` (repetitions) is reached.
- The maximum amount of `time` is exceeded.
- Performance is minimized to the `goal`.
- The performance gradient falls below `min_grad`.
- Validation performance has increased more than `max_fail` times since the last time it decreased (when using validation).

7.4.8 trainoss: One-step secant backpropagation

Syntax

```
net.trainFcn = 'trainoss'
[net,tr] = train(net,...)
```

Description

`trainoss` is a network training function that updates weight and bias values according to the one-step secant method.

`net.trainFcn = 'trainoss'` sets the network `trainFcn` property.

`[net,tr] = train(net,...)` trains the network with `trainoss`.

Training occurs according to `trainoss` training parameters, shown here with their default values:

`net.trainParam.epochs`	`1000`	Maximum number of epochs to train
`net.trainParam.goal`	`0`	Performance goal
`net.trainParam.max_fail`	`6`	Maximum validation failures
`net.trainParam.min_grad`	`1e-10`	Minimum performance gradient
`net.trainParam.searchFcn`	`'srchbac'`	Name of line search routine to use
`net.trainParam.show`	`25`	Epochs between displays (`NaN` for no displays)
`net.trainParam.showCommandLine`	`false`	Generate command-line output
`net.trainParam.showWindow`	`true`	Show training GUI
`net.trainParam.time`	`inf`	Maximum time to train in seconds

Parameters related to line search methods (not all used for all methods):

`net.trainParam.scal_tol`	`20`	Divide into `delta` to determine tolerance for linear search.
`net.trainParam.alpha`	`0.001`	Scale factor that determines sufficient reduction in `perf`
`net.trainParam.beta`	`0.1`	Scale factor that determines sufficiently large step size
`net.trainParam.delta`	`0.01`	Initial step size in interval location step
`net.trainParam.gama`	`0.1`	Parameter to avoid small reductions in performance, usually set to `0.1`(see `srch_cha`)
`net.trainParam.low_lim`	`0.1`	Lower limit on change in step size
`net.trainParam.up_lim`	`0.5`	Upper limit on change in step size
`net.trainParam.maxstep`	`100`	Maximum step length

`net.trainParam.minstep`	`1.0e-6`	Minimum step length
`net.trainParam.bmax`	`26`	Maximum step size

Network Use

You can create a standard network that uses `trainoss` with `feedforwardnet` or `cascadeforwardnet`. To prepare a custom network to be trained with `trainoss`:

- Set `net.trainFcn` to `'trainoss'`. This sets `net.trainParam` to `trainoss's` default parameters.
- Set `net.trainParam` properties to desired values.

In either case, calling `train` with the resulting network trains the network with `trainoss`.

Examples

Here a neural network is trained to predict median house prices.

```
[x,t] = house_dataset;

net = feedforwardnet(10,'trainoss');

net = train(net,x,t);

y = net(x)
```

Definitions

Because the BFGS algorithm requires more storage and computation in each iteration than the conjugate gradient algorithms, there is need for a secant approximation with smaller storage and computation requirements. The one step secant (OSS) method is an attempt to bridge the gap between the conjugate gradient algorithms and the quasi-Newton (secant) algorithms. This algorithm does not store the complete Hessian matrix; it assumes that at each iteration, the previous Hessian was the identity matrix. This has the additional advantage that the new search direction can be calculated without computing a matrix inverse.

The one step secant method is described in [Batt92]. This algorithm requires less storage and computation per epoch than the BFGS algorithm. It requires slightly more storage and computation per epoch than the conjugate gradient algorithms. It can be considered a compromise between full quasi-Newton algorithms and conjugate gradient algorithms.

Algorithms

`trainoss` can train any network as long as its weight, net input, and transfer functions have derivative functions.

Backpropagation is used to calculate derivatives of performance `perf` with respect to the weight and bias variables X. Each variable is adjusted according to the following:

```
X = X + a*dX;
```

where dX is the search direction. The parameter a is selected to minimize the performance along the search direction. The line search function `searchFcn` is used to locate the minimum point. The first search direction is the negative of the gradient of performance. In succeeding iterations the search direction is computed from the new gradient and the previous steps and gradients, according to the following formula:

```
dX = -gX + Ac*X_step + Bc*dgX;
```

where gX is the gradient, `X_step` is the change in the weights on the previous iteration, and dgX is the change in the gradient from the last iteration. See Battiti (*Neural Computation,* Vol. 4, 1992, pp. 141–166) for a more detailed discussion of the one-step secant algorithm.

Training stops when any of these conditions occurs:

- The maximum number of `epochs` (repetitions) is reached.
- The maximum amount of `time` is exceeded.
- Performance is minimized to the `goal`.
- The performance gradient falls below `min_grad`.
- Validation performance has increased more than `max_fail` times since the last time it decreased (when using validation).

7.4.9 traingdx: Gradient descent with momentum and adaptive learning rate backpropagation

Syntax

```
net.trainFcn = 'traingdx'
[net,tr] = train(net,...)
```

Description

`traingdx` is a network training function that updates weight and bias values according to gradient descent momentum and an adaptive learning rate.

`net.trainFcn = 'traingdx'` sets the network `trainFcn` property.

`[net,tr] = train(net,...)` trains the network with `traingdx`.

Training occurs according to `traingdx` training parameters, shown here with their default values:

`net.trainParam.epochs`	`1000`	Maximum number of epochs to train
`net.trainParam.goal`	`0`	Performance goal
`net.trainParam.lr`	`0.01`	Learning rate
`net.trainParam.lr_inc`	`1.05`	Ratio to increase learning rate
`net.trainParam.lr_dec`	`0.7`	Ratio to decrease learning rate
`net.trainParam.max_fail`	`6`	Maximum validation failures
`net.trainParam.max_perf_inc`	`1.04`	Maximum performance increase
`net.trainParam.mc`	`0.9`	Momentum constant
`net.trainParam.min_grad`	`1e-5`	Minimum performance gradient
`net.trainParam.show`	`25`	Epochs between displays (`NaN` for no displays)
`net.trainParam.showCommandLine`	`false`	Generate command-line output
`net.trainParam.showWindow`	`true`	Show training GUI
`net.trainParam.time`	`inf`	Maximum time to train in seconds

Network Use

You can create a standard network that uses `traingdx` with `feedforwardnet` or `cascadeforwardnet`. To prepare a custom network to be trained with `traingdx`,

- Set `net.trainFcn` to `'traingdx'`. This sets `net.trainParam` to `traingdx`'s default parameters.
- Set `net.trainParam` properties to desired values.

In either case, calling `train` with the resulting network trains the network with `traingdx`.

See `help feedforwardnet` and `help cascadeforwardnet` for examples.

Definitions

The function `traingdx` combines adaptive learning rate with momentum training. It is invoked in the same way as `traingda`, except that it has the momentum coefficient `mc` as an additional training parameter.

Algorithms

`traingdx` can train any network as long as its weight, net input, and transfer functions have derivative functions.

Backpropagation is used to calculate derivatives of performance `perf` with respect to the weight and bias variables `X`. Each variable is adjusted according to gradient descent with momentum,

```
dX = mc*dXprev + lr*mc*dperf/dX
```

where `dXprev` is the previous change to the weight or bias.

For each epoch, if performance decreases toward the goal, then the learning rate is increased by the factor `lr_inc`. If performance increases by more than the factor `max_perf_inc`, the learning rate is adjusted by the factor `lr_dec` and the change that increased the performance is not made.

Training stops when any of these conditions occurs:

- The maximum number of `epochs` (repetitions) is reached.
- The maximum amount of `time` is exceeded.
- Performance is minimized to the `goal`.
- The performance gradient falls below `min_grad`.
- Validation performance has increased more than `max_fail` times since the last time it decreased (when using validation).

7.4.10 traingdm: Gradient descent with momentum backpropagation

Syntax

```
net.trainFcn = 'traingdm'
[net,tr] = train(net,...)
```

Description

`traingdm` is a network training function that updates weight and bias values according to gradient descent with momentum.

`net.trainFcn = 'traingdm'` sets the network `trainFcn` property.

`[net,tr] = train(net,...)` trains the network with `traingdm`.

Training occurs according to `traingdm` training parameters, shown here with their default values:

net.trainParam.epochs	1000	Maximum number of epochs to train
net.trainParam.goal	0	Performance goal
net.trainParam.lr	0.01	Learning rate
net.trainParam.max_fail	6	Maximum validation failures
net.trainParam.mc	0.9	Momentum constant
net.trainParam.min_grad	1e-5	Minimum performance gradient
net.trainParam.show	25	Epochs between showing progress
net.trainParam.showCommandLine	false	Generate command-line output
net.trainParam.showWindow	true	Show training GUI
net.trainParam.time	inf	Maximum time to train in seconds

Network Use

You can create a standard network that uses `traingdm` with `feedforwardnet` or `cascadeforwardnet`. To prepare a custom network to be trained with `traingdm`,

1. Set `net.trainFcn` to `'traingdm'`. This sets `net.trainParam` to `traingdm`'s default parameters.
2. Set `net.trainParam` properties to desired values.

In either case, calling `train` with the resulting network trains the network with `traingdm`.

See `help feedforwardnet` and `help cascadeforwardnet` for examples.

Definitions

In addition to `traingd`, there are three other variations of gradient descent.

Gradient descent with momentum, implemented by `traingdm`, allows a network to respond not only to the local gradient, but also to recent trends in the error surface. Acting like a lowpass filter, momentum allows the network to ignore small features in the error surface. Without momentum a network can get stuck in a shallow local minimum. With momentum a network can slide through such a minimum. See page 12–9 of [HDB96] for a discussion of momentum.

Gradient descent with momentum depends on two training parameters. The parameter `lr` indicates the learning rate, similar to the simple gradient descent. The parameter `mc` is the momentum constant that defines the amount of momentum. `mc` is set between 0 (no momentum) and values close to 1 (lots of momentum). A momentum constant of 1 results in a network that is completely insensitive to the local gradient and, therefore, does not learn properly.)

```
p = [-1 -1 2 2; 0 5 0 5];

t = [-1 -1 1 1];
```

```
net = feedforwardnet(3,'traingdm');

net.trainParam.lr = 0.05;

net.trainParam.mc = 0.9;

net = train(net,p,t);

y = net(p)
```

Try the *Neural Network Design* demonstration `nnd12mo` [HDB96] for an illustration of the performance of the batch momentum algorithm.

Algorithms

`traingdm` can train any network as long as its weight, net input, and transfer functions have derivative functions.

Backpropagation is used to calculate derivatives of performance `perf` with respect to the weight and bias variables `X`. Each variable is adjusted according to gradient descent with momentum,

```
dX = mc*dXprev + lr*(1-mc)*dperf/dX
```

where `dXprev` is the previous change to the weight or bias.

Training stops when any of these conditions occurs:

- The maximum number of `epochs` (repetitions) is reached.
- The maximum amount of `time` is exceeded.
- Performance is minimized to the `goal`.
- The performance gradient falls below `min_grad`.
- Validation performance has increased more than `max_fail` times since the last time it decreased (when using validation).

7.4.11 traingd: Gradient descent backpropagation

Syntax

```
net.trainFcn = 'traingd'
[net,tr] = train(net,...)
```

Description

`traingd` is a network training function that updates weight and bias values according to gradient descent.

`net.trainFcn = 'traingd'` sets the network `trainFcn` property.

`[net,tr] = train(net,...)` trains the network with `traingd`.

Training occurs according to `traingd` training parameters, shown here with their default values:

`net.trainParam.epochs`	`1000`	Maximum number of epochs to train
`net.trainParam.goal`	`0`	Performance goal
`net.trainParam.showCommandLine`	`false`	Generate command-line output
`net.trainParam.showWindow`	`true`	Show training GUI
`net.trainParam.lr`	`0.01`	Learning rate
`net.trainParam.max_fail`	`6`	Maximum validation failures
`net.trainParam.min_grad`	`1e-5`	Minimum performance gradient
`net.trainParam.show`	`25`	Epochs between displays (`NaN` for no displays)
`net.trainParam.time`	`inf`	Maximum time to train in seconds

Network Use

You can create a standard network that uses `traingd` with `feedforwardnet` or `cascadeforwardnet`. To prepare a custom network to be trained with `traingd`,

- Set `net.trainFcn` to `'traingd'`. This sets `net.trainParam` to `traingd`'s default parameters.
- Set `net.trainParam` properties to desired values.

In either case, calling `train` with the resulting network trains the network with `traingd`.

See `help feedforwardnet` and `help cascadeforwardnet` for examples.

Definitions

The batch steepest descent training function is `traingd`. The weights and biases are updated in the direction of the negative gradient of the performance function. If you want to train a network using batch steepest descent, you should set the network `trainFcn` to `traingd`, and then call the function `train`. There is only one training function associated with a given network.

There are seven training parameters associated with `traingd`:

- `epochs`
- `show`
- `goal`
- `time`

- `min_grad`
- `max_fail`
- `lr`

The learning rate `lr` is multiplied times the negative of the gradient to determine the changes to the weights and biases. The larger the learning rate, the bigger the step. If the learning rate is made too large, the algorithm becomes unstable. If the learning rate is set too small, the algorithm takes a long time to converge. See page 12-8 of [HDB96] for a discussion of the choice of learning rate.

The training status is displayed for every `show` iterations of the algorithm. (If `show` is set to `NaN`, then the training status is never displayed.) The other parameters determine when the training stops. The training stops if the number of iterations exceeds `epochs`, if the performance function drops below `goal`, if the magnitude of the gradient is less than `mingrad`, or if the training time is longer than `time` seconds. `max_fail`, which is associated with the early stopping technique, is discussed in Improving Generalization.

The following code creates a training set of inputs p and targets `t`. For batch training, all the input vectors are placed in one matrix.

```
p = [-1 -1 2 2; 0 5 0 5];
t = [-1 -1 1 1];
```

Create the feedforward network.

```
net = feedforwardnet(3,'traingd');
```

In this simple example, turn off a feature that is introduced later.

```
net.divideFcn = '';
```

At this point, you might want to modify some of the default training parameters.

```
net.trainParam.show = 50;
net.trainParam.lr = 0.05;
net.trainParam.epochs = 300;
net.trainParam.goal = 1e-5;
```

If you want to use the default training parameters, the preceding commands are not necessary.

Now you are ready to train the network.

```
[net,tr] = train(net,p,t);
```

The training record `tr` contains information about the progress of training.

Now you can simulate the trained network to obtain its response to the inputs in the training set.

```
a = net(p)

a =

    -1.0026    -0.9962    1.0010    0.9960
```

Try the *Neural Network Design* demonstration `nnd12sd1` [HDB96] for an illustration of the performance of the batch gradient descent algorithm.

Algorithms

`traingd` can train any network as long as its weight, net input, and transfer functions have derivative functions.

Backpropagation is used to calculate derivatives of performance `perf` with respect to the weight and bias variables `X`. Each variable is adjusted according to gradient descent:

```
dX = lr * dperf/dX
```

Training stops when any of these conditions occurs:

- The maximum number of `epochs` (repetitions) is reached.
- The maximum amount of `time` is exceeded.
- Performance is minimized to the `goal`.
- The performance gradient falls below `min_grad`.
- Validation performance has increased more than `max_fail` times since the last time it decreased (when using validation).

Chapter 8

ANALYZE AND DEPLOY TRAINED NEURAL NETWORK

8.1 ANALYZE NEURAL NETWORK PERFORMANCE

When the training in Train and Apply Multilayer Neural Networks is complete, you can check the network performance and determine if any changes need to be made to the training process, the network architecture, or the data sets. First check the training record, `tr`, which was the second argument returned from the training function.

```
tr

tr =

  struct with fields:

        trainFcn: 'trainlm'
      trainParam: [1×1 struct]
      performFcn: 'mse'
    performParam: [1×1 struct]
        derivFcn: 'defaultderiv'
       divideFcn: 'dividerand'
      divideMode: 'sample'
     divideParam: [1×1 struct]
        trainInd: [1×354 double]
          valInd: [1×76 double]
         testInd: [1×76 double]
            stop: 'Validation stop.'
```

```
     num_epochs: 12
      trainMask: {[1×506 double]}
        valMask: {[1×506 double]}
       testMask: {[1×506 double]}
     best_epoch: 6
           goal: 0
         states: {1×8 cell}
          epoch: [0 1 2 3 4 5 6 7 8 9 10 11 12]
           time: [1×13 double]
           perf: [1×13 double]
          vperf: [1×13 double]
          tperf: [1×13 double]
             mu: [1×13 double]
       gradient: [1×13 double]
       val_fail: [0 0 0 0 0 1 0 1 2 3 4 5 6]
      best_perf: 7.0111
     best_vperf: 10.3333
     best_tperf: 10.6567
```

This structure contains all of the information concerning the training of the network. For example, `tr.trainInd`, `tr.valInd` and `tr.testInd` contain the indices of the data points that were used in the training, validation and test sets, respectively. If you want to retrain the network using the same division of data, you can set `net.divideFcn` to `'divideInd'`, `net.divideParam.trainInd` to `tr.trainIn d`, `net.divideParam.valInd` to `tr.valInd`, `net.divideParam.testInd` to `tr.t estInd`.

The `tr` structure also keeps track of several variables during the course of training, such as the value of the performance function, the magnitude of the gradient, etc. You can use the training record to plot the performance progress by using the `plotperf` command:

```
plotperf(tr)
```

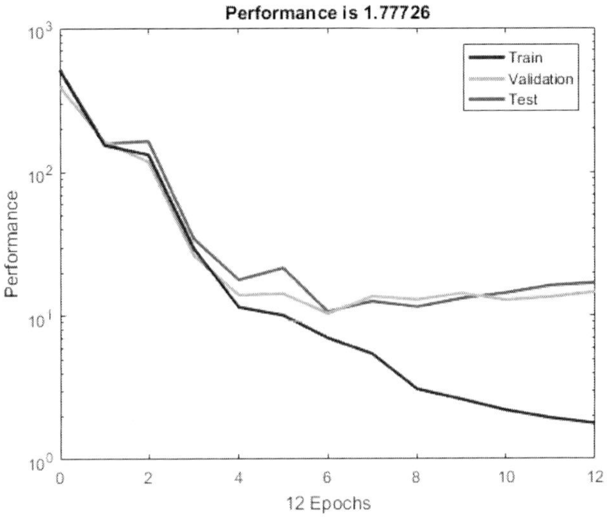

The property `tr.best_epoch` indicates the iteration at which the validation performance reached a minimum. The training continued for 6 more iterations before the training stopped.

This figure does not indicate any major problems with the training. The validation and test curves are very similar. If the test curve had increased significantly before the validation curve increased, then it is possible that some overfitting might have occurred.

The next step in validating the network is to create a regression plot, which shows the relationship between the outputs of the network and the targets. If the training were perfect, the network outputs and the targets would be exactly equal, but the relationship is rarely perfect in practice. For the housing example, we can create a regression plot with the following commands. The first command calculates the trained network response to all of the inputs in the data set. The following six commands extract the outputs and targets that belong to the training, validation and test subsets. The final command creates three regression plots for training, testing and validation.

```
houseOutputs = net(houseInputs);
trOut = houseOutputs(tr.trainInd);
vOut = houseOutputs(tr.valInd);
tsOut = houseOutputs(tr.testInd);
trTarg = houseTargets(tr.trainInd);
vTarg = houseTargets(tr.valInd);
tsTarg = houseTargets(tr.testInd);
plotregression(trTarg,trOut,'Train',vTarg,vOut,'Validation',...
tsTarg,tsOut,'Testing')
```

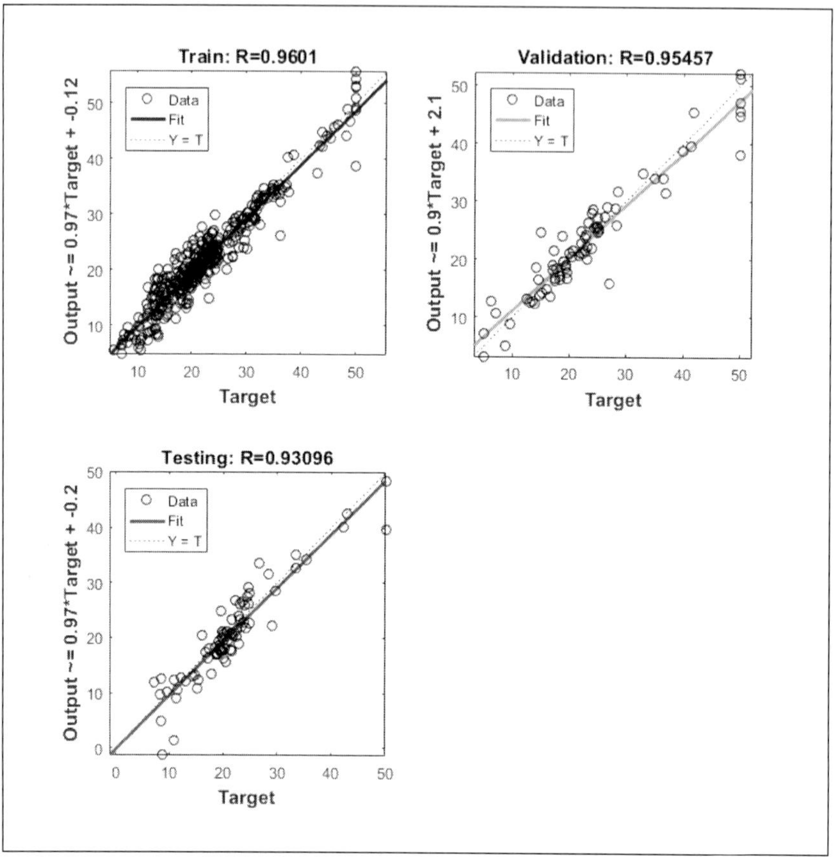

The three plots represent the training, validation, and testing data. The dashed line in each plot represents the perfect result – outputs = targets. The solid line represents the best fit linear regression line between outputs and targets. The R value is an indication of the relationship between the outputs and targets. If R = 1, this indicates that there is an exact linear relationship between outputs and targets. If R is close to zero, then there is no linear relationship between outputs and targets.

For this example, the training data indicates a good fit. The validation and test results also show R values that greater than 0.9. The scatter plot is helpful in showing that certain data points have poor fits. For example, there is a data point in the test set whose network output is close to 35, while the corresponding target value is about 12. The next step would be to investigate this data point to determine if it represents extrapolation (i.e., is it outside of the training data set). If so, then it should be included in the training set, and additional data should be collected to be used in the test set.

8.2 IMPROVING RESULTS

If the network is not sufficiently accurate, you can try initializing the network and the training again. Each time your initialize a feedforward network, the network parameters are different and might produce different solutions.

```
net = init(net);
net = train(net,houseInputs,houseTargets);
```

As a second approach, you can increase the number of hidden neurons above 20. Larger numbers of neurons in the hidden layer give the network more flexibility because the network has more parameters it can optimize. (Increase the layer size gradually. If you make the hidden layer too large, you might cause the problem to be under-characterized and the network must optimize more parameters than there are data vectors to constrain these parameters.)

A third option is to try a different training function. Bayesian regularization training with `trainbr`, for example, can sometimes produce better generalization capability than using early stopping.

Finally, try using additional training data. Providing additional data for the network is more likely to produce a network that generalizes well to new data.

8.3 DEPLOYMENT FUNCTIONS AND TOOLS FOR TRAINED NETWORKS

The function `genFunction` allows stand-alone MATLAB® functions for a trained neural network. The generated code contains all the information needed to simulate a neural network, including settings, weight and bias values, module functions, and calculations.

The generated MATLAB function can be used to inspect the exact simulation calculations that a particular neural network performs, and makes it easier to deploy neural networks for many purposes with a wide variety of MATLAB deployment products and tools.

The function `genFunction` is introduced in the deployment panels in the tools `nftool`, `nctool`, `nprtool` and `ntstool`. For information on these tool features, see Fit Data with a Neural Network, Classify Patterns with a Neural Network, Cluster Data with a Self-Organizing Map, and Neural Network Time-Series Prediction and Modeling.

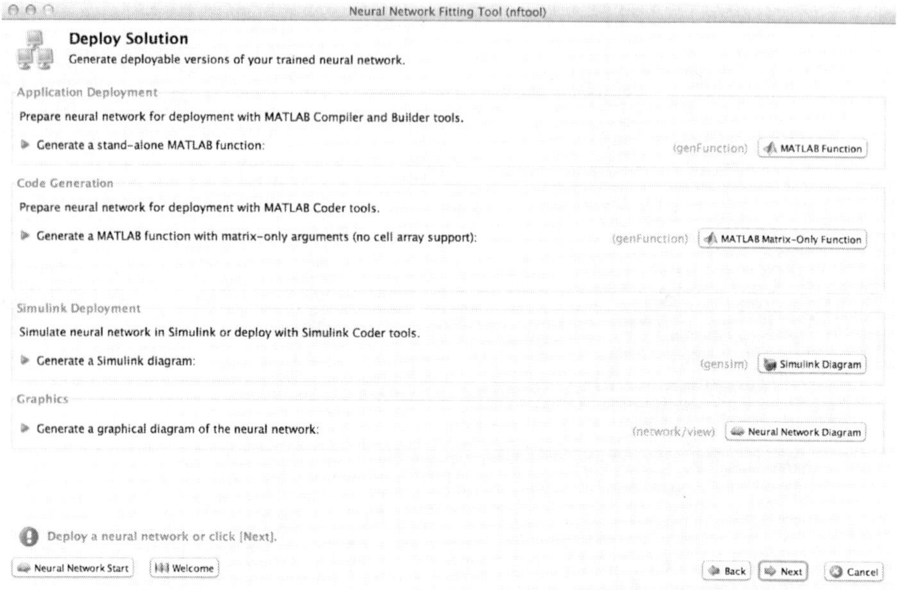

The advanced scripts generated on the Save Results panel of each of these tools includes an example of deploying networks with `genFunction`.

8.4 GENERATE NEURAL NETWORK FUNCTIONS FOR APPLICATION DEPLOYMENT

The function `genFunction` generates a stand-alone MATLAB function for simulating any trained neural network and preparing it for deployment. This might be useful for several tasks:

- Document the input-output transforms of a neural network used as a calculation template for manual reimplementations of the network
- Use the MATLAB Function block to create a Simulink® block
- Use MATLAB Compiler™ to:
    - Generate stand-alone executables
    - Generate Excel® add-ins
- Use MATLAB Compiler SDK™ to:
    - Generate C/C++ libraries
    - Generate .COM components
    - Generate Java® components
    - Generate .NET components
- Use MATLAB Coder™ to:

- Generate C/C++ code
- Generate efficient MEX-functions

`genFunction(net,'pathname')` takes a neural network and file path, and produces a standalone MATLAB function file `filename.m`.

`genFunction(...,'MatrixOnly','yes')` overrides the default cell/matrix notation and instead generates a function that uses only matrix arguments compatible with MATLAB Coder tools. For static networks, the matrix columns are interpreted as independent samples. For dynamic networks, the matrix columns are interpreted as a series of time steps. The default value is `'no'`.

`genFunction(___,'ShowLinks','no')` disables the default behavior of displaying links to generated help and source code. The default is `'yes'`.

Here a static network is trained and its outputs calculated.

```
[x,t] = house_dataset;
houseNet = feedforwardnet(10);
houseNet = train(houseNet,x,t);
y = houseNet(x);
```

The following code generates, tests, and displays a MATLAB function with the same interface as the neural network object.

```
genFunction(houseNet,'houseFcn');
y2 = houseFcn(x);
accuracy2 = max(abs(y-y2))
edit houseFcn
```

You can compile the new function with the MATLAB Compiler tools (license required) to a shared/dynamically linked library with `mcc`.

```
mcc -W lib:libHouse -T link:lib houseFcn
```

The next code generates another version of the MATLAB function that supports only matrix arguments (no cell arrays). This function is tested. Then it is used to generate a MEX-function with the MATLAB Coder tool `codegen` (license required), which is also tested.

```
genFunction(houseNet,'houseFcn','MatrixOnly','yes');
y3 = houseFcn(x);
accuracy3 = max(abs(y-y3))

x1Type = coder.typeof(double(0),[13 Inf]); % Coder type of input 1
codegen houseFcn.m -config:mex -o houseCodeGen -args {x1Type}
y4 = houseCodeGen(x);
accuracy4 = max(abs(y-y4))
```

Here a dynamic network is trained and its outputs calculated.

```
[x,t] = maglev_dataset;
maglevNet = narxnet(1:2,1:2,10);
[X,Xi,Ai,T] = preparets(maglevNet,x,{},t);
maglevNet = train(maglevNet,X,T,Xi,Ai);
[y,xf,af] = maglevNet(X,Xi,Ai);
```

Next a MATLAB function is generated and tested. The function is then used to create a shared/dynamically linked library with `mcc`.

```
genFunction(maglevNet,'maglevFcn');
[y2,xf,af] = maglevFcn(X,Xi,Ai);
accuracy2 = max(abs(cell2mat(y)-cell2mat(y2)))
mcc -W lib:libMaglev -T link:lib maglevFcn
```

The following code generates another version of the MATLAB function that supports only matrix arguments (no cell arrays). This function is tested. Then it is used to generate a MEX-function with the MATLAB Coder tool `codegen`, which is also tested.

```
genFunction(maglevNet,'maglevFcn','MatrixOnly','yes');
x1 = cell2mat(X(1,:)); % Convert each input to matrix
x2 = cell2mat(X(2,:));
xi1 = cell2mat(Xi(1,:)); % Convert each input state to matrix
xi2 = cell2mat(Xi(2,:));
[y3,xf1,xf2] = maglevFcn(x1,x2,xi1,xi2);
accuracy3 = max(abs(cell2mat(y)-y3))

x1Type = coder.typeof(double(0),[1 Inf]); % Coder type of input 1
x2Type = coder.typeof(double(0),[1 Inf]); % Coder type of input 2
xi1Type = coder.typeof(double(0),[1 2]); % Coder type of input 1
states
xi2Type = coder.typeof(double(0),[1 2]); % Coder type of input 2
states
codegen maglevFcn.m -config:mex -o maglevNetCodeGen ...
                   -args {x1Type x2Type xi1Type xi2Type}
[y4,xf1,xf2] = maglevNetCodeGen(x1,x2,xi1,xi2);
dynamic_codegen_accuracy = max(abs(cell2mat(y)-y4))
```

8.5 DEPLOY NEURAL NETWORK SIMULINK DIAGRAMS

The function `gensim` generates block descriptions of networks so you can simulate them using Simulink® software.

```
gensim(net,st)
```

The second argument to `gensim` determines the sample time, which is normally chosen to be some positive real value.

If a network has no delays associated with its input weights or layer weights, this value can be set to -1. A value of -1 causes `gensim` to generate a network with continuous sampling.

8.5.1 Example

Here is a simple problem defining a set of inputs p and corresponding targets `t`.

```
p = [1 2 3 4 5];

t = [1 3 5 7 9];
```

The code below designs a linear layer to solve this problem.

```
net = newlind(p,t)
```

You can test the network on your original inputs with `sim`.

```
y = sim(net,p)
```

The results show the network has solved the problem.

```
y =

        1.0000    3.0000    5.0000    7.0000    9.0000
```

Call `gensim` as follows to generate a Simulink version of the network.

```
gensim(net,-1)
```

The second argument is -1, so the resulting network block samples continuously.

The call to `gensim` opens the following Simulink Editor, showing a system consisting of the linear network connected to a sample input and a scope.

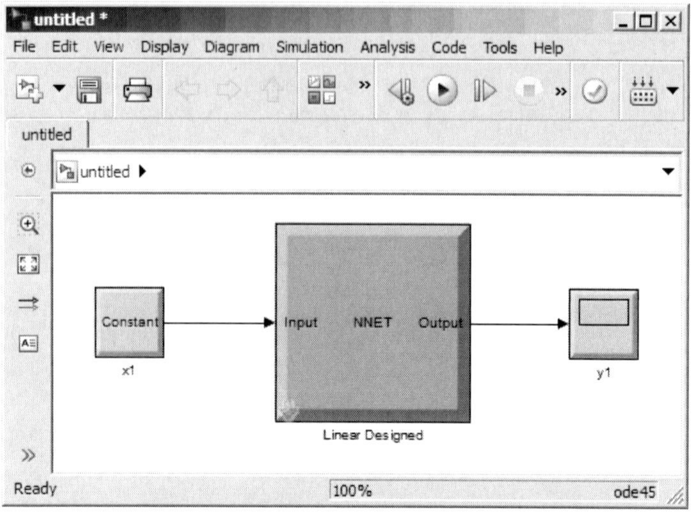

To test the network, double-click the input Constant x1 block on the left.

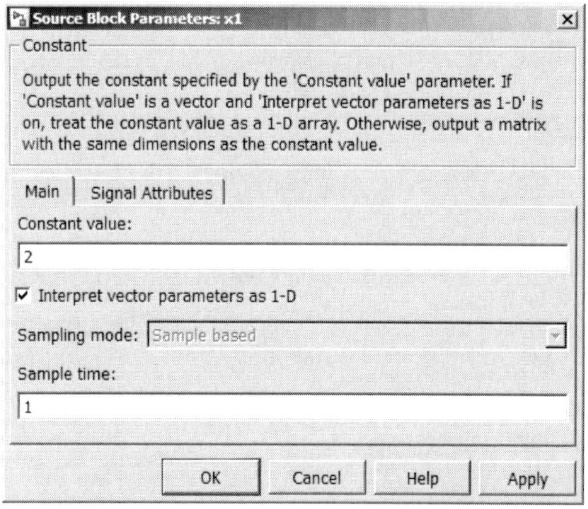

The input block is actually a standard Constant block. Change the constant value from the initial randomly generated value to 2, and then click **OK**.

Select the menu option **Simulation** > **Run**. Simulink takes a moment to simulate the system.

When the simulation is complete, double-click the output y1 block on the right to see the following display of the network's response.

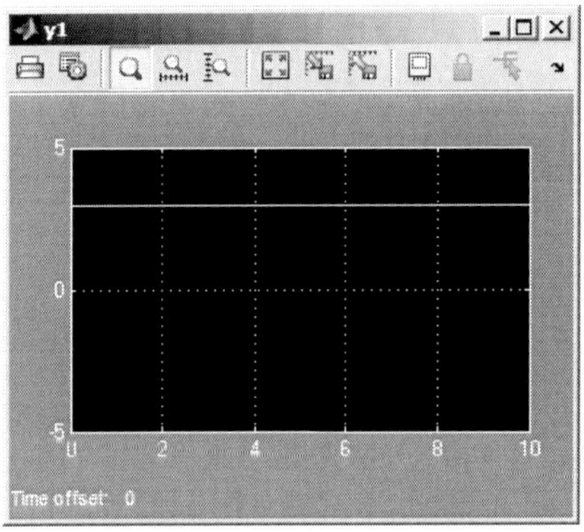

Note that the output is 3, which is the correct output for an input of 2.

8.5.2 Suggested Exercises

Here are a couple exercises you can try.

8.5.2.1.1 Change the Input Signal

Replace the constant input block with a signal generator from the standard Simulink Sources blockset. Simulate the system and view the network's response.

8.5.2.1.2 Use a Discrete Sample Time

Recreate the network, but with a discrete sample time of 0.5, instead of continuous sampling.

```
gensim(net,0.5)
```

Again, replace the constant input with a signal generator. Simulate the system and view the network's response.

8.6 DEPLOY TRAINING OF NEURAL NETWORKS

Use MATLAB® Runtime to deploy functions that can train a model. You can deploy MATLAB code that trains neural networks as described in Create Standalone Application from Command Line and Package Standalone Application with Application Compiler App.

The following methods and functions are NOT supported in deployed mode:

- Training progress dialog, `nntraintool`.
- `genFunction` and `gensim` to generate MATLAB code or Simulink® blocks
- `view` method
- `nctool`, `nftool`, `nnstart`, `nprtool`, `ntstool`

- Plot functions (such as `plotperform`, `plottrainstate`, `ploterrhist`, `plotregression`, `plotfit`, and so on)
- `perceptron`, `newlind`, `elmannet`, and `newhop` functions

Here is an example of how you can deploy training of a network. Create a script to train a neural network, for example, `mynntraining.m`:

```
% Create the predictor and response (target)
x = [0.054 0.78 0.13 0.47 0.34 0.79 0.53 0.6 0.65 0.75 0.084 0.91
0.83
     0.53 0.93 0.57 0.012 0.16 0.31 0.17 0.26 0.69 0.45 0.23 0.15
0.54];
t = [0.46 0.079 0.42 0.48 0.95 0.63 0.48 0.51 0.16 0.51 1 0.28
0.3];
% Create and display the network
net = fitnet();
disp('Training fitnet')
% Train the network using the data in x and t
net = train(net,x,t);
% Predict the responses using the trained network
y = net(x);
% Measure the performance
perf = perform(net,y,t)
```

Compile the script `mynntraining.m`, either by using the MATLAB Compiler™ interface as described in Package Standalone Application with Application Compiler App, or by using the command line:

```
mcc -m 'mynntraining.m'
```

`mcc` invokes the MATLAB Compiler to compile code at the prompt. The flag -`m` compiles a MATLAB function and generates a standalone executable. The EXE file is now in your local computer in the working directory.

To run the compiled EXE application on computers that do not have MATLAB installed, you need to download and install MATLAB Runtime. The `readme.txt` created in your working folder has more information about the deployment requirements.

Chapter 9

TRAINING SCALABILITY AND EFICIENCE

9.1 NEURAL NETWORKS WITH PARALLEL AND GPU COMPUTING

9.1.1 Modes of Parallelism

Neural networks are inherently parallel algorithms. Multicore CPUs, graphical processing units (GPUs), and clusters of computers with multiple CPUs and GPUs can take advantage of this parallelism.

Parallel Computing Toolbox™, when used in conjunction with Neural Network Toolbox (Deep Learning Toolbox from version 18)™, enables neural network training and simulation to take advantage of each mode of parallelism.

For example, the following shows a standard single-threaded training and simulation session:

```
[x,t] = house_dataset;
net1 = feedforwardnet(10);
net2 = train(net1,x,t);
y = net2(x);
```

The two steps you can parallelize in this session are the call to `train` and the implicit call to `sim` (where the network `net2`is called as a function).

In Neural Network Toolbox (Deep Learning Toolbox from version 18) you can divide any data, such as x and `t` in the previous example code, across samples. If xand `t` contain only one sample each, there is no parallelism. But if x and t contain hundreds or thousands of samples, parallelism can provide both speed and problem size benefits.

9.1.2 Distributed Computing

Parallel Computing Toolbox allows neural network training and simulation to run across multiple CPU cores on a single PC, or across multiple CPUs on multiple computers on a network using MATLAB® Distributed Computing Server™.

Using multiple cores can speed calculations. Using multiple computers can allow you to solve problems using data sets too big to fit in the RAM of a single computer. The only limit to problem size is the total quantity of RAM available across all computers.

To manage cluster configurations, use the Cluster Profile Manager from the MATLAB **Home** tab **Environment** menu **Parallel** > **Manage Cluster Profiles**.

To open a pool of MATLAB workers using the default cluster profile, which is usually the local CPU cores, use this command:

```
pool = parpool
```

```
Starting parallel pool (parpool) using the 'local' profile ...
connected to 4 workers.
```

When parpool runs, it displays the number of workers available in the pool. Another way to determine the number of workers is to query the pool:

```
pool.NumWorkers

   4
```

Now you can train and simulate the neural network with data split by sample across all the workers. To do this, set the train and sim parameter 'useParallel' to 'yes'.

```
net2 = train(net1,x,t,'useParallel','yes')
y = net2(x,'useParallel','yes')
```

Use the 'showResources' argument to verify that the calculations ran across multiple workers.

```
net2 = train(net1,x,t,'useParallel','yes','showResources','yes');
y = net2(x,'useParallel','yes','showResources','yes');
```

MATLAB indicates which resources were used. For example:

```
Computing Resources:

Parallel Workers
  Worker 1 on MyComputer, MEX on PCWIN64
```

```
  Worker 2 on MyComputer, MEX on PCWIN64
  Worker 3 on MyComputer, MEX on PCWIN64
  Worker 4 on MyComputer, MEX on PCWIN64
```

When `train` and `sim` are called, they divide the input matrix or cell array data into distributed Composite values before training and simulation. When `sim` has calculated a Composite, this output is converted back to the same matrix or cell array form before it is returned.

However, you might want to perform this data division manually if:

- The problem size is too large for the host computer. Manually defining the elements of Composite values sequentially allows much bigger problems to be defined.
- It is known that some workers are on computers that are faster or have more memory than others. You can distribute the data with differing numbers of samples per worker. This is called load balancing.

The following code sequentially creates a series of random datasets and saves them to separate files:

```
pool = gcp;
for i=1:pool.NumWorkers
  x = rand(2,1000);
  save(['inputs' num2str(i)],'x');
  t = x(1,:) .* x(2,:) + 2 * (x(1,:) + x(2,:));
  save(['targets' num2str(i)],'t');
  clear x t
end
```

Because the data was defined sequentially, you can define a total dataset larger than can fit in the host PC memory. PC memory must accommodate only a sub-dataset at a time.

Now you can load the datasets sequentially across parallel workers, and train and simulate a network on the Composite data. When `train` or `sim` is called with Composite data, the `'useParallel'` argument is automatically set to `'yes'`. When using Composite data, configure the network's input and outputs to match one of the datasets manually using the `configure` function before training.

```
xc = Composite;
tc = Composite;
for i=1:pool.NumWorkers
  data = load(['inputs' num2str(i)],'x');
  xc{i} = data.x;
  data = load(['targets' num2str(i)],'t');
  tc{i} = data.t;
  clear data
end
```

```
net2 = configure(net1,xc{1},tc{1});
net2 = train(net2,xc,tc);
yc = net2(xc);
```

To convert the Composite output returned by `sim`, you can access each of its elements, separately if concerned about memory limitations.

```
for i=1:pool.NumWorkers
  yi = yc{i}
end
```

Combined the Composite value into one local value if you are not concerned about memory limitations.

```
y = {yc{:}};
```

When load balancing, the same process happens, but, instead of each dataset having the same number of samples (1000 in the previous example), the numbers of samples can be adjusted to best take advantage of the memory and speed differences of the worker host computers.

It is not required that each worker have data. If element `i` of a Composite value is undefined, worker `i` will not be used in the computation.

9.1.3 Single GPU Computing

The number of cores, size of memory, and speed efficiencies of GPU cards are growing rapidly with each new generation. Where video games have long benefited from improved GPU performance, these cards are now flexible enough to perform general numerical computing tasks like training neural networks.

For the latest GPU requirements, see the web page for Parallel Computing Toolbox; or query MATLAB to determine whether your PC has a supported GPU. This function returns the number of GPUs in your system:

```
count = gpuDeviceCount

count =

    1
```

If the result is one or more, you can query each GPU by index for its characteristics. This includes its name, number of multiprocessors, `SIMDWidth` of each multiprocessor, and total memory.

```
gpu1 = gpuDevice(1)

gpu1 =

  CUDADevice with properties:
```

```
                   Name: 'GeForce GTX 470'
                  Index: 1
      ComputeCapability: '2.0'
         SupportsDouble: 1
          DriverVersion: 4.1000
     MaxThreadsPerBlock: 1024
       MaxShmemPerBlock: 49152
     MaxThreadBlockSize: [1024 1024 64]
            MaxGridSize: [65535 65535 1]
              SIMDWidth: 32
            TotalMemory: 1.3422e+09
        AvailableMemory: 1.1056e+09
    MultiprocessorCount: 14
           ClockRateKHz: 1215000
            ComputeMode: 'Default'
    GPUOverlapsTransfers: 1
  KernelExecutionTimeout: 1
        CanMapHostMemory: 1
         DeviceSupported: 1
          DeviceSelected: 1
```

The simplest way to take advantage of the GPU is to specify call `train` and `sim` with the parameter argument `'useGPU'`set to `'yes'` (`'no'` is the default).

```
net2 = train(net1,x,t,'useGPU','yes')
y = net2(x,'useGPU','yes')
```

If `net1` has the default training function `trainlm`, you see a warning that GPU calculations do not support Jacobian training, only gradient training. So the training function is automatically changed to the gradient training function `trainscg`. To avoid the notice, you can specify the function before training:

```
net1.trainFcn = 'trainscg';
```

To verify that the training and simulation occur on the GPU device, request that the computer resources be shown:

```
net2 = train(net1,x,t,'useGPU','yes','showResources','yes')
y = net2(x,'useGPU','yes','showResources','yes')
```

Each of the above lines of code outputs the following resources summary:

```
Computing Resources:
GPU device #1, GeForce GTX 470
```

Many MATLAB functions automatically execute on a GPU when any of the input arguments is a gpuArray. Normally you move arrays to and from the GPU with the functions gpuArray and gather. However, for neural network calculations on a GPU to be efficient, matrices need to be transposed and the columns padded so that the first element in each column aligns properly in the GPU memory. Neural Network Toolbox (Deep Learning Toolbox from version 18) provides a special function called nndata2gpu to move an array to a GPU and properly organize it:

```
xg = nndata2gpu(x);
tg = nndata2gpu(t);
```

Now you can train and simulate the network using the converted data already on the GPU, without having to specify the 'useGPU' argument. Then convert and return the resulting GPU array back to MATLAB with the complementary function gpu2nndata.

Before training with gpuArray data, the network's input and outputs must be manually configured with regular MATLAB matrices using the configure function:

```
net2 = configure(net1,x,t);  % Configure with MATLAB arrays
net2 = train(net2,xg,tg);     % Execute on GPU with NNET formatted
gpuArrays
yg = net2(xg);               % Execute on GPU
y = gpu2nndata(yg);          % Transfer array to local workspace
```

On GPUs and other hardware where you might want to deploy your neural networks, it is often the case that the exponential function exp is not implemented with hardware, but with a software library. This can slow down neural networks that use the tansig sigmoid transfer function. An alternative function is the Elliot sigmoid function whose expression does not include a call to any higher order functions:

```
    (equation)  a = n / (1 + abs(n))
```

Before training, the network's tansig layers can be converted to elliotsig layers as follows:

```
for i=1:net.numLayers
  if strcmp(net.layers{i}.transferFcn,'tansig')
    net.layers{i}.transferFcn = 'elliotsig';
  end
end
```

Now training and simulation might be faster on the GPU and simpler deployment hardware.

9.1.4 Distributed GPU Computing

Distributed and GPU computing can be combined to run calculations across multiple CPUs and/or GPUs on a single computer, or on a cluster with MATLAB Distributed Computing Server.

The simplest way to do this is to specify `train` and `sim` to do so, using the parallel pool determined by the cluster profile you use. The `'showResources'` option is especially recommended in this case, to verify that the expected hardware is being employed:

```
net2 =
train(net1,x,t,'useParallel','yes','useGPU','yes','showResources','
yes')
y =
net2(x,'useParallel','yes','useGPU','yes','showResources','yes')
```

These lines of code use all available workers in the parallel pool. One worker for each unique GPU employs that GPU, while other workers operate as CPUs. In some cases, it might be faster to use only GPUs. For instance, if a single computer has three GPUs and four workers each, the three workers that are accelerated by the three GPUs might be speed limited by the fourth CPU worker. In these cases, you can specify that `train` and `sim` use only workers with unique GPUs.

```
net2 =
train(net1,x,t,'useParallel','yes','useGPU','only','showResources',
'yes')
y =
net2(x,'useParallel','yes','useGPU','only','showResources','yes')
```

As with simple distributed computing, distributed GPU computing can benefit from manually created Composite values. Defining the Composite values yourself lets you indicate which workers to use, how many samples to assign to each worker, and which workers use GPUs.

For instance, if you have four workers and only three GPUs, you can define larger datasets for the GPU workers. Here, a random dataset is created with different sample loads per Composite element:

```
numSamples = [1000 1000 1000 300];
xc = Composite;
tc = Composite;
for i=1:4
  xi = rand(2,numSamples(i));
  ti = xi(1,:).^2 + 3*xi(2,:);
  xc{i} = xi;
  tc{i} = ti;
end
```

You can now specify that `train` and `sim` use the three GPUs available:

```
net2 = configure(net1,xc{1},tc{1});
net2 = train(net2,xc,tc,'useGPU','yes','showResources','yes');
yc = net2(xc,'showResources','yes');
```

To ensure that the GPUs get used by the first three workers, manually converting each worker's Composite elements to gpuArrays. Each worker performs this transformation within a parallel executing `spmd` block.

```
spmd
  if labindex <= 3
    xc = nndata2gpu(xc);
    tc = nndata2gpu(tc);
  end
end
```

Now the data specifies when to use GPUs, so you do not need to tell `train` and `sim` to do so.

```
net2 = configure(net1,xc{1},tc{1});
net2 = train(net2,xc,tc,'showResources','yes');
yc = net2(xc,'showResources','yes');
```

Ensure that each GPU is used by only one worker, so that the computations are most efficient. If multiple workers assign gpuArray data on the same GPU, the computation will still work but will be slower, because the GPU will operate on the multiple workers' data sequentially.

9.1.5 Deep Learning

Training a convolutional neural network (CNN, ConvNet) requires the Parallel Computing Toolbox and a CUDA®-enabled NVIDIA® GPU with compute capability 3.0 or higher. You have the option to choose the execution environment (CPU or GPU) for extracting features, predicting responses, or classifying observations (see `activations`, `predict`, and `classify`).

9.1.6 Parallel Time Series

For time series networks, simply use cell array values for `x` and `t`, and optionally include initial input delay states `xi` and initial layer delay states `ai`, as required.

```
net2 = train(net1,x,t,xi,ai,'useGPU','yes')
y = net2(x,xi,ai,'useParallel','yes','useGPU','yes')

net2 = train(net1,x,t,xi,ai,'useParallel','yes')
y = net2(x,xi,ai,'useParallel','yes','useGPU','only')

net2 = train(net1,x,t,xi,ai,'useParallel','yes','useGPU','only')
y = net2(x,xi,ai,'useParallel','yes','useGPU','only')
```

Note that parallelism happens across samples, or in the case of time series across different series. However, if the network has only input delays, with no layer delays, the delayed inputs can be precalculated so that for the purposes of computation, the time steps become different samples and can be parallelized. This is the case for networks such as `timedelaynet` and open-loop versions of `narxnet` and `narnet`. If a network has layer delays, then time cannot be "flattened" for purposes of computation, and so single series data cannot be parallelized. This is the case for networks such as `layrecnet` and closed-loop versions of `narxnet` and `narnet`. However, if the data consists of multiple sequences, it can be parallelized across the separate sequences.

9.1.7 Parallel Availability, Fallbacks, and Feedback

As mentioned previously, you can query MATLAB to discover the current parallel resources that are available.

To see what GPUs are available on the host computer:

```
gpuCount = gpuDeviceCount
for i=1:gpuCount
  gpuDevice(i)
end
```

To see how many workers are running in the current parallel pool:

```
poolSize = pool.NumWorkers
```

To see the GPUs available across a parallel pool running on a PC cluster using MATLAB Distributed Computing Server:

```
spmd
  worker.index = labindex;
  worker.name = system('hostname');
  worker.gpuCount = gpuDeviceCount;
  try
    worker.gpuInfo = gpuDevice;
  catch
    worker.gpuInfo = [];
  end
  worker
end
```

When `'useParallel'` or `'useGPU'` are set to `'yes'`, but parallel or GPU workers are unavailable, the convention is that when resources are requested, they are used if available. The computation is performed without error even if they are not. This process of falling back from requested resources to actual resources happens as follows:

- If `'useParallel'` is `'yes'` but Parallel Computing Toolbox is unavailable, or a parallel pool is not open, then computation reverts to single-threaded MATLAB.

- If 'useGPU' is 'yes' but the gpuDevice for the current MATLAB session is unassigned or not supported, then computation reverts to the CPU.
- If 'useParallel' and 'useGPU' are 'yes', then each worker with a unique GPU uses that GPU, and other workers revert to CPU.
- If 'useParallel' is 'yes' and 'useGPU' is 'only', then workers with unique GPUs are used. Other workers are not used, unless no workers have GPUs. In the case with no GPUs, all workers use CPUs.

When unsure about what hardware is actually being employed, check gpuDeviceCount, gpuDevice, and pool.NumWorkers to ensure the desired hardware is available, and call train and sim with 'showResources' set to 'yes' to verify what resources were actually used.

9.2 AUTOMATICALLY SAVE CHECKPOINTS DURING NEURAL NETWORK TRAINING

During neural network training, intermediate results can be periodically saved to a MAT file for recovery if the computer fails or you kill the training process. This helps protect the value of long training runs, which if interrupted would need to be completely restarted otherwise. This feature is especially useful for long parallel training sessions, which are more likely to be interrupted by computing resource failures.

Checkpoint saves are enabled with the optional 'CheckpointFile' training argument followed by the checkpoint file name or path. If you specify only a file name, the file is placed in the working directory by default. The file must have the .mat file extension, but if this is not specified it is automatically appended. In this example, checkpoint saves are made to the file called MyCheckpoint.mat in the current working directory.

```
[x,t] = house_dataset;
net = feedforwardnet(10);
net2 = train(net,x,t,'CheckpointFile','MyCheckpoint.mat');
22-Mar-2013 04:49:05 First Checkpoint #1:
/WorkingDir/MyCheckpoint.mat
22-Mar-2013 04:49:06 Final Checkpoint #2:
/WorkingDir/MyCheckpoint.mat
```

By default, checkpoint saves occur at most once every 60 seconds. For the previous short training example, this results in only two checkpoint saves: one at the beginning and one at the end of training.

The optional training argument 'CheckpointDelay' can change the frequency of saves. For example, here the minimum checkpoint delay is set to 10 seconds for a time-series problem where a neural network is trained to model a levitated magnet.

```
[x,t] = maglev_dataset;
```

```
net = narxnet(1:2,1:2,10);
[X,Xi,Ai,T] = preparets(net,x,{},t);
net2 =
train(net,X,T,Xi,Ai,'CheckpointFile','MyCheckpoint.mat','Checkpoint
Delay',10);
22-Mar-2013 04:59:28 First Checkpoint #1:
/WorkingDir/MyCheckpoint.mat
22-Mar-2013 04:59:38 Write Checkpoint #2:
/WorkingDir/MyCheckpoint.mat
22-Mar-2013 04:59:48 Write Checkpoint #3:
/WorkingDir/MyCheckpoint.mat
22-Mar-2013 04:59:58 Write Checkpoint #4:
/WorkingDir/MyCheckpoint.mat
22-Mar-2013 05:00:08 Write Checkpoint #5:
/WorkingDir/MyCheckpoint.mat
22-Mar-2013 05:00:09 Final Checkpoint #6:
/WorkingDir/MyCheckpoint.mat
```

After a computer failure or training interruption, you can reload the checkpoint structure containing the best neural network obtained before the interruption, and the training record. In this case, the `stage` field value is `'Final'`, indicating the last save was at the final epoch because training completed successfully. The first epoch checkpoint is indicated by `'First'`, and intermediate checkpoints by `'Write'`.

```
load('MyCheckpoint.mat')
checkpoint =

      file: '/WorkdingDir/MyCheckpoint.mat'
      time: [2013 3 22 5 0 9.0712]
    number: 6
     stage: 'Final'
       net: [1x1 network]
        tr: [1x1 struct]
```

You can resume training from the last checkpoint by reloading the dataset (if necessary), then calling train with the recovered network.

```
net = checkpoint.net;
[x,t] = maglev_dataset;
load('MyCheckpoint.mat');
[X,Xi,Ai,T] = preparets(net,x,{},t);
net2 =
train(net,X,T,Xi,Ai,'CheckpointFile','MyCheckpoint.mat','Checkpoint
Delay',10);
```

9.3 OPTIMIZE NEURAL NETWORK TRAINING SPEED AND MEMORY

9.3.1 Memory Reduction

Depending on the particular neural network, simulation and gradient calculations can occur in MATLAB® or MEX. MEX is more memory efficient, but MATLAB can be made more memory efficient in exchange for time.

To determine whether MATLAB or MEX is being used, use the `'showResources'` option, as shown in this general form of the syntax:

```
net2 = train(net1,x,t,'showResources','yes')
```

If MATLAB is being used and memory limitations are a problem, the amount of temporary storage needed can be reduced by a factor of `N`, in exchange for performing the computations `N` times sequentially on each of `N` subsets of the data.

```
net2 = train(net1,x,t,'reduction',N);
```

This is called memory reduction.

9.3.2 Fast Elliot Sigmoid

Some simple computing hardware might not support the exponential function directly, and software implementations can be slow. The Elliot sigmoid `elliotsig` function performs the same role as the symmetric sigmoid `tansig` function, but avoids the exponential function.

Here is a plot of the Elliot sigmoid:

```
n = -10:0.01:10;
a = elliotsig(n);
plot(n,a)
```

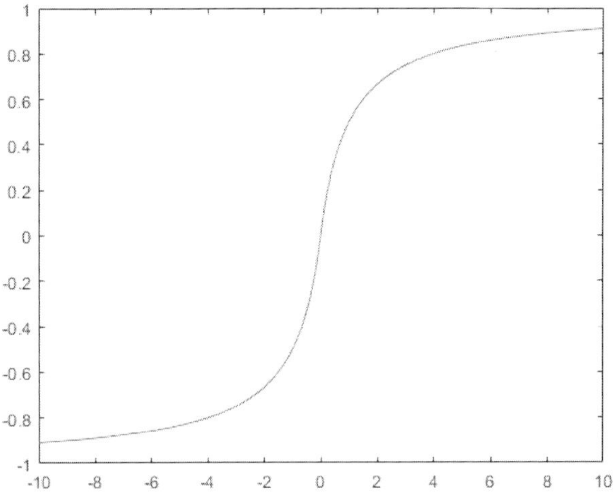

Next, `elliotsig` is compared with `tansig`.

```
a2 = tansig(n);
h = plot(n,a,n,a2);
legend(h,'elliotsig','tansig','Location','NorthWest')
```

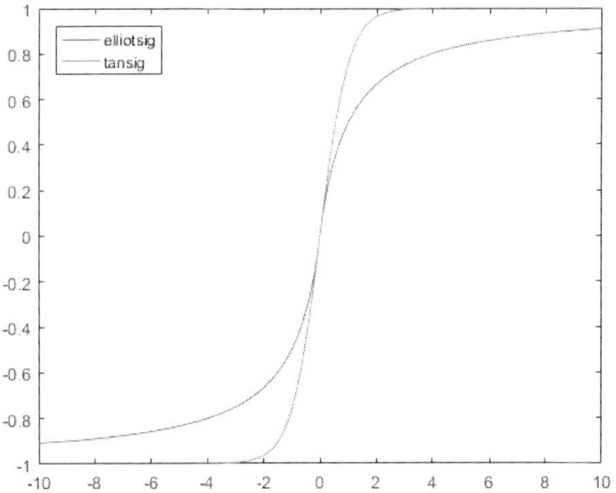

To train a neural network using `elliotsig` instead of `tansig`, transform the network's transfer functions:

```
[x,t] = house_dataset;
```

```
net = feedforwardnet;

view(net)

net.layers{1}.transferFcn = 'elliotsig';

view(net)

net = train(net,x,t);

y = net(x)
```

Here, the times to execute `elliotsig` and `tansig` are compared. `elliotsig` is approximately four times faster on the test system.

```
n = rand(1000,1000);

tic,for i=1:100,a=tansig(n); end, tansigTime = toc;

tic,for i=1:100,a=elliotsig(n); end, elliotTime = toc;

speedup = tansigTime / elliotTime

speedup =

    4.1406
```

However, while simulation is faster with `elliotsig`, training is not guaranteed to be faster, due to the different shapes of the two transfer functions. Here, 10 networks are each trained for `tansig` and `elliotsig`, but training times vary significantly even on the same problem with the same network.

```
[x,t] = house_dataset;

tansigNet = feedforwardnet;

tansigNet.trainParam.showWindow = false;

elliotNet = tansigNet;

elliotNet.layers{1}.transferFcn = 'elliotsig';

for i=1:10, tic, net = train(tansigNet,x,t); tansigTime = toc,
end

for i=1:10, tic, net = train(elliotNet,x,t), elliotTime = toc,
end
```

Chapter 10

OPTIMAL SOLUTIONS

10.1 REPRESENTING UNKNOWN OR DON'T-CARE TARGETS

10.1.1 Choose Neural Network Input-Output Processing Functions

This topic presents part of a typical multilayer network workflow.

Neural network training can be more efficient if you perform certain preprocessing steps on the network inputs and targets. This section describes several preprocessing routines that you can use. (The most common of these are provided automatically when you create a network, and they become part of the network object, so that whenever the network is used, the data coming into the network is preprocessed in the same way.)

For example, in multilayer networks, sigmoid transfer functions are generally used in the hidden layers. These functions become essentially saturated when the net input is greater than three ($\exp(-3) \cong 0.05$). If this happens at the beginning of the training process, the gradients will be very small, and the network training will be very slow. In the first layer of the network, the net input is a product of the input times the weight plus the bias. If the input is very large, then the weight must be very small in order to prevent the transfer function from becoming saturated. It is standard practice to normalize the inputs before applying them to the network.

Generally, the normalization step is applied to both the input vectors and the target vectors in the data set. In this way, the network output always falls into a normalized range. The network output can then be reverse transformed back into the units of the original target data when the network is put to use in the field.

It is easiest to think of the neural network as having a preprocessing block that appears between the input and the first layer of the network and a postprocessing block that appears between the last layer of the network and the output, as shown in the following figure.

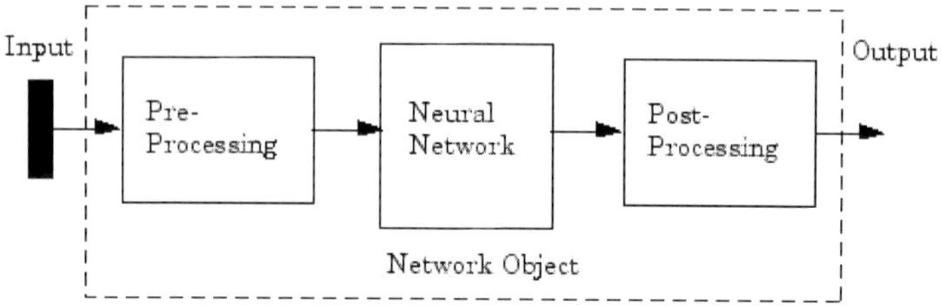

Most of the network creation functions in the toolbox, including the multilayer network creation functions, such as `feedforwardnet`, automatically assign processing functions to your network inputs and outputs. These functions transform the input and target values you provide into values that are better suited for network training.

You can override the default input and output processing functions by adjusting network properties after you create the network.

To see a cell array list of processing functions assigned to the input of a network, access this property:

```
net.inputs{1}.processFcns
```

where the index 1 refers to the first input vector. (There is only one input vector for the feedforward network.) To view the processing functions returned by the output of a two-layer network, access this network property:

```
net.outputs{2}.processFcns
```

where the index 2 refers to the output vector coming from the second layer. (For the feedforward network, there is only one output vector, and it comes from the final layer.) You can use these properties to change the processing functions that you want your network to apply to the inputs and outputs. However, the defaults usually provide excellent performance.

Several processing functions have parameters that customize their operation. You can access or change the parameters of the ith input processing function for the network input as follows:

```
net.inputs{1}.processParams{i}
```

You can access or change the parameters of the ith output processing function for the network output associated with the second layer, as follows:

```
net.outputs{2}.processParams{i}
```

For multilayer network creation functions, such as `feedforwardnet`, the default input processing functions are `removeconstantrows` and `mapminmax`. For outputs, the default processing functions are also `removeconstantrows` and `mapminmax`.

The following table lists the most common preprocessing and postprocessing functions. In most cases, you will not need to use them directly, since the preprocessing steps become part of the network object. When you simulate or train the network, the preprocessing and postprocessing will be done automatically.

Function	Algorithm
`mapminmax`	Normalize inputs/targets to fall in the range [−1, 1]
`mapstd`	Normalize inputs/targets to have zero mean and unity variance
`processpca`	Extract principal components from the input vector
`fixunknowns`	Process unknown inputs
`removeconstantrows`	Remove inputs/targets that are constant

10.1.2 Representing Unknown or Don't-Care Targets

Unknown or "don't care" targets can be represented with `NaN` values. We do not want unknown target values to have an impact on training, but if a network has several outputs, some elements of any target vector may be known while others are unknown. One solution would be to remove the partially unknown target vector and its associated input vector from the training set, but that involves the loss of the good target values. A better solution is to represent those unknown targets with `NaN` values. All the performance functions of the toolbox will ignore those targets for purposes of calculating performance and derivatives of performance.

10.2 CONFIGURE NEURAL NETWORK INPUTS AND OUTPUTS

After a neural network has been created, it must be configured. The configuration step consists of examining input and target data, setting the network's input and output sizes to match the data, and choosing settings for processing inputs and outputs that will enable best network performance. The configuration step is normally done automatically, when the training function is called. However, it can be done manually, by using the configuration function. For example, to configure the network you created previously to approximate a sine function, issue the following commands:

```
p = -2:.1:2;

t = sin(pi*p/2);

net1 = configure(net,p,t);
```

You have provided the network with an example set of inputs and targets (desired network outputs). With this information, the `configure` function can set the network input and output sizes to match the data.

After the configuration, if you look again at the weight between layer 1 and layer 2, you can see that the dimension of the weight is 1 by 20. This is because the target for this network is a scalar.

```
net1.layerWeights{2,1}

    Neural Network Weight

            delays: 0
           initFcn: (none)
        initConfig: .inputSize
             learn: true
          learnFcn: 'learngdm'
        learnParam: .lr, .mc
              size: [1 10]
         weightFcn: 'dotprod'
       weightParam: (none)
          userdata: (your custom info)
```

In addition to setting the appropriate dimensions for the weights, the configuration step also defines the settings for the processing of inputs and outputs. The input processing can be located in the `inputs` subobject:

```
net1.inputs{1}

    Neural Network Input

              name: 'Input'
    feedbackOutput: []
       processFcns: {'removeconstantrows', mapminmax}
     processParams: {1x2 cell array of 2 params}
   processSettings: {1x2 cell array of 2 settings}
    processedRange: [1x2 double]
     processedSize: 1
             range: [1x2 double]
              size: 1
          userdata: (your custom info)
```

Before the input is applied to the network, it will be processed by two functions: `removeconstantrows` and `mapminmax`. These are discussed fully in Multilayer Neural Networks and Backpropagation Training so we won't address the particulars here. These processing functions may have some processing parameters, which are contained in the subobject `net1.inputs{1}.processParam`. These have default values that you can override. The processing functions can also have configuration settings that are dependent on the sample data. These are contained in `net1.inputs{1}.processSettings` and are set during the configuration process. For example, the `mapminmax`processing function normalizes the data so that all inputs fall in the range [−1, 1]. Its configuration settings include the minimum and maximum values in the sample data, which it needs to perform the correct normalization.

As a general rule, we use the term "parameter," as in process parameters, training parameters, etc., to denote constants that have default values that are assigned by the software when the network is created (and which you can override). We use the term "configuration setting," as in process configuration setting, to denote constants that are assigned by the software from an analysis of sample data. These settings do not have default values, and should not generally be overridden.

10.3 DIVIDE DATA FOR OPTIMAL NEURAL NETWORK TRAINING

.

When training multilayer networks, the general practice is to first divide the data into three subsets. The first subset is the training set, which is used for computing the gradient and updating the network weights and biases. The second subset is the validation set. The error on the validation set is monitored during the training process. The validation error normally decreases during the initial phase of training, as does the training set error. However, when the network begins to overfit the data, the error on the validation set typically begins to rise. The network weights and biases are saved at the minimum of the validation set error.

The test set error is not used during training, but it is used to compare different models. It is also useful to plot the test set error during the training process. If the error on the test set reaches a minimum at a significantly different iteration number than the validation set error, this might indicate a poor division of the data set.

There are four functions provided for dividing data into training, validation and test sets. They are `dividerand` (the default), `divideblock`, `divideint`, and `divideind`. The data division is normally performed automatically when you train the network.

Function	Algorithm
`dividerand`	Divide the data randomly (default)
`divideblock`	Divide the data into contiguous blocks
`divideint`	Divide the data using an interleaved selection
`divideind`	Divide the data by index

You can access or change the division function for your network with this property:

```
net.divideFcn
```

Each of the division functions takes parameters that customize its behavior. These values are stored and can be changed with the following network property:

```
net.divideParam
```

The divide function is accessed automatically whenever the network is trained, and is used to divide the data into training, validation and testing subsets. If `net.divideFcn` is set to `'dividerand'` (the default), then the data is randomly divided into the three subsets using the division parameters `net.divideParam.trainRatio`, `net.divideParam.valRatio`, and `net.divideParam.testRatio`. The fraction of data that is placed in the training set is `trainRatio`/(`trainRatio`+`valRatio`+`testRatio`), with a similar formula for the other two sets. The default ratios for training, testing and validation are 0.7, 0.15 and 0.15, respectively.

If `net.divideFcn` is set to `'divideblock'`, then the data is divided into three subsets using three contiguous blocks of the original data set (training taking the first block, validation the second and testing the third). The fraction of the original data that goes into each subset is determined by the same three division parameters used for `dividerand`.

If `net.divideFcn` is set to `'divideint'`, then the data is divided by an interleaved method, as in dealing a deck of cards. It is done so that different percentages of data go into the three subsets. The fraction of the original data that goes into each subset is determined by the same three division parameters used for `dividerand`.

When `net.divideFcn` is set to `'divideind'`, the data is divided by index. The indices for the three subsets are defined by the division parameters `net.divideParam.trainInd`, `net.divideParam.valInd` and `net.divideParam.testInd`. The default assignment for these indices is the null array, so you must set the indices when using this option.

10.4 CHOOSE A MULTILAYER NEURAL NETWORK TRAINING FUNCTION

It is very difficult to know which training algorithm will be the fastest for a given problem. It depends on many factors, including the complexity of the problem, the number of data points in the training set, the number of weights and biases in the network, the error goal, and whether the network is being used for pattern recognition (discriminant analysis) or function approximation (regression). This section compares the various training algorithms. Feedforward networks are trained on six different problems. Three of the problems fall in the pattern recognition category and the three others fall in the function approximation category. Two of the problems are simple "toy" problems, while the other four are "real world" problems. Networks with a variety of different architectures and complexities are used, and the networks are trained to a variety of different accuracy levels.

The following table lists the algorithms that are tested and the acronyms used to identify them.

Acronym	Algorithm	Description
LM	`trainlm`	Levenberg-Marquardt
BFG	`trainbfg`	BFGS Quasi-Newton
RP	`trainrp`	Resilient Backpropagation
SCG	`trainscg`	Scaled Conjugate Gradient
CGB	`traincgb`	Conjugate Gradient with Powell/Beale Restarts
CGF	`traincgf`	Fletcher-Powell Conjugate Gradient
CGP	`traincgp`	Polak-Ribiére Conjugate Gradient
OSS	`trainoss`	One Step Secant
GDX	`traingdx`	Variable Learning Rate Backpropagation

The following table lists the six benchmark problems and some characteristics of the networks, training processes, and computers used.

Problem Title	Problem Type	Network Structure	Error Goal	Computer
SIN	Function approximation	1-5-1	0.002	Sun Sparc 2
PARITY	Pattern recognition	3-10-10-1	0.001	Sun Sparc 2
ENGINE	Function approximation	2-30-2	0.005	Sun Enterprise 4000
CANCER	Pattern recognition	9-5-5-2	0.012	Sun Sparc 2
CHOLESTEROL	Function approximation	21-15-3	0.027	Sun Sparc 20
DIABETES	Pattern recognition	8-15-15-2	0.05	Sun Sparc 20

10.4.1 SIN Data Set

The first benchmark data set is a simple function approximation problem. A 1-5-1 network, with `tansig` transfer functions in the hidden layer and a linear transfer function in the output layer, is used to approximate a single period of a sine wave. The following table summarizes the results of training the network using nine different training algorithms. Each entry in the table represents 30 different trials, where different random initial weights are used in each trial. In each case, the network is trained until the squared error is less than 0.002. The fastest algorithm for this problem is the Levenberg-Marquardt algorithm. On the average, it is over four times faster than the next fastest algorithm. This is the type of problem for which the LM algorithm is best suited—a function approximation problem where the network has fewer than one hundred weights and the approximation must be very accurate.

Algorithm	Mean Time (s)	Ratio	Min. Time (s)	Max. Time (s)	Std. (s)
LM	1.14	1.00	0.65	1.83	0.38
BFG	5.22	4.58	3.17	14.38	2.08
RP	5.67	4.97	2.66	17.24	3.72
SCG	6.09	5.34	3.18	23.64	3.81
CGB	6.61	5.80	2.99	23.65	3.67
CGF	7.86	6.89	3.57	31.23	4.76
CGP	8.24	7.23	4.07	32.32	5.03
OSS	9.64	8.46	3.97	59.63	9.79
GDX	27.69	24.29	17.21	258.15	43.65

The performance of the various algorithms can be affected by the accuracy required of the approximation. This is shown in the following figure, which plots the mean square error versus execution time (averaged over the 30 trials) for several representative algorithms. Here you can see that the error in the LM algorithm decreases much more rapidly with time than the other algorithms shown.

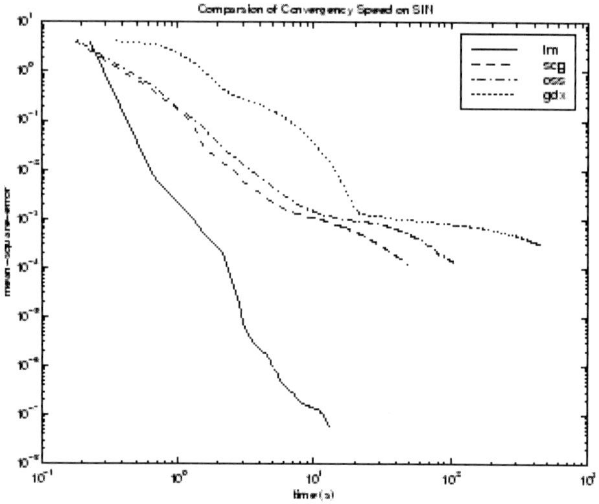

The relationship between the algorithms is further illustrated in the following figure, which plots the time required to converge versus the mean square error convergence goal. Here you can see that as the error goal is reduced, the improvement provided by the LM algorithm becomes more pronounced. Some algorithms perform better as the error goal is reduced (LM and BFG), and other algorithms degrade as the error goal is reduced (OSS and GDX).

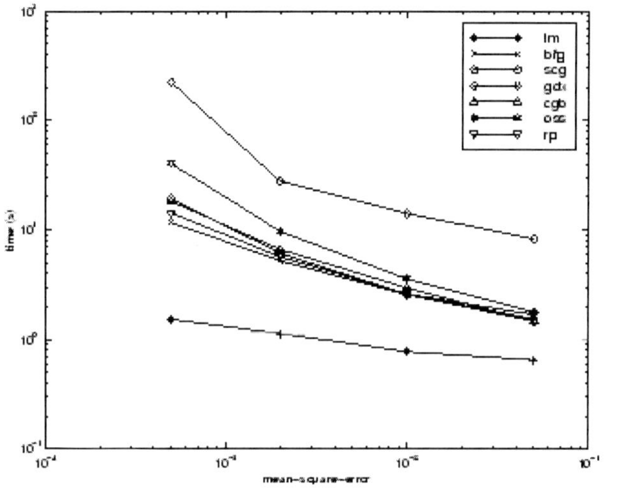

10.4.2 PARITY Data Set

The second benchmark problem is a simple pattern recognition problem—detect the parity of a 3-bit number. If the number of ones in the input pattern is odd, then the network should output a 1; otherwise, it should output a -1. The network used for this problem is a 3-10-10-1 network with tansig neurons in each layer. The following table summarizes the results of training this network with the nine different algorithms. Each entry in the table represents 30 different trials, where different random initial weights are used in each trial. In each case, the network is trained until the squared error is less than 0.001. The fastest algorithm for this problem is the resilient backpropagation algorithm, although the conjugate gradient algorithms (in particular, the scaled conjugate gradient algorithm) are almost as fast. Notice that the LM algorithm does not perform well on this problem. In general, the LM algorithm does not perform as well on pattern recognition problems as it does on function approximation problems. The LM algorithm is designed for least squares problems that are approximately linear. Because the output neurons in pattern recognition problems are generally saturated, you will not be operating in the linear region.

Algorithm	**Mean Time (s)**	**Ratio**	**Min. Time (s)**	**Max. Time (s)**	**Std. (s)**
RP	3.73	1.00	2.35	6.89	1.26
SCG	4.09	1.10	2.36	7.48	1.56
CGP	5.13	1.38	3.50	8.73	1.05
CGB	5.30	1.42	3.91	11.59	1.35
CGF	6.62	1.77	3.96	28.05	4.32
OSS	8.00	2.14	5.06	14.41	1.92
LM	13.07	3.50	6.48	23.78	4.96
BFG	19.68	5.28	14.19	26.64	2.85
GDX	27.07	7.26	25.21	28.52	0.86

As with function approximation problems, the performance of the various algorithms can be affected by the accuracy required of the network. This is shown in the following figure, which plots the mean square error versus execution time for some typical algorithms. The LM algorithm converges rapidly after some point, but only after the other algorithms have already converged.

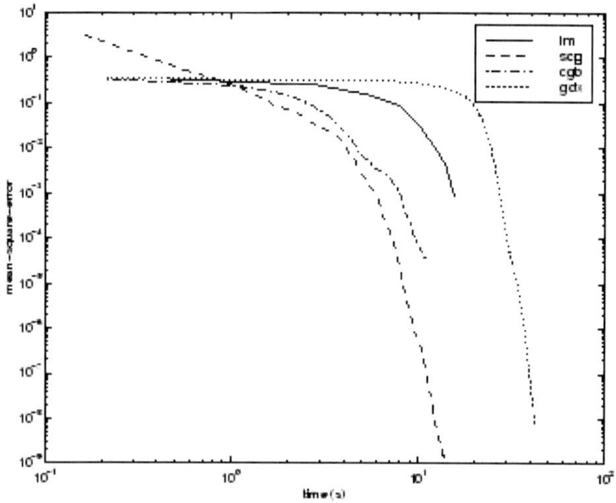

The relationship between the algorithms is further illustrated in the following figure, which plots the time required to converge versus the mean square error convergence goal. Again you can see that some algorithms degrade as the error goal is reduced (OSS and BFG).

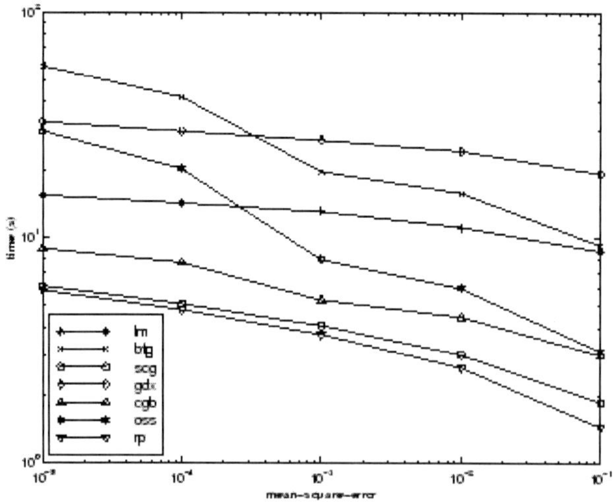

10.4.3 ENGINE Data Set

The third benchmark problem is a realistic function approximation (or nonlinear regression) problem. The data is obtained from the operation of an engine. The inputs to the network are engine speed and fueling levels and the network outputs are torque and emission levels. The network used for this problem is a 2-30-2 network with tansig neurons in the hidden layer and linear neurons in the output layer. The following table summarizes the results of training this network with the nine different algorithms. Each entry in the table represents 30 different trials (10 trials for RP and GDX because of time constraints), where different random initial weights are used in each trial. In each case, the network is trained until the squared error is less than 0.005. The fastest algorithm for this problem is the LM algorithm, although the BFGS quasi-Newton algorithm and the conjugate gradient algorithms (the scaled conjugate gradient algorithm in particular) are almost as fast. Although this is a function approximation problem, the LM algorithm is not as clearly superior as it was on the SIN data set. In this case, the number of weights and biases in the network is much larger than the one used on the SIN problem (152 versus 16), and the advantages of the LM algorithm decrease as the number of network parameters increases.

Algorithm	Mean Time (s)	Ratio	Min. Time (s)	Max. Time (s)	Std. (s)
LM	18.45	1.00	12.01	30.03	4.27
BFG	27.12	1.47	16.42	47.36	5.95
SCG	36.02	1.95	19.39	52.45	7.78
CGF	37.93	2.06	18.89	50.34	6.12
CGB	39.93	2.16	23.33	55.42	7.50
CGP	44.30	2.40	24.99	71.55	9.89
OSS	48.71	2.64	23.51	80.90	12.33
RP	65.91	3.57	31.83	134.31	34.24
GDX	188.50	10.22	81.59	279.90	66.67

The following figure plots the mean square error versus execution time for some typical algorithms. The performance of the LM algorithm improves over time relative to the other algorithms.

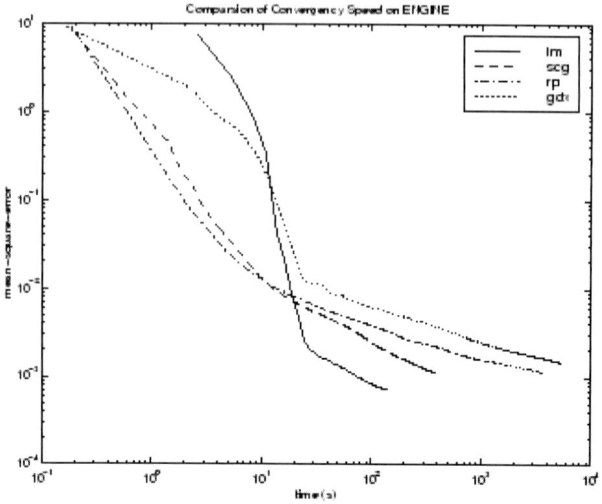

The relationship between the algorithms is further illustrated in the following figure, which plots the time required to converge versus the mean square error convergence goal. Again you can see that some algorithms degrade as the error goal is reduced (GDX and RP), while the LM algorithm improves.

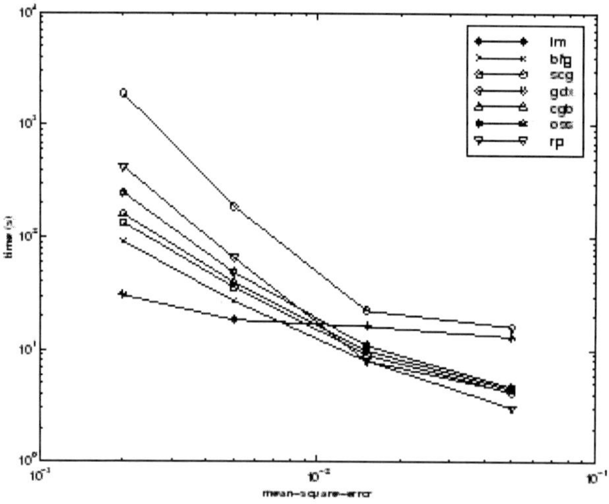

10.4.4 CANCER Data Set

The fourth benchmark problem is a realistic pattern recognition (or nonlinear discriminant analysis) problem. The objective of the network is to classify a tumor as either benign or malignant based on cell descriptions gathered by microscopic examination. Input attributes include clump thickness, uniformity of cell size and cell shape, the amount of marginal adhesion, and the frequency of bare nuclei. The data was obtained from the University of Wisconsin Hospitals, Madison, from Dr. William H. Wolberg. The network used for this problem is a 9-5-5-2 network with tansig neurons in all layers. The following table summarizes the results of training this network with the nine different algorithms. Each entry in the table represents 30 different trials, where different random initial weights are used in each trial. In each case, the network is trained until the squared error is less than 0.012. A few runs failed to converge for some of the algorithms, so only the top 75% of the runs from each algorithm were used to obtain the statistics.

The conjugate gradient algorithms and resilient backpropagation all provide fast convergence, and the LM algorithm is also reasonably fast. As with the parity data set, the LM algorithm does not perform as well on pattern recognition problems as it does on function approximation problems.

Algorithm	Mean Time (s)	Ratio	Min. Time (s)	Max. Time (s)	Std. (s)
CGB	80.27	1.00	55.07	102.31	13.17
RP	83.41	1.04	59.51	109.39	13.44
SCG	86.58	1.08	41.21	112.19	18.25
CGP	87.70	1.09	56.35	116.37	18.03
CGF	110.05	1.37	63.33	171.53	30.13
LM	110.33	1.37	58.94	201.07	38.20
BFG	209.60	2.61	118.92	318.18	58.44
GDX	313.22	3.90	166.48	446.43	75.44
OSS	463.87	5.78	250.62	599.99	97.35

The following figure plots the mean square error versus execution time for some typical algorithms. For this problem there is not as much variation in performance as in previous problems.

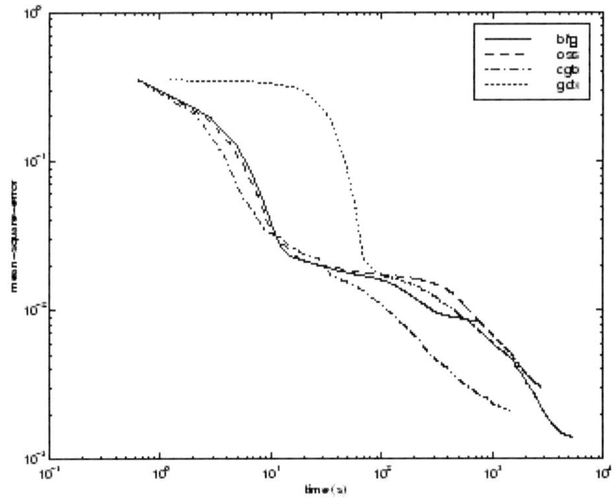

The relationship between the algorithms is further illustrated in the following figure, which plots the time required to converge versus the mean square error convergence goal. Again you can see that some algorithms degrade as the error goal is reduced (OSS and BFG) while the LM algorithm improves. It is typical of the LM algorithm on any problem that its performance improves relative to other algorithms as the error goal is reduced.

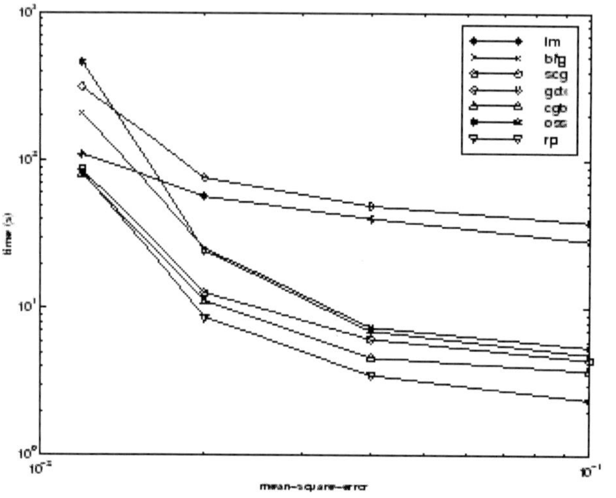

10.4.5 CHOLESTEROL Data Set

The fifth benchmark problem is a realistic function approximation (or nonlinear regression) problem. The objective of the network is to predict cholesterol levels (ldl, hdl, and vldl) based on measurements of 21 spectral components. The data was obtained from Dr. Neil Purdie, Department of Chemistry, Oklahoma State University [PuLu92]. The network used for this problem is a 21-15-3 network with tansig neurons in the hidden layers and linear neurons in the output layer. The following table summarizes the results of training this network with the nine different algorithms. Each entry in the table represents 20 different trials (10 trials for RP and GDX), where different random initial weights are used in each trial. In each case, the network is trained until the squared error is less than 0.027.

The scaled conjugate gradient algorithm has the best performance on this problem, although all the conjugate gradient algorithms perform well. The LM algorithm does not perform as well on this function approximation problem as it did on the other two. That is because the number of weights and biases in the network has increased again (378 versus 152 versus 16). As the number of parameters increases, the computation required in the LM algorithm increases geometrically.

Algorithm	Mean Time (s)	Ratio	Min. Time (s)	Max. Time (s)	Std. (s)
SCG	99.73	1.00	83.10	113.40	9.93
CGP	121.54	1.22	101.76	162.49	16.34
CGB	124.06	1.2	107.64	146.90	14.62
CGF	136.04	1.36	106.46	167.28	17.67
LM	261.50	2.62	103.52	398.45	102.06
OSS	268.55	2.69	197.84	372.99	56.79
BFG	550.92	5.52	471.61	676.39	46.59
RP	1519.00	15.23	581.17	2256.10	557.34
GDX	3169.50	31.78	2514.90	4168.20	610.52

The following figure plots the mean square error versus execution time for some typical algorithms. For this problem, you can see that the LM algorithm is able to drive the mean square error to a lower level than the other algorithms. The SCG and RP algorithms provide the fastest initial convergence.

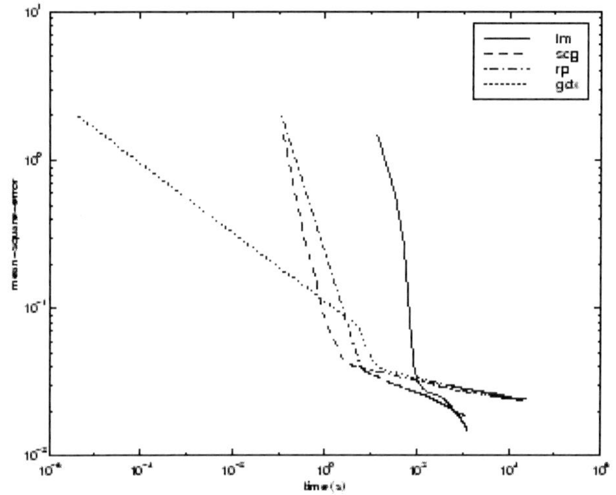

The relationship between the algorithms is further illustrated in the following figure, which plots the time required to converge versus the mean square error convergence goal. You can see that the LM and BFG algorithms improve relative to the other algorithms as the error goal is reduced.

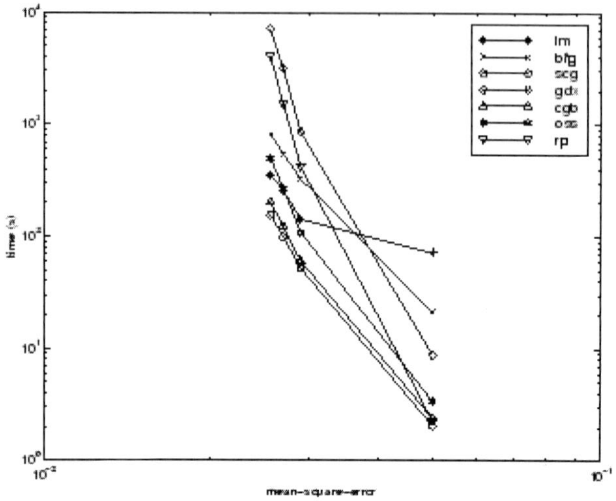

10.4.6 DIABETES Data Set

The sixth benchmark problem is a pattern recognition problem. The objective of the network is to decide whether an individual has diabetes, based on personal data (age, number of times pregnant) and the results of medical examinations (e.g., blood pressure, body mass index, result of glucose tolerance test, etc.). The data was obtained from the University of California, Irvine, machine learning data base. The network used for this problem is an 8-15-15-2 network with tansig neurons in all layers. The following table summarizes the results of training this network with the nine different algorithms. Each entry in the table represents 10 different trials, where different random initial weights are used in each trial. In each case, the network is trained until the squared error is less than 0.05.

The conjugate gradient algorithms and resilient backpropagation all provide fast convergence. The results on this problem are consistent with the other pattern recognition problems considered. The RP algorithm works well on all the pattern recognition problems. This is reasonable, because that algorithm was designed to overcome the difficulties caused by training with sigmoid functions, which have very small slopes when operating far from the center point. For pattern recognition problems, you use sigmoid transfer functions in the output layer, and you want the network to operate at the tails of the sigmoid function.

Algorithm	Mean Time (s)	Ratio	Min. Time (s)	Max. Time (s)	Std. (s)
RP	323.90	1.00	187.43	576.90	111.37
SCG	390.53	1.21	267.99	487.17	75.07
CGB	394.67	1.22	312.25	558.21	85.38
CGP	415.90	1.28	320.62	614.62	94.77
OSS	784.00	2.42	706.89	936.52	76.37
CGF	784.50	2.42	629.42	1082.20	144.63
LM	1028.10	3.17	802.01	1269.50	166.31

BFG	1821.00	5.62	1415.80	3254.50	546.36
GDX	7687.00	23.73	5169.20	10350.00	2015.00

The following figure plots the mean square error versus execution time for some typical algorithms. As with other problems, you see that the SCG and RP have fast initial convergence, while the LM algorithm is able to provide smaller final error.

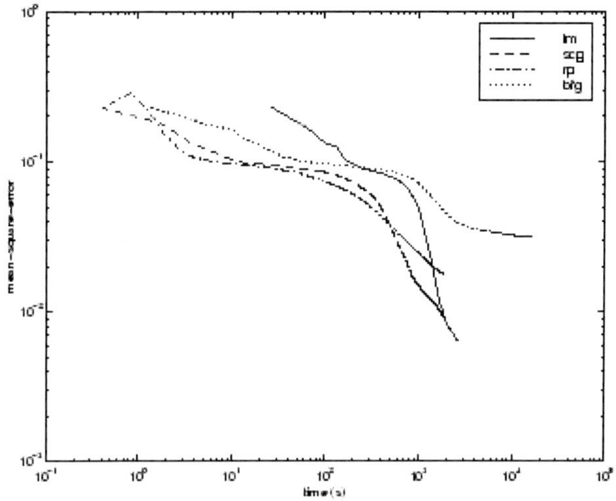

The relationship between the algorithms is further illustrated in the following figure, which plots the time required to converge versus the mean square error convergence goal. In this case, you can see that the BFG algorithm degrades as the error goal is reduced, while the LM algorithm improves. The RP algorithm is best, except at the smallest error goal, where SCG is better.

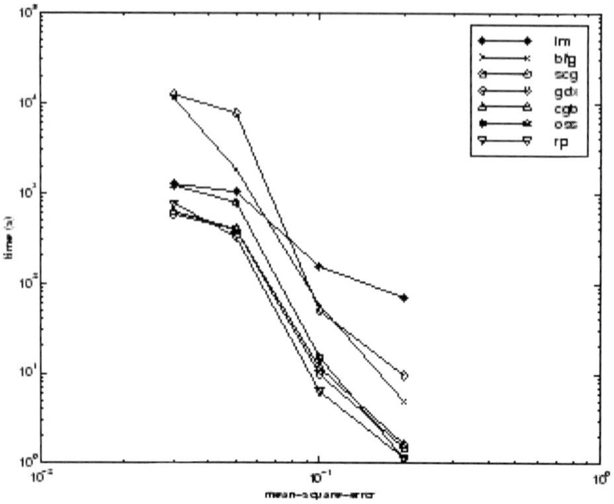

10.4.7 Summary

There are several algorithm characteristics that can be deduced from the experiments described. In general, on function approximation problems, for networks that contain up to a few hundred weights, the Levenberg-Marquardt algorithm will have the fastest convergence. This advantage is especially noticeable if very accurate training is required. In many cases, `trainlm` is able to obtain lower mean square errors than any of the other algorithms tested. However, as the number of weights in the network increases, the advantage of `trainlm` decreases. In addition, `trainlm` performance is relatively poor on pattern recognition problems. The storage requirements of `trainlm` are larger than the other algorithms tested. By adjusting the `mem_reduc` parameter, discussed earlier, the storage requirements can be reduced, but at the cost of increased execution time.

The `trainrp` function is the fastest algorithm on pattern recognition problems. However, it does not perform well on function approximation problems. Its performance also degrades as the error goal is reduced. The memory requirements for this algorithm are relatively small in comparison to the other algorithms considered.

The conjugate gradient algorithms, in particular `trainscg`, seem to perform well over a wide variety of problems, particularly for networks with a large number of weights. The SCG algorithm is almost as fast as the LM algorithm on function approximation problems (faster for large networks) and is almost as fast as `trainrp` on pattern recognition problems. Its performance does not degrade as quickly as `trainrp` performance does when the error is reduced. The conjugate gradient algorithms have relatively modest memory requirements.

The performance of `trainbfg` is similar to that of `trainlm`. It does not require as much storage as `trainlm`, but the computation required does increase geometrically with the size of the network, because the equivalent of a matrix inverse must be computed at each iteration.

The variable learning rate algorithm `traingdx` is usually much slower than the other methods, and has about the same storage requirements as `trainrp`, but it can still be useful for some problems. There are certain situations in which it is better to converge more slowly. For example, when using early stopping you can have inconsistent results if you use an algorithm that converges too quickly. You might overshoot the point at which the error on the validation set is minimized.

10.5 IMPROVE NEURAL NETWORK GENERALIZATION AND AVOID OVERFITTING

One of the problems that occur during neural network training is called overfitting. The error on the training set is driven to a very small value, but when new data is presented to the network the error is large. The network has memorized the training examples, but it has not learned to generalize to new situations.

The following figure shows the response of a 1-20-1 neural network that has been trained to approximate a noisy sine function. The underlying sine function is shown by the dotted line, the noisy measurements are given by the + symbols, and the neural network response is given by the solid line. Clearly this network has overfitted the data and will not generalize well.

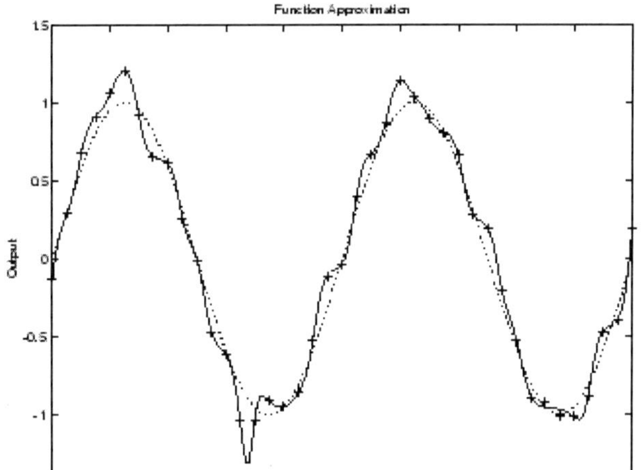

One method for improving network generalization is to use a network that is just large enough to provide an adequate fit. The larger network you use, the more complex the functions the network can create. If you use a small enough network, it will not have enough power to overfit the data. Run the *Neural Network Design* example nnd11gn [HDB96] to investigate how reducing the size of a network can prevent overfitting.

Unfortunately, it is difficult to know beforehand how large a network should be for a specific application. There are two other methods for improving generalization that are implemented in Neural Network Toolbox (Deep Learning Toolbox from version 18)™ software: regularization and early stopping. The next sections describe these two techniques and the routines to implement them.

Note that if the number of parameters in the network is much smaller than the total number of points in the training set, then there is little or no chance of overfitting. If you can easily collect more data and increase the size of the training set, then there is no need to worry about the following techniques to prevent overfitting. The rest of this section only applies to those situations in which you want to make the most of a limited supply of data.

10.5.1 Retraining Neural Networks

Typically each backpropagation training session starts with different initial weights and biases, and different divisions of data into training, validation, and test sets. These different conditions can lead to very different solutions for the same problem.

It is a good idea to train several networks to ensure that a network with good generalization is found.

Here a dataset is loaded and divided into two parts: 90% for designing networks and 10% for testing them all.

```
[x,t] = house_dataset;
Q = size(x,2);
Q1 = floor(Q*0.90);
Q2 = Q-Q1;
ind = randperm(Q);
ind1 = ind(1:Q1);
ind2 = ind(Q1+(1:Q2));
x1 = x(:,ind1);
t1 = t(:,ind1);
x2 = x(:,ind2);
t2 = t(:,ind2);
```

Next a network architecture is chosen and trained ten times on the first part of the dataset, with each network's mean square error on the second part of the dataset.

```
net = feedforwardnet(10);
numNN = 10;
NN = cell(1,numNN);
```

```
perfs = zeros(1,numNN);
for i=1:numNN
  disp(['Training ' num2str(i) '/' num2str(numNN)])
  NN{i} = train(net,x1,t1);
  y2 = NN{i}(x2);
  perfs(i) = mse(net,t2,y2);
end
```

Each network will be trained starting from different initial weights and biases, and with a different division of the first dataset into training, validation, and test sets. Note that the test sets are a good measure of generalization for each respective network, but not for all the networks, because data that is a test set for one network will likely be used for training or validation by other neural networks. This is why the original dataset was divided into two parts, to ensure that a completely independent test set is preserved.

The neural network with the lowest performance is the one that generalized best to the second part of the dataset.

10.5.2 Multiple Neural Networks

Another simple way to improve generalization, especially when caused by noisy data or a small dataset, is to train multiple neural networks and average their outputs.

For instance, here 10 neural networks are trained on a small problem and their mean squared errors compared to the means squared error of their average.

First, the dataset is loaded and divided into a design and test set.

```
[x,t] = house_dataset;
Q = size(x,2);
Q1 = floor(Q*0.90);
Q2 = Q-Q1;
ind = randperm(Q);
ind1 = ind(1:Q1);
ind2 = ind(Q1+(1:Q2));
x1 = x(:,ind1);
t1 = t(:,ind1);
x2 = x(:,ind2);
t2 = t(:,ind2);
```

Then, ten neural networks are trained.

```
net = feedforwardnet(10);
numNN = 10;
nets = cell(1,numNN);
for i=1:numNN
  disp(['Training ' num2str(i) '/' num2str(numNN)])
```

```
    nets{i} = train(net,x1,t1);
end
```

Next, each network is tested on the second dataset with both individual performances and the performance for the average output calculated.

```
perfs = zeros(1,numNN);
y2Total = 0;
for i=1:numNN
  neti = nets{i};
  y2 = neti(x2);
  perfs(i) = mse(neti,t2,y2);
  y2Total = y2Total + y2;
end
perfs
y2AverageOutput = y2Total / numNN;
perfAveragedOutputs = mse(nets{1},t2,y2AverageOutput)
```

The mean squared error for the average output is likely to be lower than most of the individual performances, perhaps not all. It is likely to generalize better to additional new data.

For some very difficult problems, a hundred networks can be trained and the average of their outputs taken for any input. This is especially helpful for a small, noisy dataset in conjunction with the Bayesian Regularization training function `trainbr`, described below.

10.5.3 Early Stopping

The default method for improving generalization is called *early stopping*. This technique is automatically provided for all of the supervised network creation functions, including the backpropagation network creation functions such as `feedforwardnet`.

In this technique the available data is divided into three subsets. The first subset is the training set, which is used for computing the gradient and updating the network weights and biases. The second subset is the validation set. The error on the validation set is monitored during the training process. The validation error normally decreases during the initial phase of training, as does the training set error. However, when the network begins to overfit the data, the error on the validation set typically begins to rise. When the validation error increases for a specified number of iterations (`net.trainParam.max_fail`), the training is stopped, and the weights and biases at the minimum of the validation error are returned.

The test set error is not used during training, but it is used to compare different models. It is also useful to plot the test set error during the training process. If the error in the test set reaches a minimum at a significantly different iteration number than the validation set error, this might indicate a poor division of the data set.

There are four functions provided for dividing data into training, validation and test sets. They are `dividerand` (the default), `divideblock`, `divideint`, and `divideind`. You can access or change the division function for your network with this property:

```
net.divideFcn
```

Each of these functions takes parameters that customize its behavior. These values are stored and can be changed with the following network property:

```
net.divideParam
```

10.5.4 Index Data Division (divideind)

Create a simple test problem. For the full data set, generate a noisy sine wave with 201 input points ranging from −1 to 1 at steps of 0.01:

```
p = [-1:0.01:1];

t = sin(2*pi*p)+0.1*randn(size(p));
```

Divide the data by index so that successive samples are assigned to the training set, validation set, and test set successively:

```
trainInd = 1:3:201
valInd = 2:3:201;
testInd = 3:3:201;
[trainP,valP,testP] = divideind(p,trainInd,valInd,testInd);
[trainT,valT,testT] = divideind(t,trainInd,valInd,testInd);
```

10.5.5 Random Data Division (dividerand)

You can divide the input data randomly so that 60% of the samples are assigned to the training set, 20% to the validation set, and 20% to the test set, as follows:

```
[trainP,valP,testP,trainInd,valInd,testInd] = dividerand(p);
```

This function not only divides the input data, but also returns indices so that you can divide the target data accordingly using `divideind`:

```
[trainT,valT,testT] = divideind(t,trainInd,valInd,testInd);
```

10.5.6 Block Data Division (divideblock)

You can also divide the input data randomly such that the first 60% of the samples are assigned to the training set, the next 20% to the validation set, and the last 20% to the test set, as follows:

```
[trainP,valP,testP,trainInd,valInd,testInd] = divideblock(p);
```

Divide the target data accordingly using `divideind`:

```
[trainT,valT,testT] = divideind(t,trainInd,valInd,testInd);
```

10.5.7 Interleaved Data Division (divideint)

Another way to divide the input data is to cycle samples between the training set, validation set, and test set according to percentages. You can interleave 60% of the samples to the training set, 20% to the validation set and 20% to the test set as follows:

```
[trainP,valP,testP,trainInd,valInd,testInd] = divideint(p);
```

Divide the target data accordingly using `divideind`.

```
[trainT,valT,testT] = divideind(t,trainInd,valInd,testInd);
```

10.5.8 Regularization

Another method for improving generalization is called regularization. This involves modifying the performance function, which is normally chosen to be the sum of squares of the network errors on the training set. The next section explains how the performance function can be modified, and the following section describes a routine that automatically sets the optimal performance function to achieve the best generalization.

10.5.9 Modified Performance Function

The typical performance function used for training feedforward neural networks is the mean sum of squares of the network errors.

$$F = mse = \frac{1}{N}\sum_{i=1}^{N}(e_i)^2 = \frac{1}{N}\sum_{i=1}^{N}(t_i - \alpha_i)^2$$

It is possible to improve generalization if you modify the performance function by adding a term that consists of the mean of the sum of squares of the network weights and biases $msereg = \gamma * msw + (1 - \gamma) * mse$, where γ is the performance ratio, and

$$msw = \frac{1}{n}\sum_{j=1}^{n} w_j^2$$

Using this performance function causes the network to have smaller weights and biases, and this forces the network response to be smoother and less likely to overfit.

The following code reinitializes the previous network and retrains it using the BFGS algorithm with the regularized performance function. Here the performance ratio is set to 0.5, which gives equal weight to the mean square errors and the mean square weights. (Data division is cancelled by setting `net.divideFcn` so that the effects of `msereg` are isolated from early stopping.)

```
[x,t] = simplefit_dataset;
net = feedforwardnet(10,'trainbfg');
net.divideFcn = '';
net.trainParam.epochs = 300;
net.trainParam.goal = 1e-5;
net.performParam.regularization = 0.5;
net = train(net,x,t);
```

The problem with regularization is that it is difficult to determine the optimum value for the performance ratio parameter. If you make this parameter too large, you might get overfitting. If the ratio is too small, the network does not adequately fit the training data. The next section describes a routine that automatically sets the regularization parameters.

10.5.10 Automated Regularization (trainbr)

It is desirable to determine the optimal regularization parameters in an automated fashion. One approach to this process is the Bayesian framework of David MacKay [MacK92]. In this framework, the weights and biases of the network are assumed to be random variables with specified distributions. The regularization parameters are related to the unknown variances associated with these distributions. You can then estimate these parameters using statistical techniques.

A detailed discussion of Bayesian regularization is beyond the scope of this user guide. A detailed discussion of the use of Bayesian regularization, in combination with Levenberg-Marquardt training, can be found in [FoHa97].

Bayesian regularization has been implemented in the function `trainbr`. The following code shows how you can train a 1-20-1 network using this function to approximate the noisy sine wave shown in the figure in Improve Neural Network Generalization and Avoid Overfitting. (Data division is cancelled by setting `net.divideFcn` so that the effects of `trainbr`are isolated from early stopping.)

```
x = -1:0.05:1;
t = sin(2*pi*x) + 0.1*randn(size(x));
net = feedforwardnet(20,'trainbr');
net = train(net,x,t);
```

One feature of this algorithm is that it provides a measure of how many network parameters (weights and biases) are being effectively used by the network. In this case, the final trained network uses approximately 12 parameters (indicated by `#Par` in the printout) out of the 61 total weights and biases in the 1-20-1 network. This effective number of parameters should remain approximately the same, no matter how large the number of parameters in the network becomes. (This assumes that the network has been trained for a sufficient number of iterations to ensure convergence.)

The `trainbr` algorithm generally works best when the network inputs and targets are scaled so that they fall approximately in the range [−1,1]. That is the case for the test problem here. If your inputs and targets do not fall in this range, you can use the function `mapminmax` or `mapstd` to perform the scaling, as described in Choose Neural Network Input-Output Processing Functions. Networks created with `feedforwardnet` include `mapminmax` as an input and output processing function by default.

The following figure shows the response of the trained network. In contrast to the previous figure, in which a 1-20-1 network overfits the data, here you see that the network response is very close to the underlying sine function (dotted line), and, therefore, the network will generalize well to new inputs. You could have tried an even larger network, but the network response would never overfit the data. This eliminates the guesswork required in determining the optimum network size.

When using `trainbr`, it is important to let the algorithm run until the effective number of parameters has converged. The training might stop with the message "Maximum MU reached." This is typical, and is a good indication that the algorithm has truly converged. You can also tell that the algorithm has converged if the sum squared error (SSE) and sum squared weights (SSW) are relatively constant over several iterations. When this occurs you might want to click the **Stop Training**button in the training window.

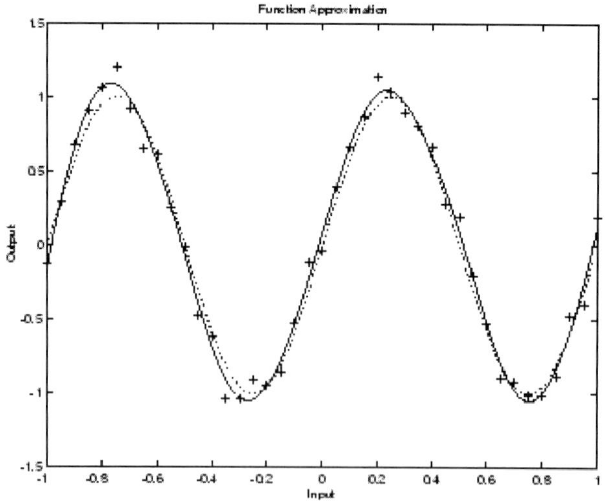

10.5.11 Summary and Discussion of Early Stopping and Regularization

Early stopping and regularization can ensure network generalization when you apply them properly.

For early stopping, you must be careful not to use an algorithm that converges too rapidly. If you are using a fast algorithm (like `trainlm`), set the training parameters so that the convergence is relatively slow. For example, set `mu` to a relatively large value, such as 1, and set `mu_dec` and `mu_inc` to values close to 1, such as 0.8 and 1.5, respectively. The training functions `trainscg` and `trainbr` usually work well with early stopping.

With early stopping, the choice of the validation set is also important. The validation set should be representative of all points in the training set.

When you use Bayesian regularization, it is important to train the network until it reaches convergence. The sum-squared error, the sum-squared weights, and the effective number of parameters should reach constant values when the network has converged.

With both early stopping and regularization, it is a good idea to train the network starting from several different initial conditions. It is possible for either method to fail in certain circumstances. By testing several different initial conditions, you can verify robust network performance.

When the data set is small and you are training function approximation networks, Bayesian regularization provides better generalization performance than early stopping. This is because Bayesian regularization does not require that a validation data set be separate from the training data set; it uses all the data.

To provide some insight into the performance of the algorithms, both early stopping and Bayesian regularization were tested on several benchmark data sets, which are listed in the following table.

Data Set Title	Number of Points	Network	Description
BALL	67	2-10-1	Dual-sensor calibration for a ball position measurement
SINE (5% N)	41	1-15-1	Single-cycle sine wave with Gaussian noise at 5% level
SINE (2% N)	41	1-15-1	Single-cycle sine wave with Gaussian noise at 2% level
ENGINE (ALL)	1199	2-30-2	Engine sensor—full data set
ENGINE (1/4)	300	2-30-2	Engine sensor—1/4 of data set
CHOLEST (ALL)	264	5-15-3	Cholesterol measurement—full data set
CHOLEST (1/2)	132	5-15-3	Cholesterol measurement—1/2 data set

These data sets are of various sizes, with different numbers of inputs and targets. With two of the data sets the networks were trained once using all the data and then retrained using only a fraction of the data. This illustrates how the advantage of Bayesian regularization becomes more noticeable when the data sets are smaller. All the data sets are obtained from physical systems except for the SINE data sets. These two were artificially created by adding various levels of noise to a single cycle of a sine wave. The performance of the algorithms on these two data sets illustrates the effect of noise.

The following table summarizes the performance of early stopping (ES) and Bayesian regularization (BR) on the seven test sets. (The `trainscg` algorithm was used for the early stopping tests. Other algorithms provide similar performance.)

Mean Squared Test Set Error

Method	Ball	Engine (All)	Engine (1/4)	Choles (All)	Choles (1/2)	Sine (5% N)	Sine (2% N)
ES	1.2e-1	1.3e-2	1.9e-2	1.2e-1	1.4e-1	1.7e-1	1.3e-1
BR	1.3e-3	2.6e-3	4.7e-3	1.2e-1	9.3e-2	3.0e-2	6.3e-3
ES/BR	92	5	4	1	1.5	5.7	21

You can see that Bayesian regularization performs better than early stopping in most cases. The performance improvement is most noticeable when the data set is small, or if there is little noise in the data set. The BALL data set, for example, was obtained from sensors that had very little noise.

Although the generalization performance of Bayesian regularization is often better than early stopping, this is not always the case. In addition, the form of Bayesian regularization implemented in the toolbox does not perform as well on pattern recognition problems as it does on function approximation problems. This is because the approximation to the Hessian that is used in the Levenberg-Marquardt algorithm is not as accurate when the network output is saturated, as would be the case in pattern recognition problems. Another disadvantage of the Bayesian regularization method is that it generally takes longer to converge than early stopping.

10.5.12 Posttraining Analysis (regression)

The performance of a trained network can be measured to some extent by the errors on the training, validation, and test sets, but it is often useful to investigate the network response in more detail. One option is to perform a regression analysis between the network response and the corresponding targets. The routine `regression` is designed to perform this analysis.

The following commands illustrate how to perform a regression analysis on a network trained.

```
x = [-1:.05:1];
t = sin(2*pi*x)+0.1*randn(size(x));
```

```
net = feedforwardnet(10);
net = train(net,x,t);
y = net(x);
[r,m,b] = regression(t,y)
r =
    0.9935
m =
    0.9874
b =
   -0.0067
```

The network output and the corresponding targets are passed to `regression`. It returns three parameters. The first two, `m`and `b`, correspond to the slope and the *y*-intercept of the best linear regression relating targets to network outputs. If there were a perfect fit (outputs exactly equal to targets), the slope would be 1, and the *y*-intercept would be 0. In this example, you can see that the numbers are very close. The third variable returned by `regression` is the correlation coefficient (R-value) between the outputs and targets. It is a measure of how well the variation in the output is explained by the targets. If this number is equal to 1, then there is perfect correlation between targets and outputs. In the example, the number is very close to 1, which indicates a good fit.

The following figure illustrates the graphical output provided by `regression`. The network outputs are plotted versus the targets as open circles. The best linear fit is indicated by a dashed line. The perfect fit (output equal to targets) is indicated by the solid line. In this example, it is difficult to distinguish the best linear fit line from the perfect fit line because the fit is so good.

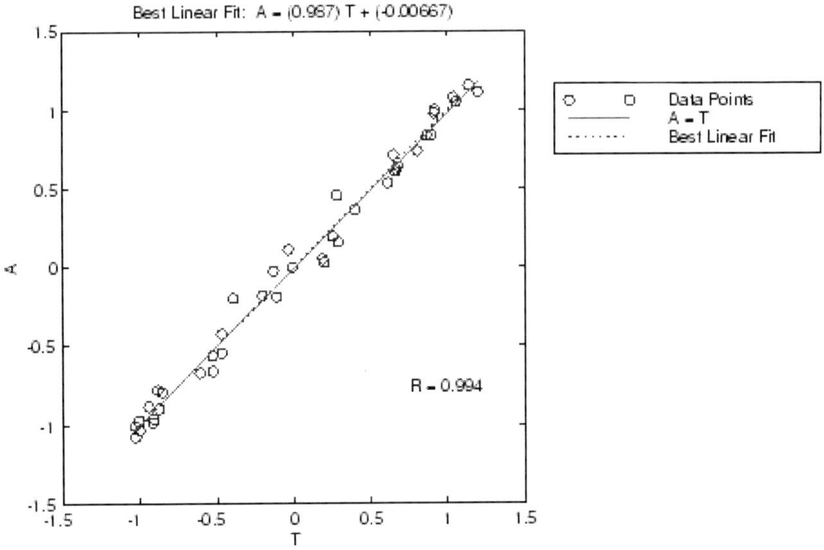

10.6 TRAIN NEURAL NETWORKS WITH ERROR WEIGHTS

In the default mean square error performance function (see Train and Apply Multilayer Neural Networks), each squared error contributes the same amount to the performance function as follows:

$$F = mse = \frac{1}{N}\sum_{i=1}^{N}(e_i)^2 = \frac{1}{N}\sum_{i=1}^{N}(t_i - a_i)^2$$

However, the toolbox allows you to weight each squared error individually as follows:

$$F = mse = \frac{1}{N}\sum_{i=1}^{N}w_i^e(e_i)^2 = \frac{1}{N}\sum_{i=1}^{N}w_i^e(t_i - a_i)^2$$

The error weighting object needs to have the same dimensions as the target data. In this way, errors can be weighted according to time step, sample number, signal number or element number. The following is an example of weighting the errors at the end of a time sequence more heavily than errors at the beginning of a time sequence. The error weighting object is passed as the last argument in the call to `train`.

```
y = laser_dataset;
y = y(1:600);
ind = 1:600;
ew = 0.99.^(600-ind);
figure
plot(ew)
ew = con2seq(ew);
ftdnn_net = timedelaynet([1:8],10);
ftdnn_net.trainParam.epochs = 1000;
ftdnn_net.divideFcn = '';
[p,Pi,Ai,t,ew1] = preparets(ftdnn_net,y,y,{},ew);
[ftdnn_net1,tr] = train(ftdnn_net,p,t,Pi,Ai,ew1);
```

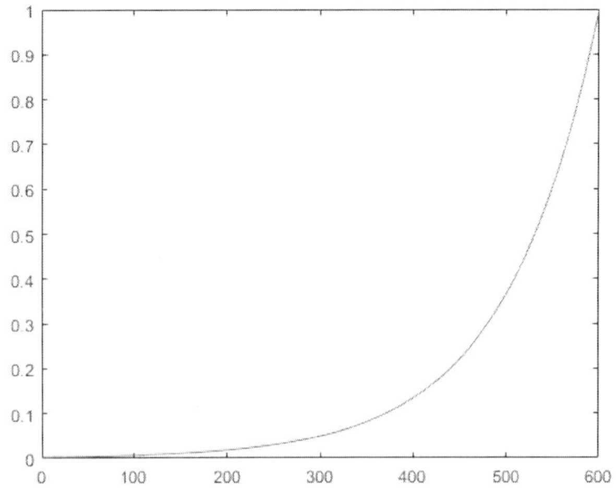

The figure illustrates the error weighting for this example. There are 600 time steps in the training data, and the errors are weighted exponentially, with the last squared error having a weight of 1, and the squared error at the first time step having a weighting of 0.0024.

The response of the trained network is shown in the following figure. If you compare this response to the response of the network that was trained without exponential weighting on the squared errors, as shown in Design Time Series Time-Delay Neural Networks, you can see that the errors late in the sequence are smaller than the errors earlier in the sequence. The errors that occurred later are smaller because they contributed more to the weighted performance index than earlier errors.

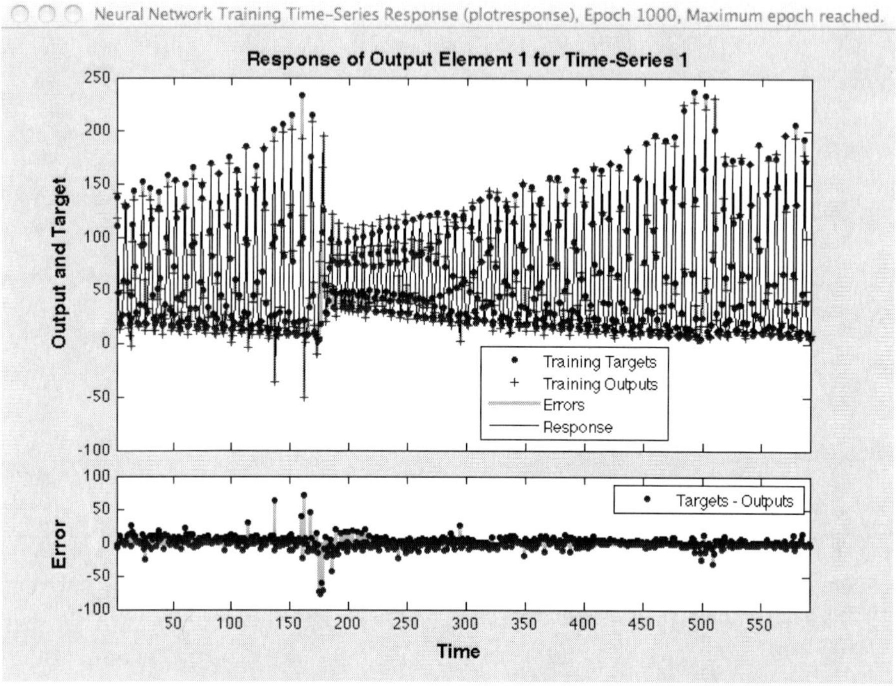

10.7 NORMALIZE ERRORS OF MULTIPLE OUTPUTS

The most common performance function used to train neural networks is mean squared error (mse). However, with multiple outputs that have different ranges of values, training with mean squared error tends to optimize accuracy on the output element with the wider range of values relative to the output element with a smaller range.

For instance, here two target elements have very different ranges:

```
x = -1:0.01:1;
t1 = 100*sin(x);
t2 = 0.01*cos(x);
t = [t1; t2];
```

The range of `t1` is 200 (from a minimum of -100 to a maximum of 100), while the range of `t2` is only 0.02 (from -0.01 to 0.01). The range of `t1` is 10,000 times greater than the range of `t2`.

If you create and train a neural network on this to minimize mean squared error, training favors the relative accuracy of the first output element over the second.

```
net = feedforwardnet(5);
net1 = train(net,x,t);
y = net1(x);
```

Here you can see that the network has learned to fit the first output element very well.

```
figure(1)
plot(x,y(1,:),x,t(1,:))
```

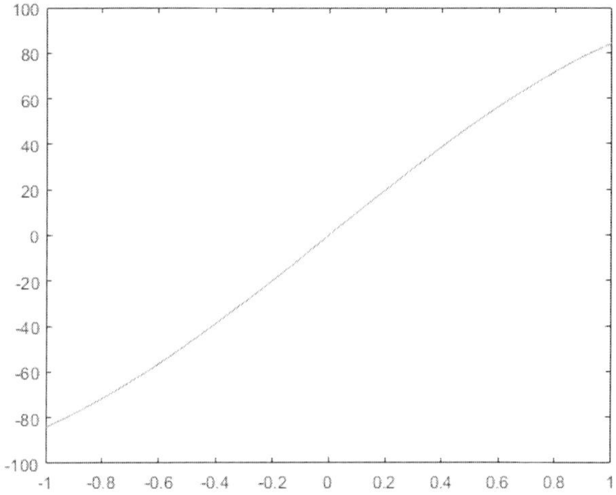

However, the second element's function is not fit nearly as well.

```
figure(2)
plot(x,y(2,:),x,t(2,:))
```

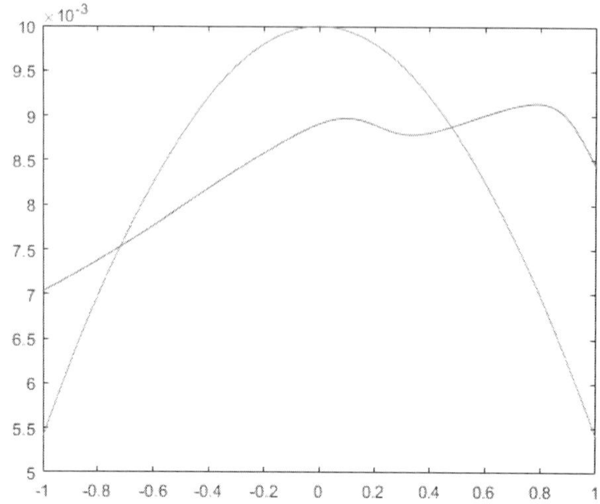

To fit both output elements equally well in a relative sense, set the `normalization` performance parameter to `'standard'`. This then calculates errors for performance measures as if each output element has a range of 2 (i.e., as if each output element's values range from -1 to 1, instead of their differing ranges).

```
net.performParam.normalization = 'standard';
net2 = train(net,x,t);
y = net2(x);
```

Now the two output elements both fit well.

```
figure(3)
plot(x,y(1,:),x,t(1,:))
```

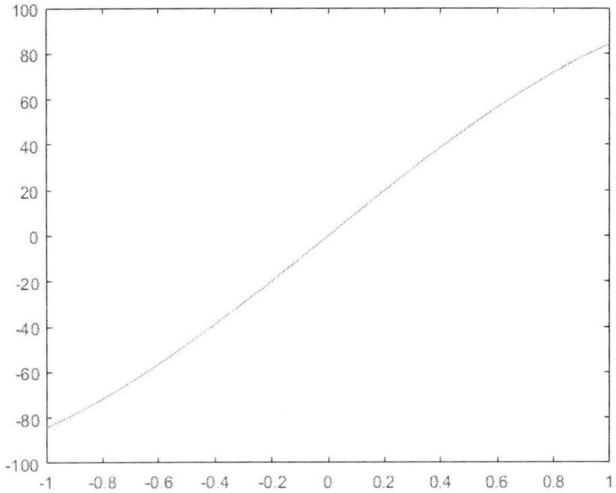


```
figure(4)
plot(x,y(2,:),x,t(2,:))
```

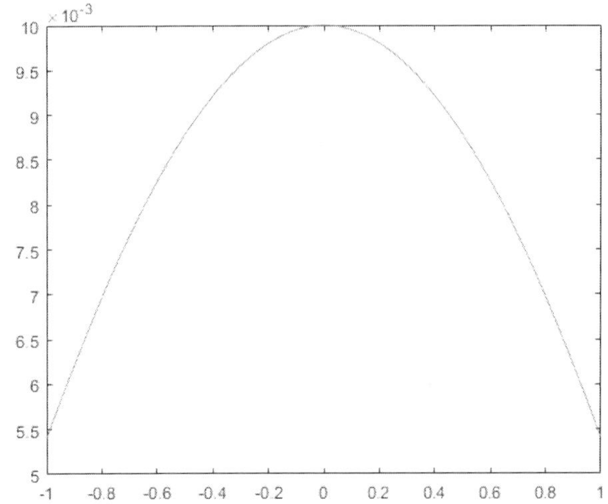

Chapter 11

CLASSIFICATION WITH NEURAL NETWORKS. EXAMPLES

11.1 CRAB CLASSIFICATION

This example illustrates using a neural network as a classifier to identify the sex of crabs from physical dimensions of the crab.

In this example we attempt to build a classifier that can identify the sex of a crab from its physical measurements. Six physical characterstics of a crab are considered: species, frontallip, rearwidth, length, width and depth. The problem on hand is to identify the sex of a crab given the observed values for each of these 6 physical characterstics.

11.1.1 Why Neural Networks?

Neural networks have proven themselves as proficient classifiers and are particularly well suited for addressing non-linear problems. Given the non-linear nature of real world phenomena, like crab classification, neural networks is certainly a good candidate for solving the problem.

The six physical characterstics will act as inputs to a neural network and the sex of the crab will be target. Given an input, which constitutes the six observed values for the physical characterstics of a crab, the neural network is expected to identify if the crab is male or female.

This is achieved by presenting previously recorded inputs to a neural network and then tuning it to produce the desired target outputs. This process is called neural network training.

11.1.2 Preparing the Data

Data for classification problems are set up for a neural network by organizing the data into two matrices, the input matrix X and the target matrix T.

Each ith column of the input matrix will have six elements representing a crabs species, fontallip, rearwidth, length, width and depth.

Each corresponding column of the target matrix will have two elements. Female crabs are reprented with a one in the first element, male crabs with a one in the second element. (All other elements are zero).

Here such the dataset is loaded.

```
[x,t] = crab_dataset;
size(x)
size(t)
ans =

     6   200


ans =

     2   200
```

11.1.3 Building the Neural Network Classifier

The next step is to create a neural network that will learn to identify the sex of the crabs.

Since the neural network starts with random initial weights, the results of this example will differ slightly every time it is run. The random seed is set to avoid this randomness. However this is not necessary for your own applications.

```
setdemorandstream(491218382)
```

Two-layer (i.e. one-hidden-layer) feed forward neural networks can learn any input-output relationship given enough neurons in the hidden layer. Layers which are not output layers are called hidden layers.

We will try a single hidden layer of 10 neurons for this example. In general, more difficult problems require more neurons, and perhaps more layers. Simpler problems require fewer neurons.

The input and output have sizes of 0 because the network has not yet been configured to match our input and target data. This will happen when the network is trained.

```
net = patternnet(10);
view(net)
```

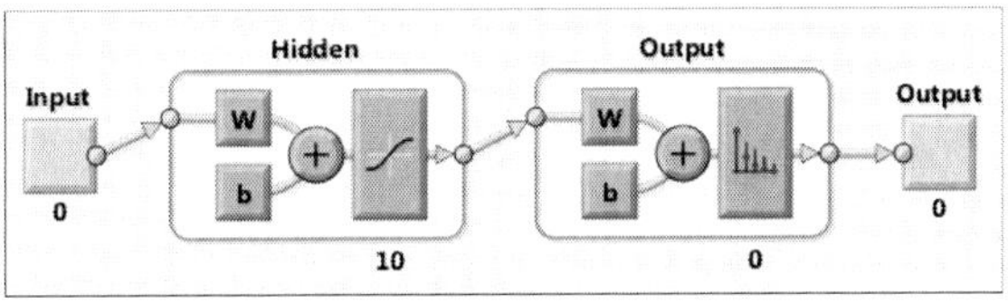

Now the network is ready to be trained. The samples are automatically divided into training, validation and test sets. The training set is used to teach the network. Training continues as long as the network continues improving on the validation set. The test set provides a completely independent measure of network accuracy.

```
[net,tr] = train(net,x,t);
Nntraintool
```

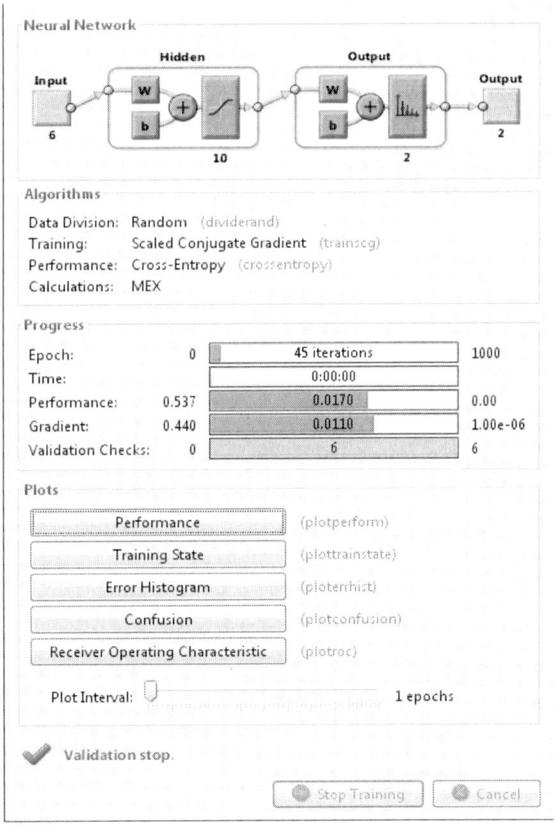

To see how the network's performance improved during training, either click the "Performance" button in the training tool, or call PLOTPERFORM.

Performance is measured in terms of mean squared error, and shown in log scale. It rapidly decreased as the network was trained.

Performance is shown for each of the training, validation and test sets. The version of the network that did best on the validation set is was after training.

```
plotperform(tr)
```

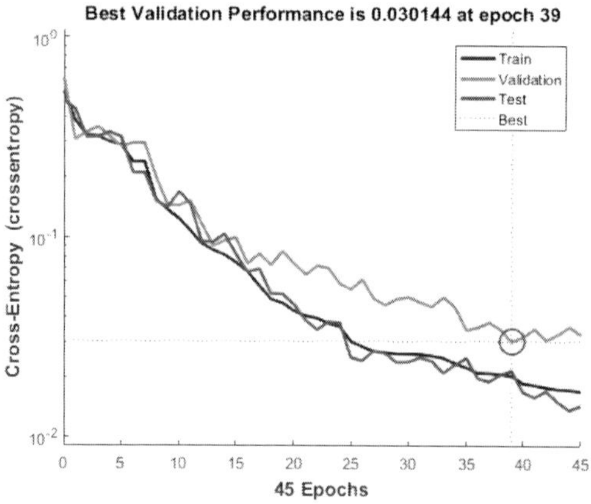

11.1.4 Testing the Classifier

The trained neural network can now be tested with the testing samples This will give us a sense of how well the network will do when applied to data from the real world.

The network outputs will be in the range 0 to 1, so we can use **vec2ind** function to get the class indices as the position of the highest element in each output vector.

```
testX = x(:,tr.testInd);
testT = t(:,tr.testInd);

testY = net(testX);
testIndices = vec2ind(testY)
testIndices =

  Columns 1 through 13

     2     2     2     1     2     2     2     1     2     2     2     2     1

  Columns 14 through 26

     1     2     2     2     1     2     2     1     2     1     1     1     1
```

```
  Columns 27 through 30

     1     2     2     1
```

One measure of how well the neural network has fit the data is the confusion plot. Here the confusion matrix is plotted across all samples.

The confusion matrix shows the percentages of correct and incorrect classifications. Correct classifications are the green squares on the matrices diagonal. Incorrect classifications form the red squares.

If the network has learned to classify properly, the percentages in the red squares should be very small, indicating few misclassifications.

If this is not the case then further training, or training a network with more hidden neurons, would be advisable.

```
plotconfusion(testT,testY)
```

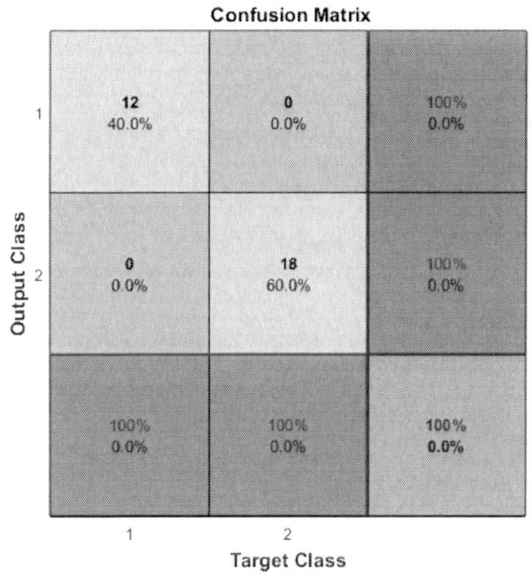

Here are the overall percentages of correct and incorrect classification.

```
[c,cm] = confusion(testT,testY)

fprintf('Percentage Correct Classification   : %f%%\n', 100*(1-c));
fprintf('Percentage Incorrect Classification : %f%%\n', 100*c);
c =

    0.0333
```

```
cm =

    12     1
     0    17

Percentage Correct Classification   : 96.666667%
Percentage Incorrect Classification : 3.333333%
```

Another measure of how well the neural network has fit data is the receiver operating characteristic plot. This shows how the false positive and true positive rates relate as the thresholding of outputs is varied from 0 to 1.

The farther left and up the line is, the fewer false positives need to be accepted in order to get a high true positive rate. The best classifiers will have a line going from the bottom left corner, to the top left corner, to the top right corner, or close to that.

```
plotroc(testT,testY)
```

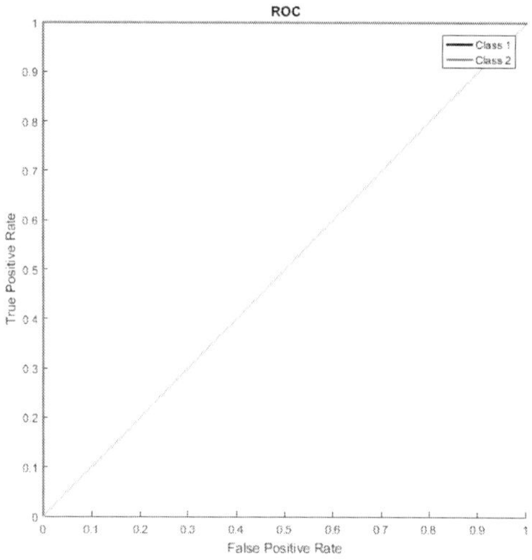

This example illustrated using a neural network to classify crabs.

11.2 WINE CLASSIFICATION

This example illustrates how a pattern recognition neural network can classify wines by winery based on its chemical characteristics.

11.2.1 The Problem: Classify Wines

In this example we attempt to build a neural network that can classify wines from three wineries by thirteen attributes:

- Alcohol
- Malic acid
- Ash
- Alcalinity of ash
- Magnesium
- Total phenols
- Flavanoids
- Nonflavanoid phenols
- Proanthocyanins
- Color intensity
- Hue
- OD280/OD315 of diluted wines
- Proline

This is an example of a pattern recognition problem, where inputs are associated with different classes, and we would like to create a neural network that not only classifies the known wines properly, but can generalize to accurately classify wines that were not used to design the solution.

11.2.2 Why Neural Networks?

Neural networks are very good at pattern recognition problems. A neural network with enough elements (called neurons) can classify any data with arbitrary accuracy. They are particularly well suited for complex decision boundary problems over many variables. Therefore neural networks are a good candidate for solving the wine classification problem.

The thirteeen neighborhood attributes will act as inputs to a neural network, and the respective target for each will be a 3-element class vector with a 1 in the position of the associated winery, #1, #2 or #3.

The network will be designed by using the attributes of neighborhoods to train the network to produce the correct target classes.

11.2.3 Preparing the Data

Data for classification problems are set up for a neural network by organizing the data into two matrices, the input matrix X and the target matrix T.

Each ith column of the input matrix will have thirteen elements representing a wine whose winery is already known.

Each corresponding column of the target matrix will have three elements, consisting of two zeros and a 1 in the location of the associated winery.

Here such a dataset is loaded.

```
[x,t] = wine_dataset;
```

We can view the sizes of inputs X and targets T.

Note that both X and T have 178 columns. These represent 178 wine sample attributes (inputs) and associated winery class vectors (targets).

Input matrix X has thirteen rows, for the thirteen attributes. Target matrix T has three rows, as for each example we have three possible wineries.

```
size(x)
size(t)
```

```
ans =

    13   178


ans =

     3   178
```

11.2.4 Pattern Recognition with a Neural Network

The next step is to create a neural network that will learn to classify the wines.

Since the neural network starts with random initial weights, the results of this example will differ slightly every time it is run. The random seed is set to avoid this randomness. However this is not necessary for your own applications.

```
setdemorandstream(391418381)
```

Two-layer (i.e. one-hidden-layer) feed forward neural networks can learn any input-output relationship given enough neurons in the hidden layer. Layers which are not output layers are called hidden layers.

We will try a single hidden layer of 10 neurons for this example. In general, more difficult problems require more neurons, and perhaps more layers. Simpler problems require fewer neurons.

The input and output have sizes of 0 because the network has not yet been configured to match our input and target data. This will happen when the network is trained.

```
net = patternnet(10);
view(net)
```

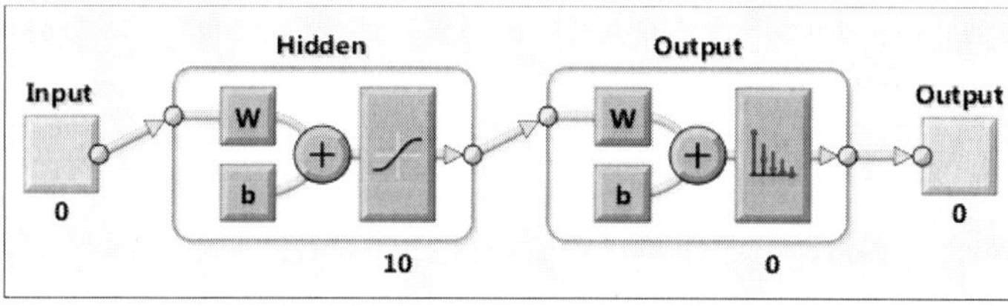

Now the network is ready to be trained. The samples are automatically divided into training, validation and test sets. The training set is used to teach the network. Training continues as long as the network continues improving on the validation set. The test set provides a completely independent measure of network accuracy.

The NN Training Tool shows the network being trained and the algorithms used to train it. It also displays the training state during training and the criteria which stopped training will be highlighted in green.

The buttons at the bottom open useful plots which can be opened during and after training. Links next to the algorithm names and plot buttons open documentation on those subjects.

```
[net,tr] = train(net,x,t);
nntraintool
```

To see how the network's performance improved during training, either click the "Performance" button in the training tool, or call PLOTPERFORM.

Performance is measured in terms of mean squared error, and shown in log scale. It rapidly decreased as the network was trained.

Performance is shown for each of the training, validation and test sets. The version of the network that did best on the validation set is was after training.

```
plotperform(tr)
```

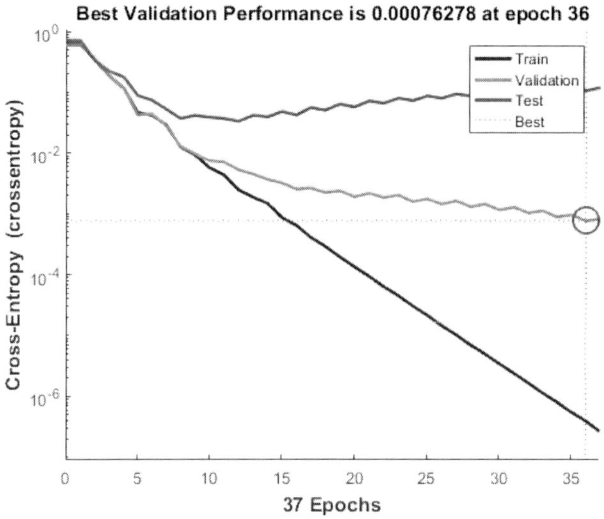

11.2.5 Testing the Neural Network

The mean squared error of the trained neural network can now be measured with respect to the testing samples. This will give us a sense of how well the network will do when applied to data from the real world.

The network outputs will be in the range 0 to 1, so we can use **vec2ind** function to get the class indices as the position of the highest element in each output vector.

```
testX = x(:,tr.testInd);
testT = t(:,tr.testInd);

testY = net(testX);
testIndices = vec2ind(testY)

testIndices =

  Columns 1 through 13

     1     1     1     2     1     1     1     1     1     1     1     2     2

  Columns 14 through 26

     2     2     2     2     2     2     3     2     3     3     3     3     3

  Column 27

     3
```

Another measure of how well the neural network has fit the data is the confusion plot. Here the confusion matrix is plotted across all samples.

The confusion matrix shows the percentages of correct and incorrect classifications. Correct classifications are the green squares on the matrices diagonal. Incorrect classifications form the red squares.

If the network has learned to classify properly, the percentages in the red squares should be very small, indicating few misclassifications.

If this is not the case then further training, or training a network with more hidden neurons, would be advisable.

```
plotconfusion(testT,testY)
```

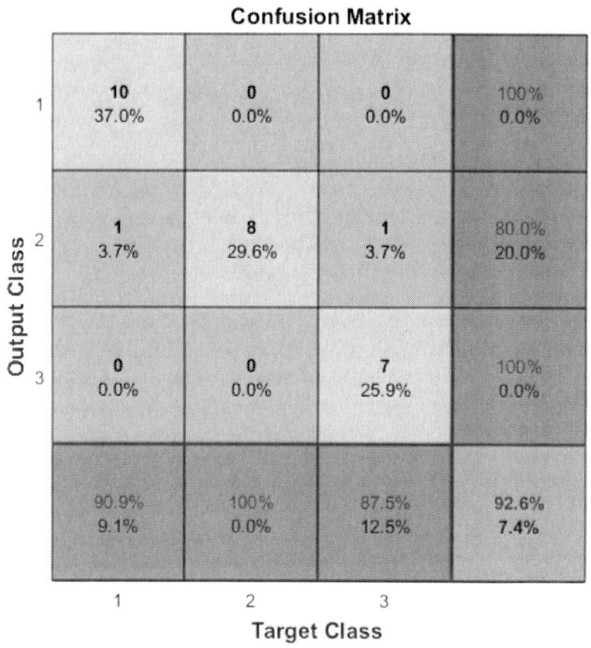

Here are the overall percentages of correct and incorrect classification.

```
[c,cm] = confusion(testT,testY)

fprintf('Percentage Correct Classification   : %f%%\n', 100*(1-c));
fprintf('Percentage Incorrect Classification : %f%%\n', 100*c);

c =
```

```
    0.0741


cm =

    10     1     0
     0     8     0
     0     1     7

Percentage Correct Classification   : 92.592593%
Percentage Incorrect Classification : 7.407407%
```

A third measure of how well the neural network has fit data is the receiver operating characteristic plot. This shows how the false positive and true positive rates relate as the thresholding of outputs is varied from 0 to 1.

The farther left and up the line is, the fewer false positives need to be accepted in order to get a high true positive rate. The best classifiers will have a line going from the bottom left corner, to the top left corner, to the top right corner, or close to that.

```
plotroc(testT,testY)
```

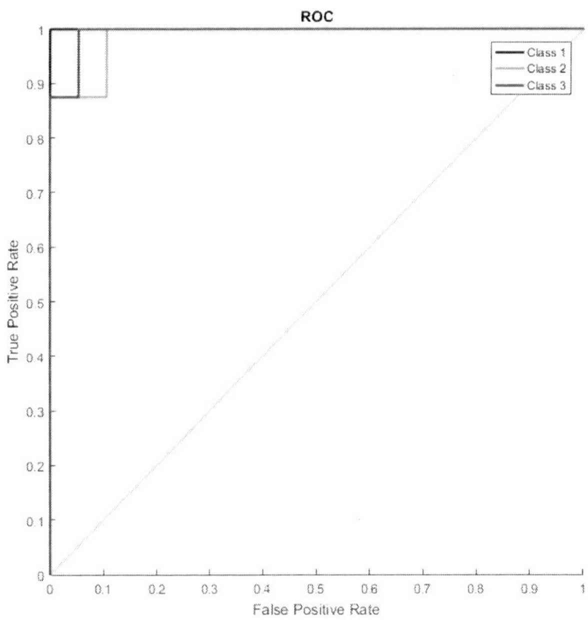

11.3 CANCER DETECTION

This example demonstrates using a neural network to detect cancer from mass spectrometry data on protein profiles.

Serum proteomic pattern diagnostics can be used to differentiate samples from patients with and without disease. Profile patterns are generated using surface-enhanced laser desorption and ionization (SELDI) protein mass spectrometry. This technology has the potential to improve clinical diagnostics tests for cancer pathologies.

The goal is to build a classifier that can distinguish between cancer and control patients from the mass spectrometry data.

The methodology followed in this example is to select a reduced set of measurements or "features" that can be used to distinguish between cancer and control patients using a classifier.

These features will be ion intensity levels at specific mass/charge values.

11.3.1 Formatting the Data

The data in this example is from the FDA-NCI Clinical Proteomics Program Databank: http://home.ccr.cancer.gov/ncifdaproteomics/ppatterns.asp

To recreate the data in **ovarian_dataset.mat** used in this example, download and uncompress the raw mass-spectrometry data from the FDA-NCI web site. Create the data file **OvarianCancerQAQCdataset.mat** by either running script **msseqprocessing** in Bioinformatics Toolbox (TM) or by following the steps in the example **biodistcompdemo** (Batch processing with parallel computing). The new file contains variables `Y`, `MZ` and `grp`.

Each column in `Y` represents measurements taken from a patient. There are `216` columns in `Y` representing `216` patients, out of which `121` are ovarian cancer patients and `95` are normal patients.

Each row in `Y` represents the ion intensity level at a specific mass-charge value indicated in `MZ`. There are `15000` mass-charge values in `MZ` and each row in `Y` represents the ion-intesity levels of the patients at that particular mass-charge value.

The variable `grp` holds the index information as to which of these samples represent cancer patients and which ones represent normal patients.

An extensive description of this data set and excellent introduction to this promising technology can be found in [1] and [2].

11.3.2 Ranking Key Features

This is a typical classification problem in which the number of features is much larger than the number of observations, but in which no single feature achieves a correct classification, therefore we need to find a classifier which appropriately learns how to weight multiple features and at the same time produce a generalized mapping which is not over-fitted.

A simple approach for finding significant features is to assume that each M/Z value is independent and compute a two-way t-test. **rankfeatures** returns an index to the most significant M/Z values, for instance 100 indices ranked by the absolute value of the test statistic.

To finish recreating the data from **ovarian_dataset.mat**, load the **OvarianCancerQAQCdataset.mat** and **rankfeatures** from Bioinformatics Toolbox to choose 100 highest ranked measurements as inputs x.

```
ind = rankfeatures(Y,grp,'CRITERION','ttest','NUMBER',100);

x = Y(ind,:);
```

Define the targets t for the two classes as follows:

```
t = double(strcmp('Cancer',grp));

t = [t; 1-t];
```

The preprocessing steps from the script and example listed above are intended to demonstrate a representative set of possible pre-processing and feature selection procedures. Using different steps or parameters may lead to different and possibly improved results of this example.

```
[x,t] = ovarian_dataset;
whos
  Name          Size              Bytes  Class     Attributes

  t             2x216              3456  double
  x           100x216            172800  double
```

Each column in x represents one of 216 different patients.

Each row in x represents the ion intensity level at one of the 100 specific mass-charge values for each patient.

The variable t has 2 rows of 216 values each of which are either [1;0], indicating a cancer patient, or [0;1] for a normal patient.

11.3.3 Classification Using a Feed Forward Neural Network

Now that you have identified some significant features, you can use this information to classify the cancer and normal samples.

Since the neural network is initialized with random initial weights, the results after training the network vary slightly every time the example is run. To avoid this randomness, the random seed is set to reproduce the same results every time. However this is not necessary for your own applications.

```
setdemorandstream(672880951)
```

A 1-hidden layer feed forward neural network with 5 hidden layer neurons is created and trained. The input and target samples are automatically divided into training, validation and test sets. The training set is used to teach the network. Training continues as long as the network continues improving on the validation set. The test set provides a completely independent measure of network accuracy.

The input and output have sizes of 0 because the network has not yet been configured to match our input and target data. This will happen when the network is trained.

```
net = patternnet(5);
view(net)
```

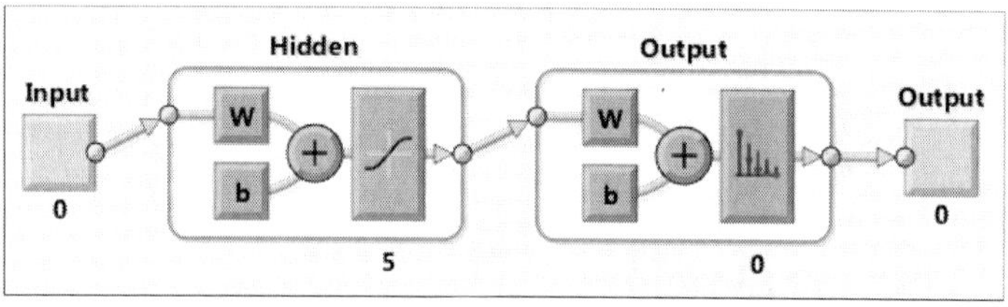

Now the network is ready to be trained. The samples are automatically divided into training, validation and test sets. The training set is used to teach the network. Training continues as long as the network continues improving on the validation set. The test set provides a completely independent measure of network accuracy.

The NN Training Tool shows the network being trained and the algorithms used to train it. It also displays the training state during training and the criteria which stopped training will be highlighted in green.

The buttons at the bottom open useful plots which can be opened during and after training. Links next to the algorithm names and plot buttons open documentation on those subjects.

```
[net,tr] = train(net,x,t);
```

To see how the network's performance improved during training, either click the "Performance" button in the training tool, or call PLOTPERFORM.

Performance is measured in terms of mean squared error, and shown in log scale. It rapidly decreased as the network was trained.

Performance is shown for each of the training, validation and test sets. The version of the network that did best on the validation set is was after training.

```
plotperform(tr)
```

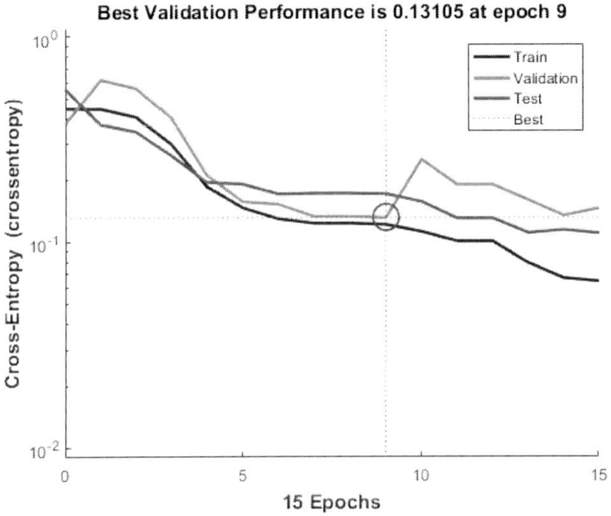

The trained neural network can now be tested with the testing samples we partitioned from the main dataset. The testing data was not used in training in any way and hence provides an "out-of-sample" dataset to test the network on. This will give us a sense of how well the network will do when tested with data from the real world.

The network outputs will be in the range 0 to 1, so we threshold them to get 1's and 0's indicating cancer or normal patients respectively.

```
testX = x(:,tr.testInd);
testT = t(:,tr.testInd);

testY = net(testX);
testClasses = testY > 0.5
testClasses =

  2×32 logical array

  Columns 1 through 19

   0   1   1   0   1   1   1   1   1   1   1   1   1   1   1   1   1   1   0
   1   0   0   1   0   0   0   0   0   0   0   0   0   0   0   0   0   0   1
```

```
  Columns 20 through 32

     0     0     0     1     0     0     0     0     0     0     0     0     0
     1     1     1     0     1     1     1     1     1     1     1     1     1
```

One measure of how well the neural network has fit the data is the confusion plot. Here the confusion matrix is plotted across all samples.

The confusion matrix shows the percentages of correct and incorrect classifications. Correct classifications are the green squares on the matrices diagonal. Incorrect classifications form the red squares.

If the network has learned to classify properly, the percentages in the red squares should be very small, indicating few misclassifications.

If this is not the case then further training, or training a network with more hidden neurons, would be advisable.

```
plotconfusion(testT,testY)
```

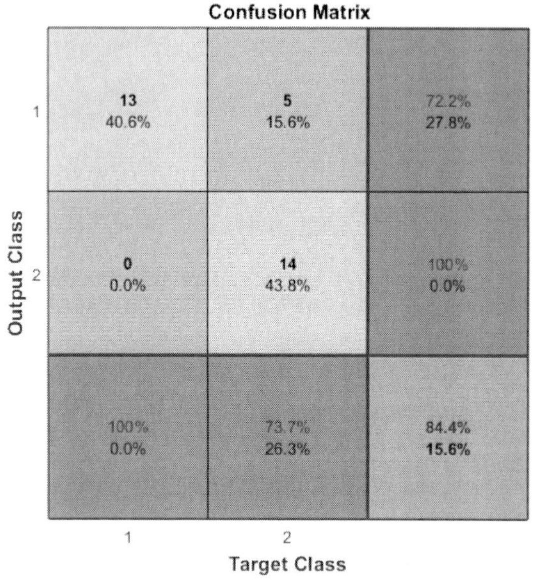

Here are the overall percentages of correct and incorrect classification.

```
[c,cm] = confusion(testT,testY)

fprintf('Percentage Correct Classification   : %f%%\n', 100*(1-c));
fprintf('Percentage Incorrect Classification : %f%%\n', 100*c);
c =
```

```
    0.0938

cm =

    16     2
     1    13

Percentage Correct Classification   : 90.625000%
Percentage Incorrect Classification : 9.375000%
```

Another measure of how well the neural network has fit data is the receiver operating characteristic plot. This shows how the false positive and true positive rates relate as the thresholding of outputs is varied from 0 to 1.

The farther left and up the line is, the fewer false positives need to be accepted in order to get a high true positive rate. The best classifiers will have a line going from the bottom left corner, to the top left corner, to the top right corner, or close to that.

Class 1 indicate cancer patiencts, class 2 normal patients.

```
plotroc(testT,testY)
```

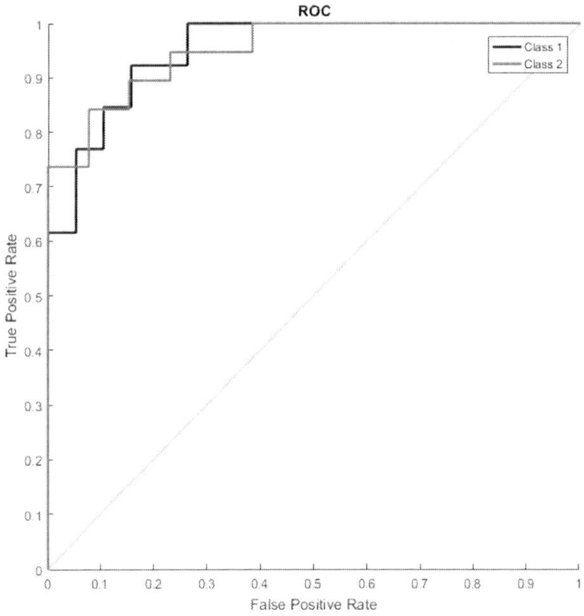

This example illustrated how neural networks can be used as classifiers for cancer detection. One can also experiment using techniques like principal component analysis to reduce the dimensionality of the data to be used for building neural networks to improve classifier performance.

11.4 CHARACTER RECOGNITION

This example illustrates how to train a neural network to perform simple character recognition.

The script **prprob** defines a matrix X with 26 columns, one for each letter of the alphabet. Each column has 35 values which can either be 1 or 0. Each column of 35 values defines a 5x7 bitmap of a letter.

The matrix T is a 26x26 identity matrix which maps the 26 input vectors to the 26 classes.

```
[X,T] = prprob;
```

Here A, the first letter, is plotted as a bit map.

```
plotchar(X(:,1))
```

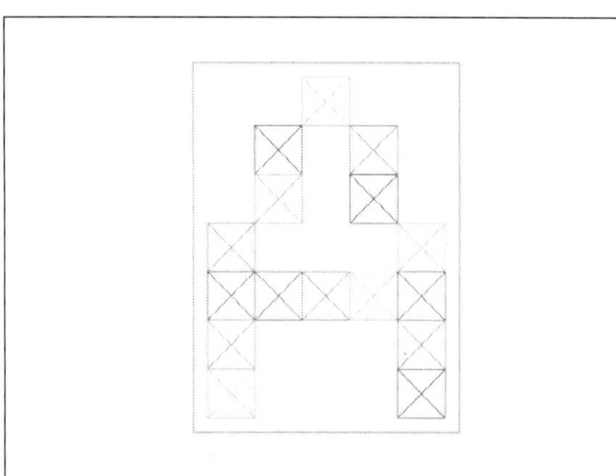

11.4.1 Creating the First Neural Network

To solve this problem we will use a feedforward neural network set up for pattern recognition with 25 hidden neurons.

Since the neural network is initialized with random initial weights, the results after training vary slightly every time the example is run. To avoid this randomness, the random seed is set to reproduce the same results every time. This is not necessary for your own applications.

```
setdemorandstream(pi);

net1 = feedforwardnet(25);
view(net1)
```

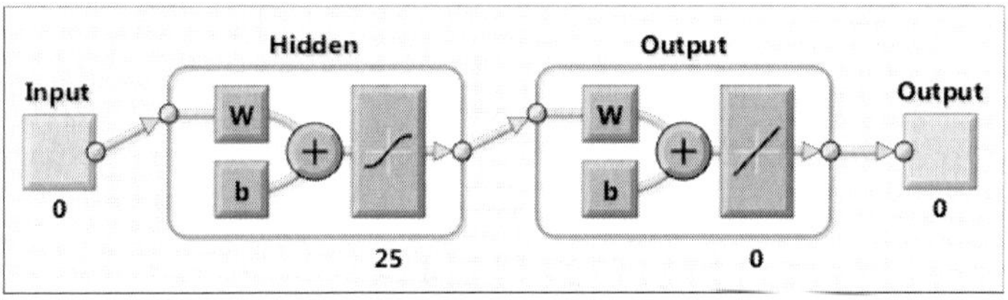

11.4.2 Training the first Neural Network

The function **train** divides up the data into training, validation and test sets. The training set is used to update the network, the validation set is used to stop the network before it overfits the training data, thus preserving good generalization. The test set acts as a completely independent measure of how well the network can be expected to do on new samples.

Training stops when the network is no longer likely to improve on the training or validation sets.

```
net1.divideFcn = '';
net1 = train(net1,X,T,nnMATLAB);


Computing Resources:
MATLAB on GLNXA64
```

11.4.3 Training the Second Neural Network

We would like the network to not only recognize perfectly formed letters, but also noisy versions of the letters. So we will try training a second network on noisy data and compare its ability to genearlize with the first network.

Here 30 noisy copies of each letter Xn are created. Values are limited by **min** and **max** to fall between 0 and 1. The corresponding targets Tn are also defined.

```
numNoise = 30;
Xn = min(max(repmat(X,1,numNoise)+randn(35,26*numNoise)*0.2,0),1);
Tn = repmat(T,1,numNoise);
```

Here is a noise version of A.

```
figure
```

```
plotchar(Xn(:,1))
```

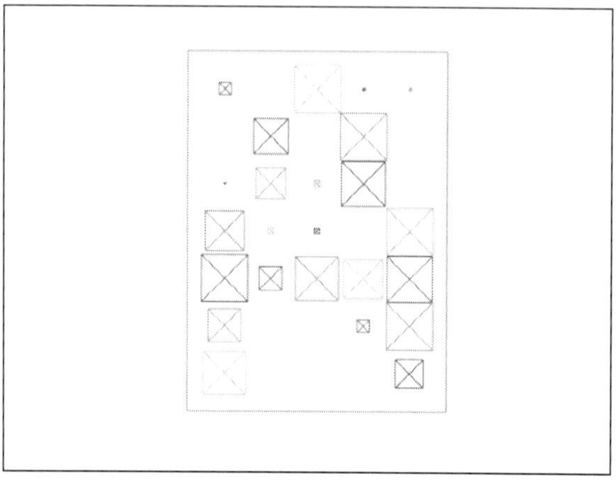

Here the second network is created and trained.

```
net2 = feedforwardnet(25);
net2 = train(net2,Xn,Tn,nnMATLAB);
```

```
Computing Resources:
MATLAB on GLNXA64
```

11.4.4 Testing Both Neural Networks

```
noiseLevels = 0:.05:1;
numLevels = length(noiseLevels);
percError1 = zeros(1,numLevels);
percError2 = zeros(1,numLevels);
for i = 1:numLevels
  Xtest =
min(max(repmat(X,1,numNoise)+randn(35,26*numNoise)*noiseLevels(i),0
),1);
  Y1 = net1(Xtest);
  percError1(i) = sum(sum(abs(Tn-compet(Y1))))/(26*numNoise*2);
  Y2 = net2(Xtest);
  percError2(i) = sum(sum(abs(Tn-compet(Y2))))/(26*numNoise*2);
end

figure
plot(noiseLevels,percError1*100,'--',noiseLevels,percError2*100);
title('Percentage of Recognition Errors');
xlabel('Noise Level');
ylabel('Errors');
```

```
legend('Network 1','Network 2','Location','NorthWest')
```

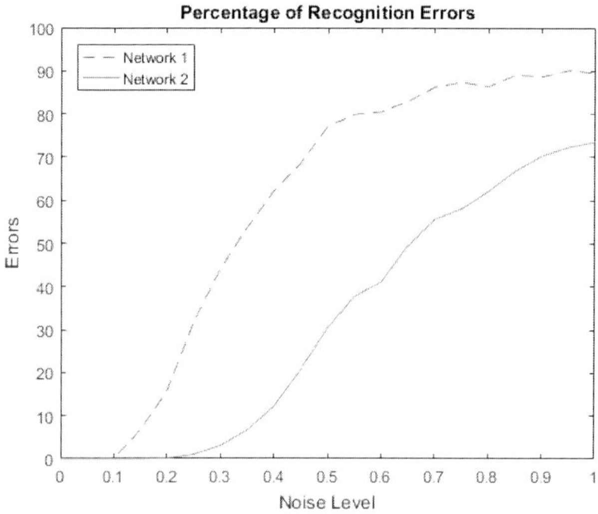

Network 1, trained without noise, has more errors due to noise than does Network 2, which was trained with noise.

Chapter 12

AUTOENCODERS AND CLUSTERING WITH NEURAL NETWORKS. EXAMPLES

12.1 TRAIN STACKED AUTOENCODERS FOR IMAGE CLASSIFICATION

This example shows how to use Neural Network Toolbox (Deep Learning Toolbox from version 18) autoencoders functionality for training a deep neural network to classify images of digits.

Neural networks with multiple hidden layers can be useful for solving classification problems with complex data, such as images. Each layer can learn features at a different level of abstraction. However, training neural networks with multiple hidden layers can be difficult in practice.

One way to effectively train a neural network with multiple layers is by training one layer at a time. You can achieve this by training a special type of network known as an autoencoder for each desired hidden layer.

This example shows you how to train a neural network with two hidden layers to classify digits in images. First you train the hidden layers individually in an unsupervised fashion using autoencoders. Then you train a final softmax layer, and join the layers together to form a deep network, which you train one final time in a supervised fashion.

12.1.1 Data set

This example uses synthetic data throughout, for training and testing. The synthetic images have been generated by applying random affine transformations to digit images created using different fonts.

Each digit image is 28-by-28 pixels, and there are 5,000 training examples. You can load the training data, and view some of the images.

```
% Load the training data into memory
[xTrainImages,tTrain] = digitTrainCellArrayData;

% Display some of the training images
clf
for i = 1:20
    subplot(4,5,i);
    imshow(xTrainImages{i});
end
```

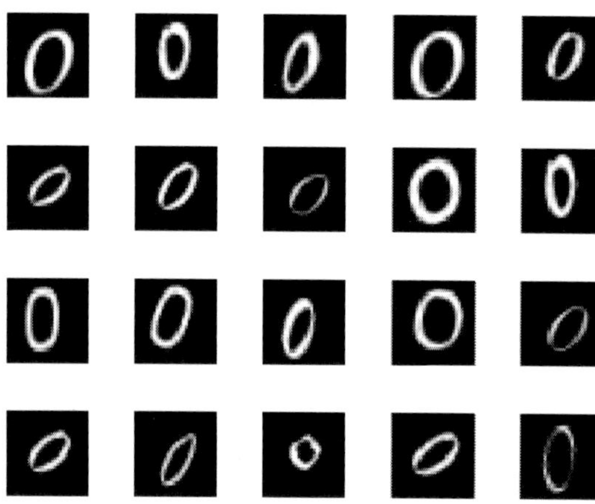

The labels for the images are stored in a 10-by-5000 matrix, where in every column a single element will be 1 to indicate the class that the digit belongs to, and all other elements in the column will be 0. It should be noted that if the tenth element is 1, then the digit image is a zero.

12.1.2 Training the first autoencoder

Begin by training a sparse autoencoder on the training data without using the labels.

An autoencoder is a neural network which attempts to replicate its input at its output. Thus, the size of its input will be the same as the size of its output. When the number of neurons in the hidden layer is less than the size of the input, the autoencoder learns a compressed representation of the input.

Neural networks have weights randomly initialized before training. Therefore the results from training are different each time. To avoid this behavior, explicitly set the random number generator seed.

```
rng('default')
```

Set the size of the hidden layer for the autoencoder. For the autoencoder that you are going to train, it is a good idea to make this smaller than the input size.

```
hiddenSize1 = 100;
```

The type of autoencoder that you will train is a sparse autoencoder. This autoencoder uses regularizers to learn a sparse representation in the first layer. You can control the influence of these regularizers by setting various parameters:

- `L2WeightRegularization` controls the impact of an L2 regularizer for the weights of the network (and not the biases). This should typically be quite small.
- `SparsityRegularization` controls the impact of a sparsity regularizer, which attempts to enforce a constraint on the sparsity of the output from the hidden layer. Note that this is different from applying a sparsity regularizer to the weights.
- `SparsityProportion` is a parameter of the sparsity regularizer. It controls the sparsity of the output from the hidden layer. A low value for `SparsityProportion` usually leads to each neuron in the hidden layer "specializing" by only giving a high output for a small number of training examples. For example, if `SparsityProportion` is set to 0.1, this is equivalent to saying that each neuron in the hidden layer should have an average output of 0.1 over the training examples. This value must be between 0 and 1. The ideal value varies depending on the nature of the problem.

Now train the autoencoder, specifying the values for the regularizers that are described above.

```
autoenc1 = trainAutoencoder(xTrainImages,hiddenSize1, ...
    'MaxEpochs',400, ...
    'L2WeightRegularization',0.004, ...
    'SparsityRegularization',4, ...
    'SparsityProportion',0.15, ...
    'ScaleData', false);
```

You can view a diagram of the autoencoder. The autoencoder is comprised of an encoder followed by a decoder. The encoder maps an input to a hidden representation, and the decoder attempts to reverse this mapping to reconstruct the original input.

```
view(autoenc1)
```

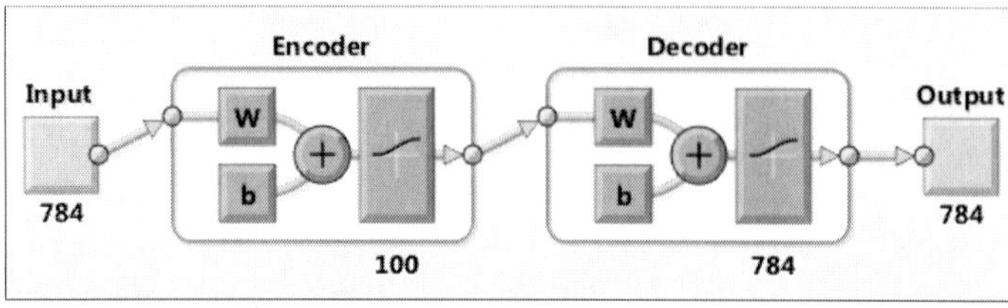

12.1.3 Visualizing the weights of the first autoencoder

The mapping learned by the encoder part of an autoencoder can be useful for extracting features from data. Each neuron in the encoder has a vector of weights associated with it which will be tuned to respond to a particular visual feature. You can view a representation of these features.

```
figure()
plotWeights(autoenc1);
```

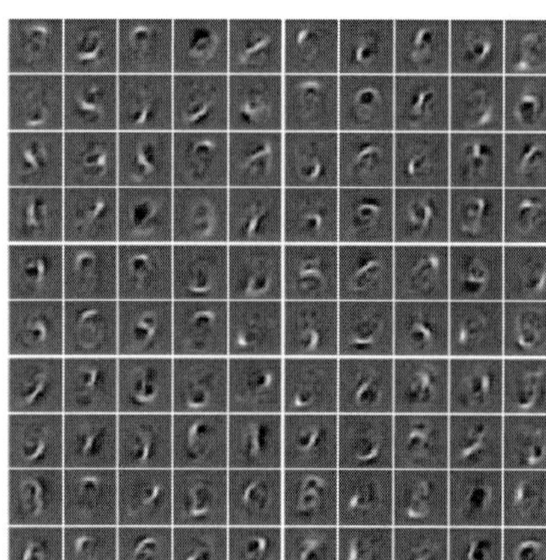

You can see that the features learned by the autoencoder represent curls and stroke patterns from the digit images.

The 100-dimensional output from the hidden layer of the autoencoder is a compressed version of the input, which summarizes its response to the features visualized above. Train the next autoencoder on a set of these vectors extracted from the training data. First, you must use the encoder from the trained autoencoder to generate the features.

```
feat1 = encode(autoenc1,xTrainImages);
```

12.1.4 Training the second autoencoder

After training the first autoencoder, you train the second autoencoder in a similar way. The main difference is that you use the features that were generated from the first autoencoder as the training data in the second autoencoder. Also, you decrease the size of the hidden representation to 50, so that the encoder in the second autoencoder learns an even smaller representation of the input data.

```
hiddenSize2 = 50;
autoenc2 = trainAutoencoder(feat1,hiddenSize2, ...
    'MaxEpochs',100, ...
    'L2WeightRegularization',0.002, ...
    'SparsityRegularization',4, ...
    'SparsityProportion',0.1, ...
    'ScaleData', false);
```

Once again, you can view a diagram of the autoencoder with the `view` function.

```
view(autoenc2)
```

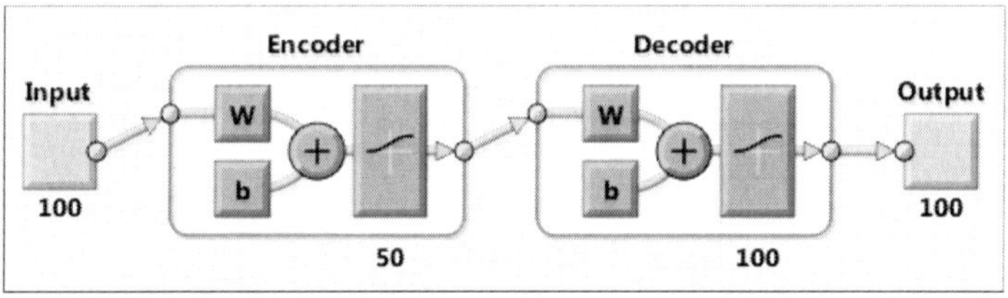

You can extract a second set of features by passing the previous set through the encoder from the second autoencoder.

```
feat2 = encode(autoenc2,feat1);
```

The original vectors in the training data had 784 dimensions. After passing them through the first encoder, this was reduced to 100 dimensions. After using the second encoder, this was reduced again to 50 dimensions. You can now train a final layer to classify these 50-dimensional vectors into different digit classes.

12.1.5 Training the final softmax layer

Train a softmax layer to classify the 50-dimensional feature vectors. Unlike the autoencoders, you train the softmax layer in a supervised fashion using labels for the training data.

```
softnet = trainSoftmaxLayer(feat2,tTrain,'MaxEpochs',400);
```

You can view a diagram of the softmax layer with the `view` function.

```
view(softnet)
```

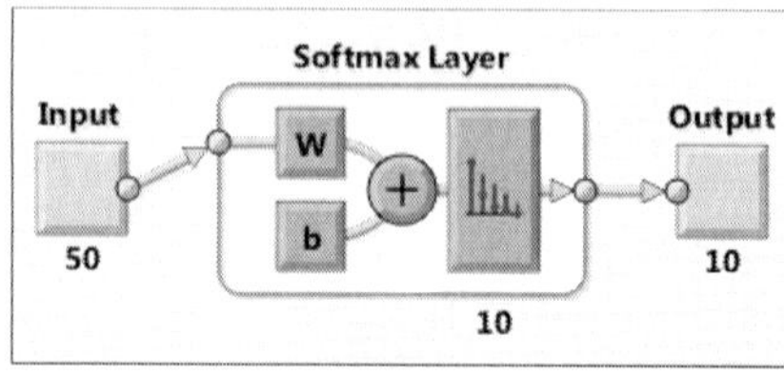

12.1.6 Forming a stacked neural network

You have trained three separate components of a deep neural network in isolation. At this point, it might be useful to view the three neural networks that you have trained. They are `autoenc1`, `autoenc2`, and `softnet`.

```
view(autoenc1)
view(autoenc2)
view(softnet)
```

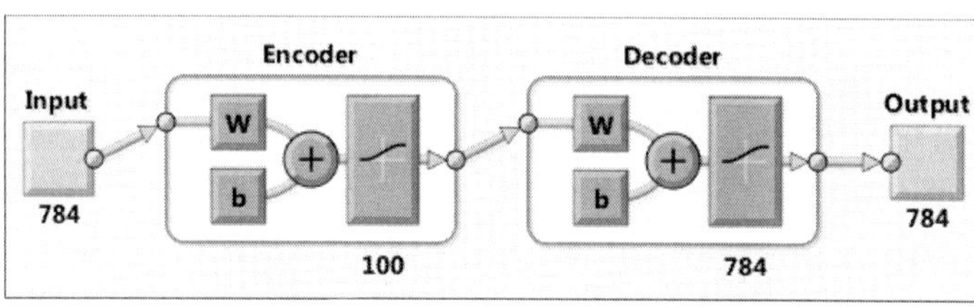

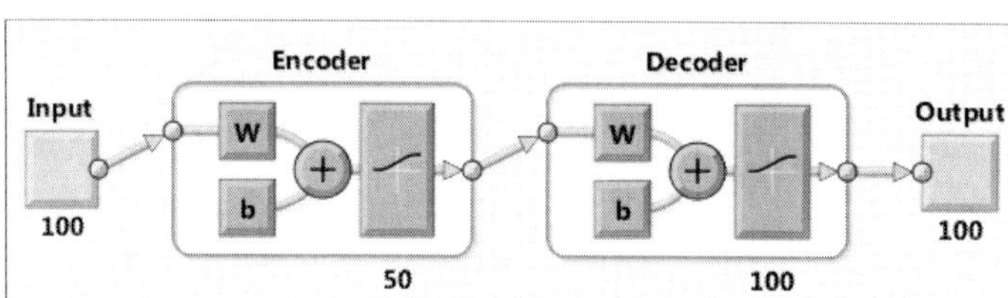

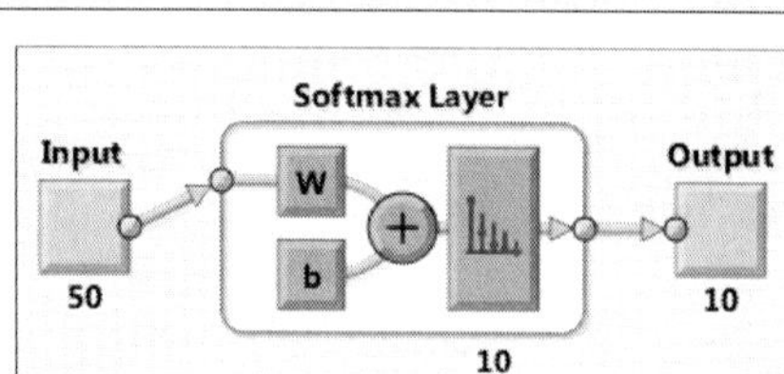

As was explained, the encoders from the autoencoders have been used to extract features. You can stack the encoders from the autoencoders together with the softmax layer to form a deep network.

```
deepnet = stack(autoenc1,autoenc2,softnet);
```

You can view a diagram of the stacked network with the `view` function. The network is formed by the encoders from the autoencoders and the softmax layer.

```
view(deepnet)
```

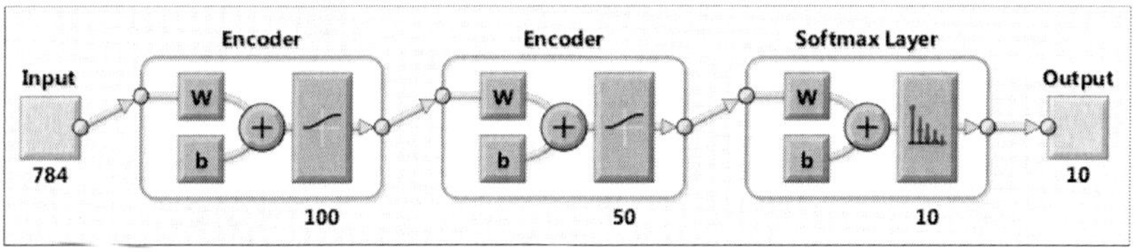

With the full deep network formed, you can compute the results on the test set. To use images with the stacked network, you have to reshape the test images into a matrix. You can do this by stacking the columns of an image to form a vector, and then forming a matrix from these vectors.

```
% Get the number of pixels in each image
imageWidth = 28;
imageHeight = 28;
inputSize = imageWidth*imageHeight;

% Load the test images
[xTestImages,tTest] = digitTestCellArrayData;

% Turn the test images into vectors and put them in a matrix
xTest = zeros(inputSize,numel(xTestImages));
for i = 1:numel(xTestImages)
    xTest(:,i) = xTestImages{i}(:);
end
```

You can visualize the results with a confusion matrix. The numbers in the bottom right-hand square of the matrix give the overall accuracy.

```
y = deepnet(xTest);
plotconfusion(tTest,y);
```

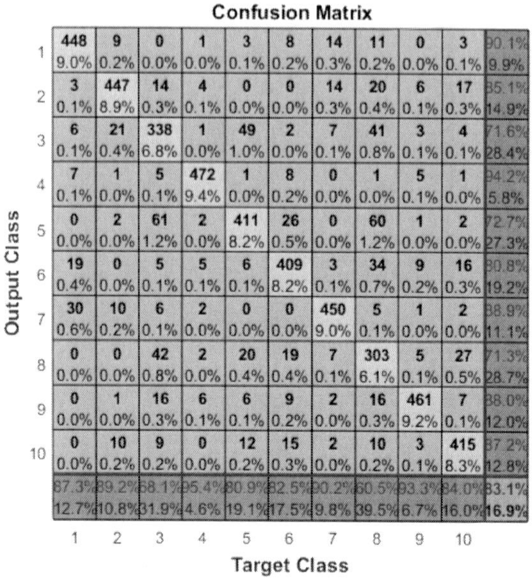

12.1.7 Fine tuning the deep neural network

The results for the deep neural network can be improved by performing backpropagation on the whole multilayer network. This process is often referred to as fine tuning.

You fine tune the network by retraining it on the training data in a supervised fashion. Before you can do this, you have to reshape the training images into a matrix, as was done for the test images.

```
% Turn the training images into vectors and put them in a matrix
xTrain = zeros(inputSize,numel(xTrainImages));
for i = 1:numel(xTrainImages)
    xTrain(:,i) = xTrainImages{i}(:);
end

% Perform fine tuning
deepnet = train(deepnet,xTrain,tTrain);
```

You then view the results again using a confusion matrix.

```
y = deepnet(xTest);
plotconfusion(tTest,y);
```

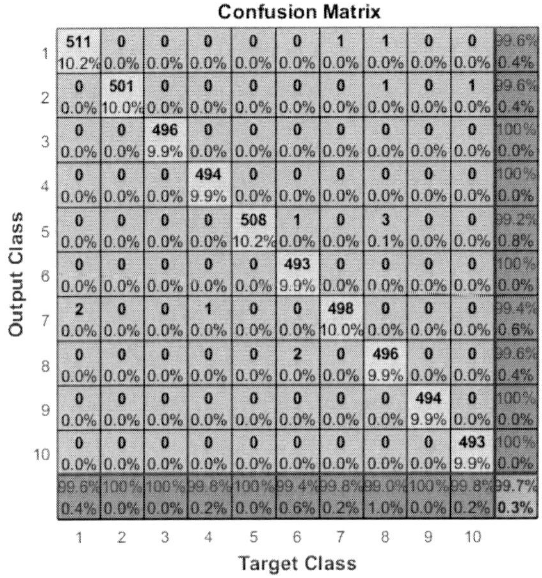

12.1.8 Summary

This example showed how to train a deep neural network to classify digits in images using Neural Network Toolbox (Deep Learning Toolbox from version 18)™. The steps that have been outlined can be applied to other similar problems, such as classifying images of letters, or even small images of objects of a specific category.

12.2 TRANSFER LEARNING USING CONVOLUTIONAL NEURAL NETWORKS

Fine-tune a convolutional neural network pretrained on digit images to learn the features of letter images. Transfer learning is considered as the transfer of knowledge from one learned task to a new task in machine learning [1]. In the context of neural networks, it is transferring learned features of a pretrained network to a new problem. Training a convolutional neural network from the beginning in each case usually is not effective when there is not sufficient amount of training data. The common practice in deep learning for such cases is to use a network that is trained on a large data set for a new problem. While the initial layers of the pretrained network can be fixed, the last few layers must be fine-tuned to learn the specific features of the new data set. Transfer learning usually results in faster training times than training a new convolutional neural network because you do not need to estimate all the parameters in the new network.

NOTE: Training a convolutional neural network requires Parallel Computing Toolbox™ and a CUDA®-enabled NVIDIA® GPU with compute capability 3.0 or higher.

Load the sample data as an `ImageDatastore`.

```
digitDatasetPath =
fullfile(matlabroot,'toolbox','nnet','nndemos',...
    'nndatasets','DigitDataset');
digitData = imageDatastore(digitDatasetPath,...
        'IncludeSubfolders',true,'LabelSource','foldernames');
```

The data store contains 10000 synthetic images of digits 0–9. The images are generated by applying random transformations to digit images created using different fonts. Each digit image is 28-by-28 pixels.

Display some of the images in the datastore.

```
for i = 1:20
    subplot(4,5,i);
    imshow(digitData.Files{i});
end
```

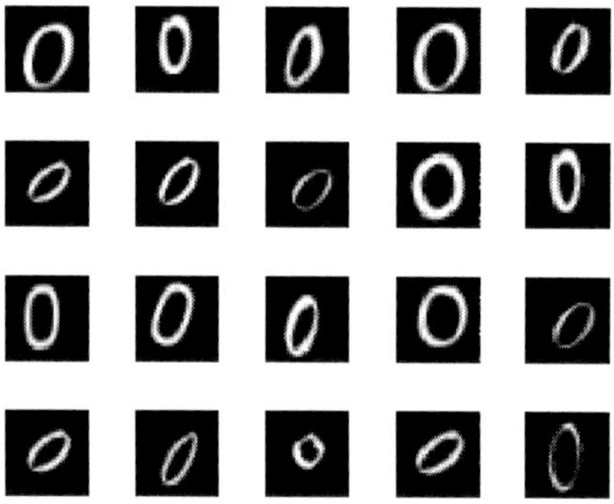

Check the number of images in each digit category.

```
digitData.countEachLabel
```

```
ans =

    Label    Count
    _____    _____
```

```
0          988
1         1026
2         1003
3          993
4          991
5         1017
6          992
7          999
8         1003
9          988
```

The data contains an unequal number of images per category.

To balance the number of images for each digit in the training set, first find the minimum number of images in a category.

```
minSetCount = min(digitData.countEachLabel{:,2})
```

```
minSetCount =

   988
```

Divide the dataset so that each category in the training set has 494 images and the testing set has the remaining images from each label.

```
trainingNumFiles = round(minSetCount/2);
rng(1) % For reproducibility
[trainDigitData,testDigitData] = splitEachLabel(digitData,...
                                 trainingNumFiles,'randomize');
```

`splitEachLabel` splits the image files in `digitData` into two new datastores, `trainDigitData` and `testDigitData`.

Create the layers for the convolutional neural network.

```
layers = [imageInputLayer([28 28 1])
          convolution2dLayer(5,20)
          reluLayer()
          maxPooling2dLayer(2,'Stride',2)
          fullyConnectedLayer(10)
          softmaxLayer()
          classificationLayer()];
```

Create the training options. Set the maximum number of epochs at 20, and start the training with an initial learning rate of 0.001.

```
options = trainingOptions('sgdm','MaxEpochs',20,...
```

```
        'InitialLearnRate',0.001);
```

Train the network using the training set and the options you defined in the previous step.

```
convnet = trainNetwork(trainDigitData,layers,options);
```

Epoch	Iteration	Time Elapsed (seconds)	Mini-batch Loss	Mini-batch Accuracy	Base Learning Rate
2	50	0.71	0.2233	92.97%	0.001000
3	100	1.37	0.0182	99.22%	0.001000
4	150	2.02	0.0395	99.22%	0.001000
6	200	2.70	0.0105	99.22%	0.001000
7	250	3.35	0.0026	100.00%	0.001000
8	300	4.00	0.0004	100.00%	0.001000
10	350	4.67	0.0002	100.00%	0.001000
11	400	5.32	0.0001	100.00%	0.001000
12	450	5.95	0.0001	100.00%	0.001000
14	500	6.60	0.0002	100.00%	0.001000
15	550	7.23	0.0001	100.00%	0.001000
16	600	7.87	0.0001	100.00%	0.001000
18	650	8.52	0.0001	100.00%	0.001000
19	700	9.15	0.0001	100.00%	0.001000
20	750	9.79	0.0000	100.00%	0.001000

Test the network using the testing set and compute the accuracy.

```
YTest = classify(convnet,testDigitData);
TTest = testDigitData.Labels;
accuracy = sum(YTest == TTest)/numel(YTest)

accuracy =

    0.9976
```

Accuracy is the ratio of the number of true labels in the test data matching the classifications from `classify`, to the number of images in the test data. In this case 99.78% of the digit estimations match the true digit values in the test set.

Now, suppose you would like to use the trained network `net` to predict classes on a new set of data. Load the letters training data.

```
load lettersTrainSet.mat
```

`XTrain` contains 1500 28-by-28 grayscale images of the letters A, B, and C in a 4-D array. `TTrain` contains the categorical array of the letter labels.

Display some of the letter images.

```
figure;
for j = 1:20
    subplot(4,5,j);
    selectImage = datasample(XTrain,1,4);
    imshow(selectImage,[]);
```

```
end
```

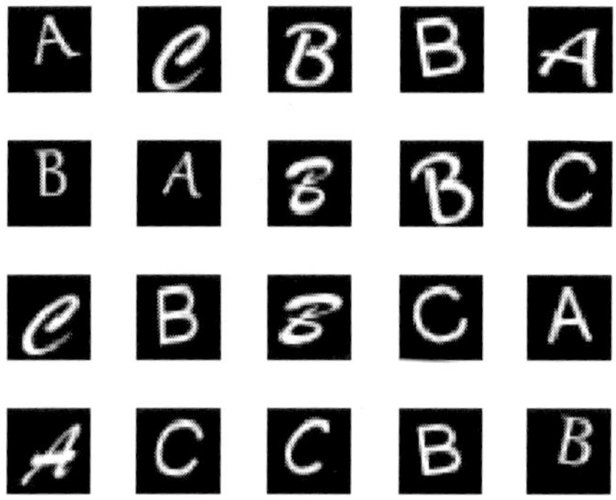

The pixel values in `XTrain` are in the range [0 1]. The digit data used in training the network `net` were in [0 255]; scale the letters data between [0 255].

```
XTrain = XTrain*255;
```

The last three layers of the trained network `net` are tuned for the digit dataset, which has 10 classes. The properties of these layers depend on the classification task. Display the fully connected layer (`fullyConnectedLayer`).

```
convnet.Layers(end-2)

ans =

  FullyConnectedLayer with properties:

          Name: 'fc'

   Hyperparameters
     InputSize: 2880
    OutputSize: 10

   Learnable Parameters
       Weights: [10×2880 single]
          Bias: [10×1 single]

Use properties method to see a list of all properties.
```

Display the last layer (`classificationLayer`).

```
convnet.Layers(end)
```

```
ans =

  ClassificationOutputLayer with properties:

            Name: 'classoutput'
      ClassNames: {10×1 cell}
      OutputSize: 10

   Hyperparameters
    LossFunction: 'crossentropyex'
```

These three layers must be fine-tuned for the new classification problem. Extract all the layers but the last three from the trained network, `net`.

```
layersTransfer = convnet.Layers(1:end-3);
```

The letters data set has three classes. Add a new fully connected layer for three classes, and increase the learning rate for this layer.

```
layersTransfer(end+1) = fullyConnectedLayer(3,...
              'WeightLearnRateFactor',10,...
                  'BiasLearnRateFactor',20);
```

`WeightLearnRateFactor` and `BiasLearnRateFactor` are multipliers of the global learning rate for the fully connected layer.

Add a softmax layer and a classification output layer.

```
layersTransfer(end+1) = softmaxLayer();
layersTransfer(end+1) = classificationLayer();
```

Create the options for transfer learning. You do not have to train for many epochs (`MaxEpochs` can be lower than before). Set the `InitialLearnRate` at a lower rate than used for training `net` to improve convergence by taking smaller steps.

```
optionsTransfer = trainingOptions('sgdm',...
         'MaxEpochs',5,...
         'InitialLearnRate',0.000005,...
         'Verbose',true);
```

Perform transfer learning.

```
convnetTransfer = trainNetwork(XTrain,TTrain,...
                    layersTransfer,optionsTransfer);
```

```
|=========================================================================================|
|     Epoch     |   Iteration   | Time Elapsed |  Mini-batch  |  Mini-batch  | Base Learning|
|               |               |  (seconds)   |     Loss     |   Accuracy   |     Rate     |
|=========================================================================================|
|             5 |            50 |         0.43 |       0.0011 |      100.00% |     0.000005 |
|=========================================================================================|
```

Load the letters test data. Similar to the letters training data, scale the testing data between [0 255], because the training data were between that range.

```
load lettersTestSet.mat
XTest = XTest*255;
```

Test the accuracy.

```
YTest = classify(convnetTransfer,XTest);
accuracy = sum(YTest == TTest)/numel(TTest)
```

```
accuracy =

    0.9587
```

12.3 IRIS CLUSTERING

This example illustrates how a self-organizing map neural network can cluster iris flowers into classes topologically, providing insight into the types of flowers and a useful tool for further analysis.

In this example we attempt to build a neural network that clusters iris flowers into natural classes, such that similar classes are grouped together. Each iris is described by four features:

- Sepal length in cm
- Sepal width in cm
- Petal length in cm
- Petal width in cm

This is an example of a clustering problem, where we would like to group samples into classes based on the similarity between samples. We would like to create a neural network which not only creates class definitions for the known inputs, but will let us classify unknown inputs accordingly.

12.3.1 Why Self-Organizing Map Neural Networks?

Self-organizing maps (SOMs) are very good at creating classifications. Further, the classifications retain topological information about which classes are most similar to others. Self-organizing maps can be created with any desired level of detail. They are particularly well suited for clustering data in many dimensions and with complexly shaped and connected feature spaces. They are well suited to cluster iris flowers.

The four flower attributes will act as inputs to the SOM, which will map them onto a 2-dimensional layer of neurons.

12.3.2 Preparing the Data

Data for clustering problems are set up for a SOM by organizing the data into an input matrix X.

Each ith column of the input matrix will have four elements representing the four measurements taken on a single flower.

Here such a dataset is loaded.

```
x = iris_dataset;
```

We can view the size of inputs X.

Note that X has 150 columns. These represent 150 sets of iris flower attributes. It has four rows, for the four measurements.

```
size(x)
ans =

     4   150
```

12.3.3 Clustering with a Neural Network

The next step is to create a neural network that will learn to cluster.

selforgmap creates self-organizing maps for classify samples with as as much detailed as desired by selecting the number of neurons in each dimension of the layer.

We will try a 2-dimension layer of 64 neurons arranged in an 8x8 hexagonal grid for this example. In general, greater detail is achieved with more neurons, and more dimensions allows for the modelling the topology of more complex feature spaces.

The input size is 0 because the network has not yet been configured to match our input data. This will happen when the network is trained.

```
net = selforgmap([8 8]);
view(net)
```

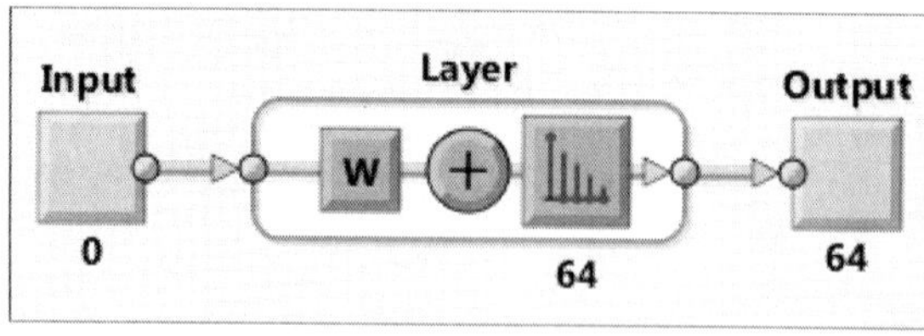

Now the network is ready to be optimized with **train**.

The NN Training Tool shows the network being trained and the algorithms used to train it. It also displays the training state during training and the criteria which stopped training will be highlighted in green.

The buttons at the bottom open useful plots which can be opened during and after training. Links next to the algorithm names and plot buttons open documentation on those subjects.

```
[net,tr] = train(net,x);
nntraintool
```

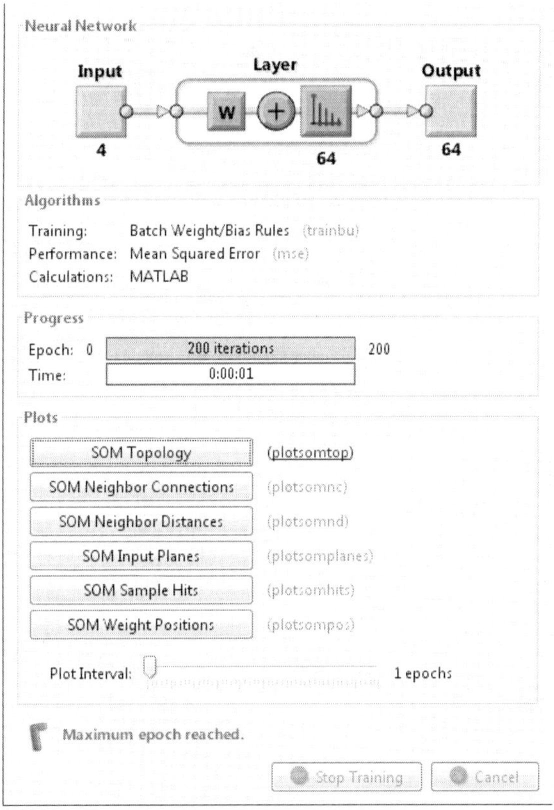

Here the self-organizing map is used to compute the class vectors of each of the training inputs. These classfications cover the feature space populated by the known flowers, and can now be used to classify new flowers accordingly. The network output will be a 64x150 matrix, where each ith column represents the jth cluster for each ith input vector with a 1 in its jth element.

The function **vec2ind** returns the index of the neuron with an output of 1, for each vector. The indices will range between 1 and 64 for the 64 clusters represented by the 64 neurons.

```
y = net(x);
cluster_index = vec2ind(y);
```

plotsomtop plots the self-organizing maps topology of 64 neurons positioned in an 8x8 hexagonal grid. Each neuron has learned to represent a different class of flower, with adjecent neurons typically representing similar classes.

```
plotsomtop(net)
```

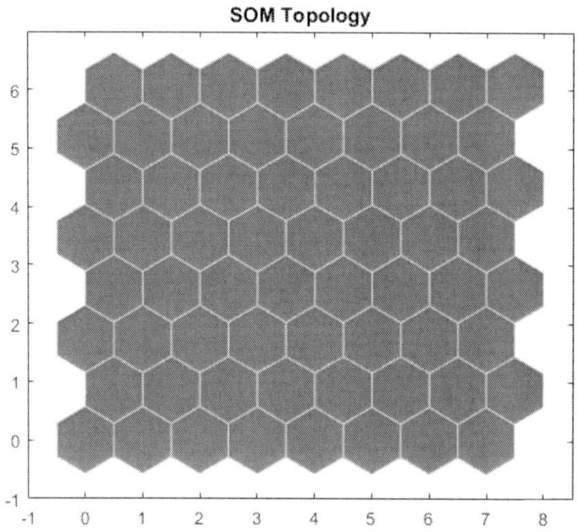

plotsomhits calculates the classes for each flower and shows the number of flowers in each class. Areas of neurons with large numbers of hits indicate classes representing similar highly populated regions of the feature space. Wheras areas with few hits indicate sparsely populated regions of the feature space.

```
plotsomhits(net,x)
```

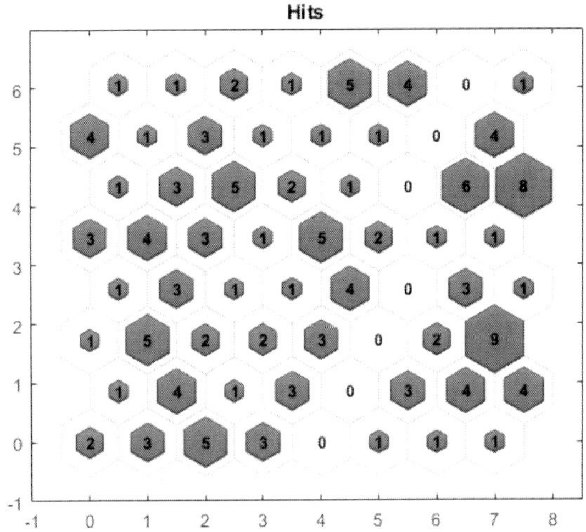

plotsomnc shows the neuron neighbor connections. Neighbors typically classify similar samples.

```
plotsomnc(net)
```

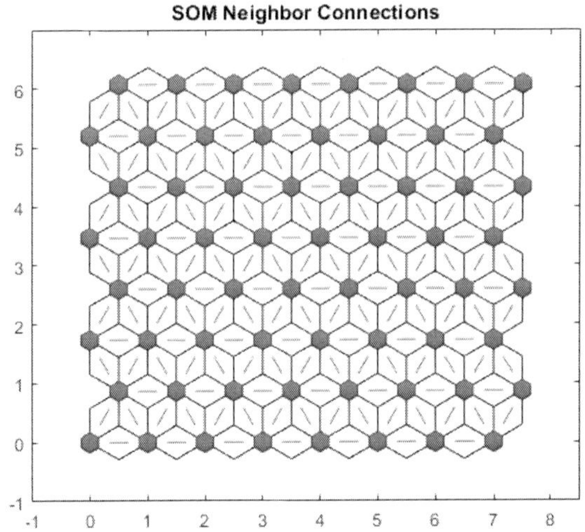

plotsomnd shows how distant (in terms of Euclidian distance) each neuron's class is from its neighbors. Connections which are bright indicate highly connected areas of the input space. While dark connections indicate classes representing regions of the feature space which are far apart, with few or no flowers between them.

Long borders of dark connections separating large regions of the input space indicate that the classes on either side of the border represent flowers with very different features.

```
plotsomnd(net)
```

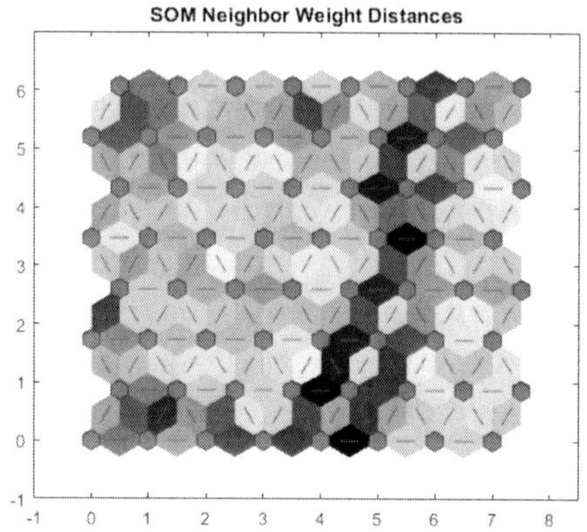

plotsomplanes shows a weight plane for each of the four input features. They are visualizations of the weights that connect each input to each of the 64 neurons in the 8x8 hexagonal grid. Darker colors represent larger weights. If two inputs have similar weight planes (their color gradients may be the same or in reverse) it indicates they are highly correlated.

```
plotsomplanes(net)
```

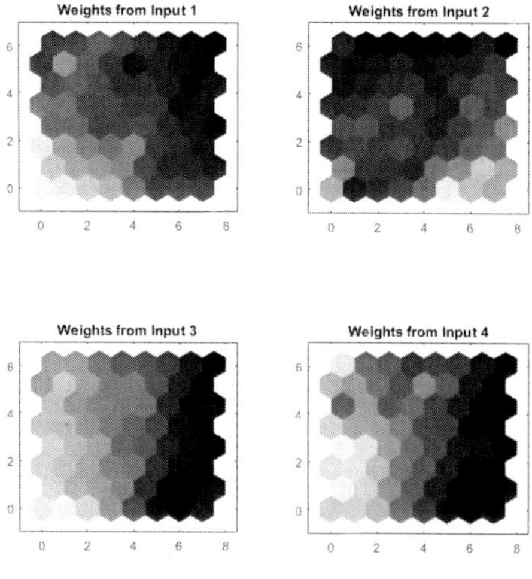

This example illustrated how to design a neural network that clusters iris flowers based on four of their characteristics.

12.4 GENE EXPRESSION ANALYSIS

This example demonstrates looking for patterns in gene expression profiles in baker's yeast using neural networks.

12.4.1 The Problem: Analyzing Gene Expressions in Baker's Yeast (Saccharomyces Cerevisiae)

The goal is to gain some understanding of gene expressions in Saccharomyces cerevisiae, which is commonly known as baker's yeast or brewer's yeast. It is the fungus that is used to bake bread and ferment wine from grapes.

Saccharomyces cerevisiae, when introduced in a medium rich in glucose, can convert glucose to ethanol. Initially, yeast converts glucose to ethanol by a metabolic process called "fermentation". However once supply of glucose is exhausted yeast shifts from anaerobic fermentation of glucose to aerobic respiraton of ethanol. This process is called diauxic shift. This process is of considerable interest since it is accompanied by major changes in gene expression.

The example uses DNA microarray data to study temporal gene expression of almost all genes in Saccharomyces cerevisiae during the diauxic shift.

You need Bioinformatics Toolbox™ to run this example.

```
if ~nnDependency.bioInfoAvailable
  errordlg('This example requires Bioinformatics Toolbox.');
  return;
end
```

12.4.2 The Data

This example uses data from DeRisi, JL, Iyer, VR, Brown, PO. "Exploring the metabolic and genetic control of gene expression on a genomic scale." Science. 1997 Oct 24;278(5338):680-6. PMID: 9381177

The full data set can be downloaded from the Gene Expression Omnibus website: http://www.yeastgenome.org

Start by loading the data into MATLAB®.

```
load yeastdata.mat
```

Gene expression levels were measured at seven time points during the diauxic shift. The variable `times` contains the times at which the expression levels were measured in the experiment. The variable `genes` contains the names of the genes whose expression levels were measured. The variable yeastvalues contains the "VALUE" data or LOG_RAT2N_MEAN, or log2 of ratio of CH2DN_MEAN and CH1DN_MEAN from the seven time steps in the experiment.

To get an idea of the size of the data you can use **numel(genes)** to show how many genes there are in the data set.

```
numel(genes)

ans =

        6400
```

genes is a cell array of the gene names. You can access the entries using MATLAB cell array indexing:

```
genes{15}

ans =

YAL054C
```

This indicates that the 15th row of the variable **yeastvalues** contains expression levels for the ORF YAL054C. You can use the web command to access information about this ORF in the Saccharomyces Genome Database (SGD).

```
url = sprintf(...
        'http://www.yeastgenome.org/cgi-bin/locus.fpl?locus=%s',...
        genes{15});
web(url);
```

12.4.3 Filtering the Genes

The data set is quite large and a lot of the information corresponds to genes that do not show any interesting changes during the experiment. To make it easier to find the interesting genes, the first thing to do is to reduce the size of the data set by removing genes with expression profiles that do not show anything of interest. There are 6400 expression profiles. You can use a number of techniques to reduce this to some subset that contains the most significant genes.

If you look through the gene list you will see several spots marked as 'EMPTY'. These are empty spots on the array, and while they might have data associated with them, for the purposes of this example, you can consider these points to be noise. These points can be found using the **strcmp** function and removed from the data set with indexing commands.

```
emptySpots = strcmp('EMPTY',genes);
yeastvalues(emptySpots,:) = [];
```

```
genes(emptySpots) = [];
numel(genes)

ans =

        6314
```

In the yeastvalues data you will also see several places where the expression level is marked as NaN. This indicates that no data was collected for this spot at the particular time step. One approach to dealing with these missing values would be to impute them using the mean or median of data for the particular gene over time. This example uses a less rigorous approach of simply throwing away the data for any genes where one or more expression level was not measured.

The function **isnan** is used to identify the genes with missing data and indexing commands are used to remove the genes with missing data.

```
nanIndices = any(isnan(yeastvalues),2);
yeastvalues(nanIndices,:) = [];
genes(nanIndices) = [];
numel(genes)

ans =

        6276
```

If you were to plot the expression profiles of all the remaining profiles, you would see that most profiles are flat and not significantly different from the others. This flat data is obviously of use as it indicates that the genes associated with these profiles are not significantly affected by the diauxic shift; however, in this example, you are interested in the genes with large changes in expression accompanying the diauxic shift. You can use filtering functions in the Bioinformatics Toolbox™ to remove genes with various types of profiles that do not provide useful information about genes affected by the metabolic change.

You can use the **genevarfilter** function to filter out genes with small variance over time. The function returns a logical array of the same size as the variable genes with ones corresponding to rows of yeastvalues with variance greater than the 10th percentile and zeros corresponding to those below the threshold.

```
mask = genevarfilter(yeastvalues);
% Use the mask as an index into the values to remove the filtered
genes.
yeastvalues = yeastvalues(mask,:);
genes = genes(mask);
numel(genes)
```

```
ans =

        5648
```

The function **genelowvalfilter** removes genes that have very low absolute expression values. Note that the gene filter functions can also automatically calculate the filtered data and names.

```
[mask, yeastvalues, genes] = ...
  genelowvalfilter(yeastvalues,genes,'absval',log2(3));
numel(genes)

ans =

   822
```

Use **geneentropyfilter** to remove genes whose profiles have low entropy:

```
[mask, yeastvalues, genes] = ...
  geneentropyfilter(yeastvalues,genes,'prctile',15);
numel(genes)

ans =

   614
```

12.4.4 Principal Component Analysis

Now that you have a manageable list of genes, you can look for relationships between the profiles.

Normalizing the standard deviation and mean of data allows the network to treat each input as equally important over its range of values.

Principal-component analysis (PCA) is a useful technique that can be used to reduce the dimensionality of large data sets, such as those from microarray analysis. This technique isolates the principal components of the dataset eliminating those components that contribute the least to the variation in the data set.

The two settings variables can be used to apply **mapstd** and **processpca** to other data to consistently when the network is applied to new data.

```
[x,std_settings] = mapstd(yeastvalues');  % Normalize data
[x,pca_settings] = processpca(x,0.15);    % PCA
```

The input vectors are first normalized, using `mapstd`, so that they have zero mean and unity variance. `processpca` is the function that implements the PCA algorithm. The second argument passed to `processpca` is 0.15. This means that `processpca` eliminates those principal components that contribute less than 15% to the total variation in the data set. The variable `pc` now contains the principal components of the yeastvalues data.

The principal components can be visiualized using the **scatter** function.

```
figure
scatter(x(1,:),x(2,:));
xlabel('First Principal Component');
ylabel('Second Principal Component');
title('Principal Component Scatter Plot');
```

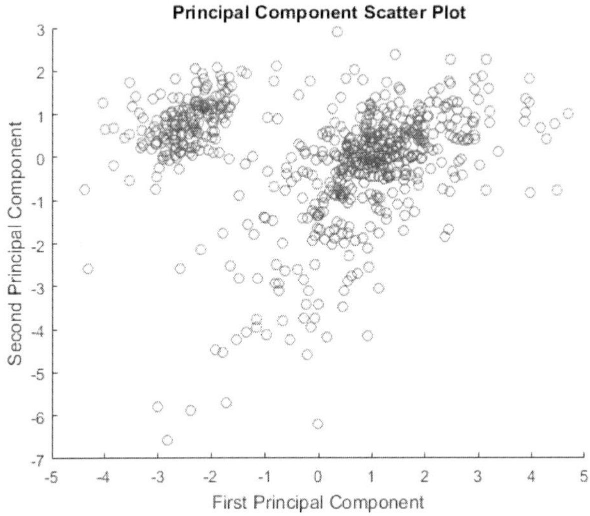

12.4.5 Cluster Analysis: Self-Organizing Maps

The principal components can be now be clustered using the Self-Organizing map (SOM) clustering algorithm available in Neural Network Toolbox (Deep Learning Toolbox from version 18) software.

The **selforgmap** function creates a Self-Organizing map network which can then be trained with the **train** function.

The input size is 0 because the network has not yet been configured to match our input data. This will happen when the network is trained.

```
net = selforgmap([5 3]);
view(net)
```

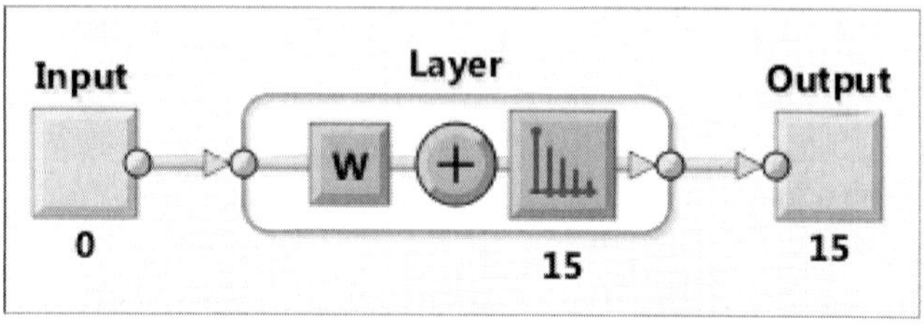

Now the network is ready to be trained.

The NN Training Tool shows the network being trained and the algorithms used to train it. It also displays the training state during training and the criteria which stopped training will be highlighted in green.

The buttons at the bottom open useful plots which can be opened during and after training. Links next to the algorithm names and plot buttons open documentation on those subjects.

```
net = train(net,x);
nntraintool
```

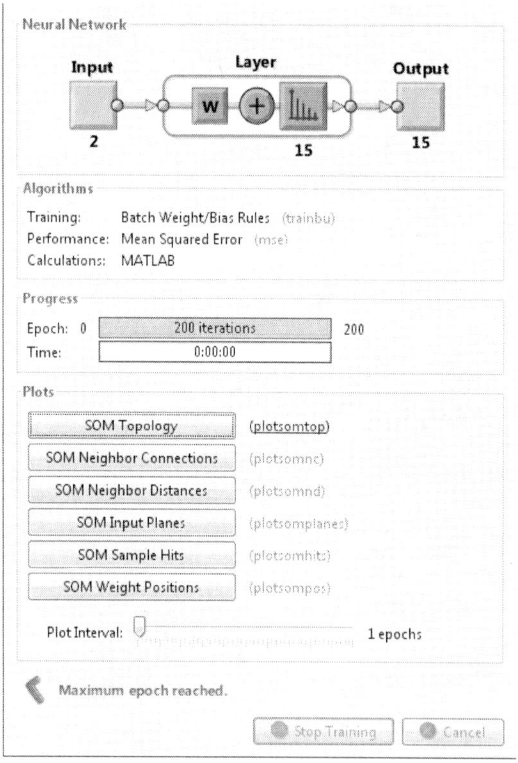

Use **plotsompos** to display the network over a scatter plot of the first two dimensions of the data.

```
figure
plotsompos(net,x);
```

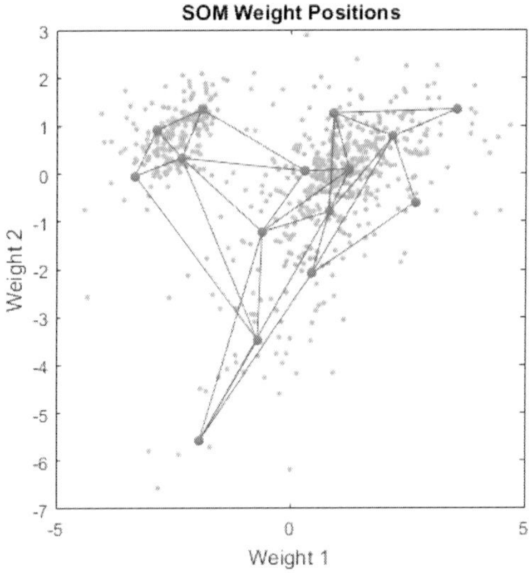

You can assign clusters using the SOM by finding the nearest node to each point in the data set.

```
y = net(x);
cluster_indices = vec2ind(y);
```

Use **plotsomhits** to see how many vectors are assigned to each of the neurons in the map.

```
figure
plotsomhits(net,x);
```

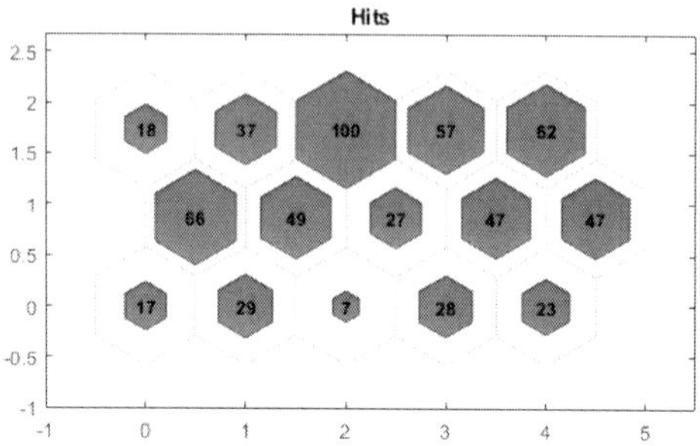

You can also use other clustering algorithms like Hierarchical clustering and K-means, available in the Statistics and Machine Learning Toolbox™ for cluster analysis.

Made in United States
North Haven, CT
17 August 2025

71810119R00192